PROFESSIONALISM
IN THE EARLY YEARS

PROFESSIONALISM
IN THE EARLY YEARS

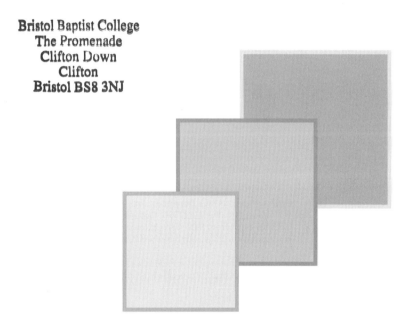

Editors: Linda Miller & Carrie Cable

HODDER
EDUCATION
AN HACHETTE UK COMPANY

Orders: please contact Bookpoint Ltd, 130 Milton Park, Abingdon, Oxon OX14 4SB.
Telephone: (44) 01235 827720. Fax: (44) 01235 400454.
Lines are open from 9.00–5.00, Monday to Saturday, with a 24-hour message answering service.
You can also order through our website www.hoddereducation.co.uk.

British Library Cataloguing in Publication Data
A catalogue record for this title is available from the British Library.

ISBN: 978 0 340 94834 7

First Published 2008
Impression number   10 9 8 7 6 5 4 3 2
Year   2012 2011 2010

Copyright © 2008 Linda Miller and Carrie Cable

Hachette Livre UK's policy is to use papers that are natural, renewable and recyclable products and
made from wood grown in sustainable forests. The logging and manufacturing processes are
expected to conform to the environmental regulations of the country of origin.

Cover photo © Andersen Ross/Getty Images.
Typeset by Servis Filmsetting Ltd, Manchester.

Printed in India for Hodder Education, an Hachette UK Company, 338 Euston Road,
London NW1 3BH.

CONTENTS

LIST OF CONTRIBUTORS

CARRIE CABLE is a Senior Lecturer in Education at the Open University where she is involved in developing courses for teaching assistants and early years practitioners. She has published a number of articles, co-edited a book on teaching assistants and co-edited *Developing Early Years Practice* (2005) with Linda Miller and Jane Devereux (David Fulton/Open University Press).

PAMELA CALDER is Honorary Visiting Research Fellow at London South Bank University and Chair of the Early Childhood Studies Degrees Network. Her most recent publications include a chapter in the (2007) *International Encyclopedia of Early Childhood Education* (Rebecca New and Moncrieff Cochran (eds), Westport.Praeger/Greenwood Press).

ANNA CRAFT is Professor at the University of Exeter and Open University and Government Advisor on creative and cultural education. Recent books: *Reflective Practice in the Early Years* with Alice Paige-Smith (Open University Press 2008), *Creative Learning 3–11* with Teresa Cremin and Pamela Burnard (Trentham 2008), *Creativity, Wisdom and Trusteeship* with Howard Gardner and Guy Claxton (Corwin Press 2008).

CARMEN DALLI is Associate Professor in the School of Education Studies and Director of the Institute for Early Childhood Studies at Victoria University of Wellington in New Zealand. She combines a research interest in the development of under 3-year-olds in early childhood services with research on professionalism and ethical practice.

JANE DEVEREUX was formerly a Senior Lecturer at The Open University working on the Foundation Degree in Early Years and also Director for the Teacher Education in Sub-Saharan Africa (TESSA) project. Recent publications include *Developing Subject Knowledge: Primary Science* (2007) (2nd edition) (Paul Chapman Publishing/Open University Press).

GILL GOODLIFF is a Lecturer in Early Years at the Open University where she teaches on the Foundation Degree in Early Years and is Lead Assessor for Early Years Professional Status. Her research focuses on the professional identities of early years practitioners and young children's spirituality.

SUE GRIFFIN is former National Training and Quality Assurance Manager at the National Childminding Association and now works as a consultant and writer. Her book *Getting Started in Home-based Childcare* for new childminders and nannies was published in 2006 (Heinemann).

GILL HAYNES OBE Gill Haynes is a consultant and is currently the independent chair of a New Deal for Communities programme in South London and Vice Chair of the Children's Workforce Development Council (England). She was formerly the Chief Executive of the National Childminding Association.

CAROLINE JONES is course leader for the Early Years Foundation Degree at the University of Warwick, an educational trainer and consultant and director of a group of early childhood settings. She has published widely including *Leadership and Management in the Early Years* with Linda Pound (2008) (McGraw Hill, in press).

LINDA MILLER is Professor of Early Years at the Open University and from 2003 to 2008 Chair of the Sector Endorsed Foundation Degrees in Early Years Network. She has written and co-edited a wide range of books for early years practitioners, including *Developing Early Years Practice* (2005) with Carrie Cable and Jane Devereux (David Fulton/Open University Press).

PETER MOSS is Professor of Early Childhood Provision at the Institute of Education University of London. He is also editor of *Children in Europe* and co-editor, with Gunilla Dahlberg, of the book series *Contesting Early Childhood* (published by Routledge). Much of his work over the last 20 years has been cross-national, in particular in Europe.

PAMELA OBERHUEMER is a researcher at the State Institute of Early Childhood Research in Munich, Germany. She has focused on cross-national issues for many years. Recent publications include (in German) 'Training and staffing policies for early childhood work in an expanded European Union', in a volume edited by the Deutsches Jugendinstitut (2006) entitled *Reform or end of the training route for Erzieherinnen? Contributions to a controversial debate*.

SUE OWEN is Director of the Early Childhood Unit at the National Children's Bureau and takes part in consultations and advisory groups on training, qualifications and workforce issues. Her most recent publication is *Authentic Relationships in Group Care for Infants and Toddlers* with Stephanie Petrie (London: Jessica Kingsley 2005).

ALICE PAIGE-SMITH is a Lecturer in Early Years Education at the Open University, where she teaches on the Foundation Degree in Early Years. Her most recent publication is *Reflective Practice in the Early Years* with Anna Craft (Open University Press 2007).

LINDA POUND is an education consultant providing training for early years practitioners in the UK and overseas. Linda writes extensively for a range of audiences – her most recent book is a second edition of *Supporting Mathematical Development in the Early Years* (Open University Press 2006).

PETER TWINING is the Head of the Department of Education at the Open University and Director of schome (the education system for the information age) – see http://www.schome.ac.uk/ for further information. Recent publications include 'Talking about schools: Towards a typology for future education', *Educational Research*, 49(4), 329–341, 2007, with Jonathan Rix.

MARTIN WOODHEAD is Professor of Childhood Studies at the Open University. He has published extensively over 30 years, including co-editing three of the *Childhood* textbook series published by Wiley in 2003. He is also co-editor of *Children & Society*. During 2005 he advised the United Nations Committee on the Rights of the Child on the preparation of General Comment 7 on realising child rights in early childhood.

What does 'the expert choice' mean for you?

We work with more examiners and experts than any other publisher

- Because we work with more experts and examiners than any other publisher, the very latest curriculum requirements are built into this course and there is a perfect match between your course and the resources that you need to succeed. We make it easier for you to gain the skills and knowledge that you need for the best results.

- We have chosen the best team of experts – including the people that mark the exams – to give you the very best chance of success; look out for their advice throughout this book: this is content that you can trust.

More direct contact with teachers and students than any other publisher

- We talk with more than 100 000 students every year through our student conferences, run by Philip Allan Updates. We hear at first hand what you need to make a success of your A-level studies and build what we learn into every new course. Learn more about our conferences at www.philipallan.co.uk

- Our new materials are trialled in classrooms as we develop them, and the feedback built into every new book or resource that we publish. You can be part of that. If you have comments that you would like to make about this book, please email us at: feedback@hodder.co.uk

More collaboration with Subject Associations than any other publisher

- Subject Associations sit at the heart of education. We work closely with more Associations than any other publisher. This means that our resources support the most creative teaching and learning, using the skills of the best teachers in their field to create resources for you.

More opportunities for your teachers to stay ahead than with any other publisher

- Through our Philip Allan Updates Conferences, we offer teachers access to Continuing Professional Development. Our focused and practical conferences ensure that your teachers have access to the best presenters, teaching materials and training resources. Our presenters include experienced teachers, Chief and Principal Examiners, leading educationalists, authors and consultants. This course is built on all of this expertise.

INTRODUCTION TO PROFESSIONALISM IN THE EARLY YEARS

Linda Miller and Carrie Cable

INTRODUCTION

The focus for this book is professionalism in the early years. In England, early years is emerging as the term to encompass the bringing together of education and care services for young children, but as Sue Own and Gill Haynes note in the first chapter, it is impossible to educate without caring, or care without promoting children's learning. However, the title of the OECD (2006a) report *Starting Strong II: Early Childhood Education and Care* reflects the terminology more commonly used to describe early years policy and provision within the 20 countries reviewed. Both terms will be found in this book. Our aim is to reflect a range of voices and perspectives on what constitutes professionalism in the early years, how this can be developed and what it means for those working in the field. It brings together work by key authorities and those involved in the training and professional development of the early years workforce in England and beyond.

The idea for the book stemmed from the involvement of the editors with policy developments relating to the reform of the early years workforce in England and our membership of an international group of trainers and researchers concerned with exploring the notion of professionalism in early childhood. Through our dialogue with colleagues, both at a national and international level, we became increasingly aware of common themes in the debates about the expansion of early years education and care systems, underpinned by the drive to create a new professional workforce to bring about the envisaged changes. The chapters in this book are a unique attempt to bring together some of these developments and to draw together different perspectives and viewpoints relating to the professional development of early years practitioners. The book includes both critical reviews and accounts of research and practice. Key themes are presented in relation to both localised and international contexts; these include routes to professionalism, developing professional practice and rethinking professionalism.

As the OECD Executive summary report notes (OECD 2006b), the provision of quality early childhood education and care has remained as a high priority on government agendas in recent years. However, the review shows a mixed picture of professional education standards, a continuing gap between child care staff and teachers in relation to training and levels of pay, and gender and diversity imbalances. It is significant to note that the debate about the types of skills that are most appropriate for working in early childhood education is taking place in many countries.

In England the government has committed to the reform of the children's workforce through a reform agenda (DfES 2006). One of government's key policy objectives is to increase the skills, confidence and competence of the early years workforce, which is seen as critical to its success in providing quality provision and positive outcomes for young children and their families. This agenda is enshrined in a series of major policy documents (see Chapter 1) and in the establishment of a Children's Workforce Development Council (CWDC), one of whose stated aims is: 'to improve the lives of children, young people, their families and carers by ensuring that all people working with them have the best possible training, qualifications, support and advice' (http://www.cwdcouncil.org.uk/index.asp).

Although this reform agenda is bringing to fruition many of the developments that those working in this field have striven for, for many years, in opening up new routes to training and professionalism, it is not without its critics. The degree of prescription and regulation is seen by some to threaten the empowerment of early years practitioners (Osgood 2006; see also Chapter 11). One of the key themes running through this book is the need to develop reflective and critical practitioners who can actively engage with these developments and contribute to shaping notions of professionalism in the early years.

The government agenda in England is broad and aims to be far reaching, encompassing health and social care as well as numerous other workforce groups. In one book it would be impossible to do justice to all those working in the children's workforce and we have chosen to focus on the field of early years. At the same time, the key aim of government policy is to develop an integrated workforce based around a Common Core of Skills (DfES 2005) and an Integrated Qualifications Framework which will enable movement between and across the workforce, and this aim is reflected in many chapters.

The developments briefly discussed above have heightened debates around professionalism, professional practice and professional development for early years practitioners in England. Such debates include: the different roles undertaken by those working in the early years and what should they be in the future; questions about the knowledge, understanding, skills and attributes needed to carry out these varying roles; issues relating to pathways and progression routes for the workforce and what constitutes professionalism and professional practice. Throughout the book we explore these questions and consider the range of early years professionals that will be needed to implement this government agenda. We explore notions of professionalism in both a national and international context in the belief that all practitioners need to be able to engage critically, reflectively and reflexively with policy agendas, as well as with theory, practice and research.

PROFESSIONALISM IN THE EARLY YEARS

The chapters in this book recognise that early years practitioners will be at various points in their professional journey, depending upon their age, stage in their career and level of training and qualifications. A number of chapters explore professionalism from the perspectives of different professional roles and from different starting points and consider how these contribute to our knowledge and understanding of the field and our understanding of professionalism and professional practice. New professional development opportunities, such as those leading to Early Years Professional Status in England, have the potential to establish a new graduate-led workforce, and we examine how this may also contribute to establishing a new professionalism. We acknowledge that barriers still exist, for example in relation to status, pay and levels of empowerment and that resolution of these issues will be crucial in developing this new professionalism.

The book begins with an overview of the English context in relation to policy, practice and routes to higher level education and training for early years practitioners. Subsequent chapters consider how professional practice can be developed and the part that reflection and critical engagement can play. In parallel with the developments in England, there is international interest in developing professionals who can work at a high level with young children and who can take a leadership role with colleagues. Later chapters offer views from Europe and New Zealand, where evidence from research shows that early years professionals, working within vastly different systems, share the view that their work is important for young children, families and for society at large. In the final chapter, we look to the future and consider the implications of the issues around professionalism raised in this book.

In the first section of the book, 'Routes to Professionalism', Sue Owen and Gill Haynes in their chapter, 'Developing professionalism in the early years: from policy to practice', set the scene for the chapters that follow. The chapter offers an overview of the progress that has been made in developing national policy in England in early years services over the last decade and then focuses more specifically on workforce policy developments.

The next four chapters examine different routes to professionalism for the early years workforce. In Chapter 2, Linda Miller reviews policy developments underpinning the implementation of two new professional roles in England: Senior Practitioner and the Early Years Professional. She considers the implications of these roles in the context of proposals for a graduate-led professional workforce and discusses whether a regulatory framework and externally defined standards might inhibit the development of professionalism, or whether they are part of the professionalism agenda.

Early Childhood Studies (ECS) degrees are established training routes which aim to achieve a well qualified and graduate early years workforce. In Chapter 3, Pamela Calder considers the conceptual base for these degrees and their relationship with the Early Years Professional role. She discusses the development of ECS degrees as a specialist subject area in universities and how they stem from a campaigning past, to improve provision and to change the education, training, attitudes, status and pay of those who work with young children and the esteem in which they are held. She argues that the development of ECS degrees is part of a wider context, which involves how society views children, the role of women, families and employment.

In Chapter 4, 'The early years teacher', Jane Devereux and Carrie Cable discuss a range of current issues related to the role and training of early years specialist teachers. These issues are considered in relation to a variety of early years specialist routes at undergraduate and postgraduate levels and recent policy initiatives in the UK. The chapter examines key features of the current situation and considers how the challenges of reconceptualising an early years specialist teacher in relation to inter-disciplinary and cross-sector working, in both initial training and continuing professional development might be achieved. Finally, they argue for the urgent need to clarify understandings of the roles of and relationship between the Early Years Professional and the early years teacher.

'Teaching assistants in the early years' is the title of Chapter 5. In this chapter, Carrie Cable describes how the last 10 years have seen a rapid growth in the numbers and roles of teaching assistants in primary schools, where teaching assistants with a wide variety of training and qualifications are now employed in ever-increasing numbers to support the learning and development of young children. The chapter explores the professionalisation of this group of early years practitioners through the development of specific occupational standards and additional standards for Higher Level Teaching Assistants, which relate to standards for Qualified Teacher Status (QTS). The chapter considers how the role can be interpreted very differently in early years classes in schools (and between schools) and explores some of the attributes that teaching assistants consider are an important part of their professional practice.

In Chapter 6, Sue Griffin explores how home-based childcarers choose to promote themselves as 'professional' and what inhibits others from using the word. The chapter considers how childminders enter the children's workforce from many backgrounds, which can include professional status in another role in the sector. The chapter reflects on how the role of the National Childminding Association has been to encourage childminders to have a sense of pride in the value of the work they do and to recognise the significance of the skills they use in that work, dispelling the idea that childminders are 'mother substitutes'. The chapter also explores why others often do not perceive these workers as 'professional'; working alone and being home based is not seen as a professional context. The chapter considers how the growth of training opportunities for childminders has developed their perception of themselves as professionals, and also the part played by quality assurance in developing understanding and skills for reflective practice.

Early years practitioners work with the youngest and most vulnerable members of society, so strong and effective leadership must be a key element of early years settings. In Chapter 7, 'Leadership in the early years', Linda Pound argues that everyone who works with young children has to assume responsibilities and make judgements which require them to demonstrate the characteristics of leaders throughout their working day. She explores the roles, styles and characteristics of leaders in the early years and the different forms that leadership can take. This chapter also explores the policy agenda around leadership in early years settings as multi-agency working and inter-professional collaboration become the norm, and looks at initiatives such as the National Professional Qualification in Integrated Centre Leadership (NPQICL).

In the next section of the book, 'Developing Professional Practice', the authors of the three chapters explore some of the ways in which students studying for early years qualifications can develop reflection on practice to further their professional development. The importance of early years professionals reflecting on their practice is now widely acknowledged (Schön 1987). In Chapter 8, Anna Craft and Alice Paige-Smith consider the nature of reflective practice in early years settings, why it is important and what it involves. As the early years workforce is required to develop increasingly multi-agency and inter-professional working practices, communities of practice are changing. The notion of reflective practice is discussed against these rapidly changing working contexts and professional practices, and the potential and challenges for reflection and enquiry, documenting, interpreting and sharing perspectives in contributing to these developments are explored.

In Chapter 9, 'Computer mediated communication: using e-learning to support professional development', Gill Goodliff and Peter Twining consider ways of using computer mediated communication (CMC) to enhance practice and professional development. They start by exploring the potential role and significance of ICT for early years professional practice. Drawing on their experience of using CMC in the context of the Open University Foundation Degree in Early Years, they examine how computer conferencing can be used to support professional learning and reduce isolation, as part of a developing community of practice.

In Chapter 10 we hear 'students' voices'. Caroline Jones draws on students' experience of studying for the Early Years Foundation Degree at Warwick University. The chapter draws on data from a number of sources including students' reflective journals, learning diaries and course evaluations. It discusses the impact of the course on students' professional and personal development and the challenge of combining study, work and family commitments. A key theme explored in the chapter is 'change', as the experience of studying for the foundation degree is seen to have the power to change lives, not only of the students themselves but of the children and adults they work with.

In the final section, 'Rethinking professionalism', we draw together a range of perspectives on what it means to be a professional and on professionalism in the early years.

The chapter by Peter Moss focuses on rethinking and reforming the early years workforce and sets the scene for this section. He considers how, as early childhood services move up the policy agenda, so too does the early childhood workforce. Its members are recognised as the main resource for such services, and there is an increasing recognition that the work is complex and requires enhanced education. But despite this recognition, the situation in many countries – where the early childhood workforce remains split between a minority of teachers and a growing majority of childcare workers with lower qualifications and poorer work conditions – is highly problematic. The chapter considers what forms change might take, both structurally and in terms of how the worker and their work is understood, arguing for the need to connect restructuring with rethinking to re-envision the workforce. It also examines how understandings of the workforce are produced from different discourses and how different understandings relate to concepts of professionalism, proposing a politics of occupational identity and values that moves beyond the dualistic 'non-professional/professional' divide. It concludes by arguing that although strong forces are involved, there is scope for contestation and change.

In Chapter 12, Pamela Oberhuemer offers a European perspective on the early childhood professional. In a context of expansion, increasing access and ever-changing demands across Europe, the professional preparation and in-service support of those working with young children are critical quality issues. The chapter outlines selected policy approaches towards professionalisation and links these to inherent understandings of professionalism. In conclusion, it is suggested that recent moves towards conceptualising early childhood centres as multi-purpose sites and 'spaces' for both children and adults require a reappraisal of our constructions of professional knowledge, competencies and dispositions.

In Chapter 13, Carmen Dali discusses the New Zealand government's 10-year strategic plan for the early childhood education sector, *Pathways to the Future: Ngā Huarahi Arataki* (2002), which envisages a fully trained early childhood workforce by 2012. This chapter outlines the political and industrial context of this policy alongside an emerging discourse of professionalism within the local scholarly and practice scene. This includes debates about the meaning of professionalism in a sector that is very diverse. The chapter argues that as early childhood teachers take their place as professionals alongside teachers in the broader education sector, it is time for a new definition of professionalism that responds to the lived reality of early childhood work. Data from an ongoing study of early childhood teachers' views of professionalism and professional behavior are used to support this argument and to propose a grounds-up definition of the new professional teacher in New Zealand.

In Chapter 14, Martin Woodhead argues that the United Nations Convention on the Rights of the Child (UNCRC) is one of the most significant documents shaping research, policy and practice for all children throughout the world. He explores the significance of the UNCRC for rights-based perspective for professional work in the early years and the implications for the development of policy and services in England, in particular the Common Core of Skills and Knowledge for the Children's Workforce (DfES 2005). In the second part of the chapter he draws attention to the tension between universalistic theories and the plurality of pathways through childhood. The chapter explores concepts of 'normal' development, development as a 'natural' process, and an emphasis on 'needs' (what he terms the 3 Ns) and proposes an alternative way of thinking which recognises that development is 'contextual', 'cultural' and about respecting children's 'competencies' (3 Cs).

The final chapter, 'Looking to the Future', brings together some key themes and issues raised in the preceding chapters as we consider the way forward for professionalism in the early years.

REFERENCES

DfES (2005) *Common Core of Skills and Knowledge for the Children's Workforce.* Nottingham: DfES

DfES (2006) *Children's Workforce Strategy.* Nottingham: DfES

(http://www.cwdcouncil.org.uk/index.asp – accessed 2/11/2007)

OECD (2006a) *Starting Strong II. Early Childhood Education and Care.* Paris: Organisation for Economic Co-operation and Development

OECD (2006b) *Executive Summary.* Paris: Organisation for Economic Co-operation and Development

Osgood, J. (2006) 'Deconstructing professionalism in early childhood education: resisting the regulatory gaze,' *Contemporary Issues in Early Childhood*, 7, 15–14

Schön D (1987) *Educating the Reflective Practitioner.* San Francisco: Josey Bass

1

ROUTES TO PROFESSIONALISM

DEVELOPING PROFESSIONALISM IN THE EARLY YEARS: FROM POLICY TO PRACTICE

1

Sue Owen and Gill Haynes

INTRODUCTION

In this chapter we look briefly at the policy context of early years services over the past 10 years, before concentrating on the recent policy and strategy developments linked to the *Every Child Matters* agenda. This general survey then leads into a more specific focus on the policy related to workforce development in England as the context for the latest discussions of professionalism in the early years.

BACKGROUND TO EARLY YEARS SERVICES

Early years services in the UK have, until recently, lacked any form of national financial support or policy direction. Until 1996 when the Conservative Government introduced a voucher scheme to pay for part-time nursery education places for 4-year-olds, the extent of provision was determined by the commitment of individual local authorities or the purchasing power of parents. This led to patchy provision in which some areas had maintained neither nursery education nor any social services day nurseries at all, while others, such as Manchester, had a strong tradition of both. Equally, voluntary sector provision was dependent on the willingness of local councils to subsidise its costs and support training and advisory services for its staff. Both the voluntary sector and the growing full-time day care sector in childminding and private day nurseries were dependent on demand and the ability of parents to pay. This structural diversity was always reflected in the profile of the various workforces, with the statutory services employing 'professional' teachers and nursery nurses (even if they were unequal in status) and the voluntary and independent sector developing their own training and qualifications to meet the needs and characteristics of their own practitioners.

When the National Childcare Strategy was brought in by the Labour Government in 1997–8, early years services gradually came under the jurisdiction of local education authorities and, at national level, the Department for Education (now the Department for Children, Schools and Families, DCSF) rather than their traditional home in health and social care (Jamieson and Owen 2000; Randall and Fisher 2001). This was a popular move with national early years' organisations which had fought for young children's services to be integrated under one department and for children's learning to be seen as the central element of universal services. The widespread adoption of the generic term 'early years services' was brought about by this long-standing campaign to eliminate the historic 'care/education'. Even though we have different professional profiles for practitioners it is still, it is argued, impossible to educate without caring, or care without promoting children's learning.

Early years services are also essential for working parents and, since 1997, children's day care has become a significant element in government economic policies designed to reduce social exclusion and child poverty. The National Childcare Strategy was based on extending free part-time nursery education to all 4-year-old and then 3-year-old children whose parents wanted to use it, but full day care is still the responsibility of parents. Although the government has put in place measures to help extend availability, most notably a system of tax credits which can be accessed by working parents using regulated day care, individual parents still have to pay for their own day care (Jamieson and Owen 2000; Randall and Fisher 2001).

THE EVERY CHILD MATTERS AGENDA

. . .we are proposing here a range of measures to reform and improve children's care – crucially, for the first time ever requiring local authorities to bring together in one place under one person services for children, and at the same time suggesting real changes in the way those we ask to do this work carry out their tasks on our and our children's behalf.

(From the Prime Minister's Foreword to the Green Paper: *Every Child Matters*, HM Treasury 2003:1)

The Green Paper *Every Child Matters* was launched on the 8 September 2003 by the Chief Secretary to the Treasury, thus showing that the Treasury as well as the service ministries of Education and Health, was behind this radical restructuring of services for children. The Foreword by the Prime Minister hinted at one of the programme's central features, the creation of structures which would ensure service integration; and it is this which is having one of the most transformative effects on the concept of professionalism for the workforce.

Although arising specifically from the case of an abused child (Victoria Climbié) Every Child Matters aims to do more than make recommendations to local authorities about how to improve their child protection systems. Instead it was designed to reform the entire system of children's services in England, placing them within an ethos based on children's rights and entitlements and on positive outcomes for children. These are to be planned and delivered by local authorities according to their knowledge of the needs in their areas, but assessed and inspected nationally through performance indicators. Although these outcomes are for all children, the focus of the strategy is very firmly on children who are at risk, and the contributing policies and guidance are designed to ensure that local authorities narrow the gap between such children and those who traditionally do well.

Every Child Matters: Next Steps (DfES 2004a) was published six months after the Green Paper and outlined the government's response to the consultation's findings. The wider strategy which it outlined included some key areas relating to early years services and it was supported by the 10 Year Childcare Strategy which was published six months later. The government stressed the important role which early years services have to play in Every Child Matters and that they should be a priority area within local authorities' Children and Young People's Plans. In this way the government's existing programme of expansion of early years services was brought into the fold of Every Child Matters and a new project was announced to create Sure Start Children's Centres in the most disadvantaged areas, combining health, family and parenting support and information services with integrated childcare and education for children from birth onwards. Doing well at school, avoiding social exclusion and contributing to the economy and society are all recognised here as being underpinned by the work done in a child's earliest years.

The final document, *Every Child Matters: Change for Children* (DfES 2004b), was published on 1 December 2004. It introduced the legislative changes in the Children Act 2004, and emphasised that the whole programme of reform was designed 'to shift the focus of services from dealing with the consequences of difficulties in children's lives to preventing things from going wrong in the first place' (DfES 2004b: 2). This transformation is to be effected by local authorities working in partnership with their communities and supported by the government through a programme of change management which includes Local Area Agreements negotiated between central and local government in order to 'achieve a balance between national and local priorities' (DfES 2004b: 22).

A policy 'umbrella' such as Every Child Matters will inevitably have something to say about the workforce which has to implement it, especially when, as this one does, it attempts to integrate a range of services which have arisen in very different circumstances and to meet different needs. Are the existing workforces trained and qualified in the skills and knowledge which they need to do this different task? Do they understand how to work effectively with the other professions they are expected to work alongside? Is there a direct relationship between training and education processes and the desired outcomes for children? Is there a core of 'professional' competence (i.e. knowledge twinned with skills) which an early years worker needs, and at what level should that be pitched?

Workforce reform has been an important element in the government's approach to services for young children since 1997. *Next Steps* announced a consultation document on a pay and workforce strategy which would begin to rationalise the existing, complicated situation of the children's workforce as a whole (DfES 2004a). The 'pay' element of the strategy was later dropped, although it was still being referred to in the 10 Years Strategy document published in December 2004. The document did, however, place a great deal of emphasis on the early years workforce as being key to the Every Child Matters reforms and as being particularly in need of change.

Interestingly, a very similar debate is taking place in the United States where the policy 'umbrella' of the *Good Start, Grow Smart* initiative in 2002 has instituted just such a review:

> *There is increased public attention to the professional development of the early childhood workforce given the renewed policy focus on the early childhood years as*

laying the groundwork for school readiness and the specific emphasis in the Good Start, Grow Smart initiative on professional development of the early childhood workforce as a factor that can contribute to early learning and school readiness.

(Zaslow and Martinez-Beck 2006: 9)

The 10 Year Childcare Strategy and its underpinning legislation, The Childcare Act 2006, is the key early years vehicle for taking forward Every Child Matters. It was published in December 2004 and its full title, *Choice for Parents: the Best Start for Children, a Ten Year Strategy for Childcare* (HM Treasury et al. 2004) clearly indicates the focus of the strategy which is on moving children out of poverty via the workforce participation of their parents. Having said this, the strategy also places an emphasis on the needs of vulnerable children, whether or not their parents are in the workforce, and on the needs of children from groups who have traditionally not fully benefited from early years services, such as disabled children and children from black and other minority ethnic groups. In essence, the 10 year childcare strategy is designed to rationalise, redesign and re-badge the existing early years initiatives so that they fit within the Every Child Matters framework.

The Childcare Act 2006 underpins the Strategy by giving certain duties to local authorities, including a duty to make sure that there is 'sufficient' childcare for children up to the September after they are 14 (18 for disabled children) which will be fulfilled if the local childcare market allows parents to make a choice about working. However, there is an emphasis on the needs of parents for whom the market is seen not to have provided for in the past: lower-income families and families with disabled children. The government stressed that making these responsibilities statutory would enshrine them within local authority performance assessment systems and ensure that they were taken seriously (McAuliffe, Linsey and Fowler 2006).

The Strategy does not just deal with expansion of places, but also with quality, and here there is to be a three-pronged approach. There will be the new single-quality framework for all children from birth: the Early Years Foundation Stage (DfES 2007), which will guide the approaches and activities within settings; the independent registration and inspection framework of Ofsted (Ofsted 2007); and, most importantly for this discussion, workforce reform designed to provide practitioners who are better trained and qualified to support young children and their families in reaching the desired outcomes of the policy.

A central aspect of the Strategy is that all full-day care settings will be 'professionally' led, i.e. by a graduate professional (DfES 2005) and this has been contentious for an early years workforce which, as we have seen above, is slowly being forged out of a very diverse range of practitioners with varied training, qualifications, service histories and career pathways. Some have argued, for example, that we need to maintain a non-graduate route into the profession for less academic workers who have strong skills in the care and education of young children and, moreover, that not all staff want to go on to obtain a degree. Others feel very strongly that higher education should be required for anyone who is charged with the learning of young children because this is such an important phase of education that requirements for it should be as high, if not higher, than for teachers of other phases.

It is the specific policy focus on the professionalisation of this workforce which we will turn to now.

*With the emphasis firmly on professionalism in the workforce, it's good to see that
opportunities for training are growing.*

(Nursery World, Summer 2007: 3)

Nursery World's annual training supplement, 'Training Today', captures the extent to
which policy initiatives in the early years have transformed training and
qualifications since the National Council for Vocational Qualifications (NCVQ) was
set up in 1986 to develop a national system of vocational awards for both young people and adults. The supplement details the range of opportunities now available for
people working in early years and integrated childcare settings, from new school-
based awards, to full-time diploma and degree courses, sector endorsed foundation
degrees and accredited units to support the delivery of the Early Years Foundation
Stage.

However, although the supplement tracks recent developments in the funding
and availability of training and qualifications, it masks some crucial issues in the
long-standing debate about what professionalism in the early years workforce really
means, as debated in this book. Nor does it convey the scale of the task facing governments if the goal of 'creating a world class workforce' for the early years is to be
realised in our lifetime (HM Treasury et al. 2004).

Although early years services lacked significant national financial support or policy direction before 1996, the importance of workforce development opportunities
for practitioners had not been completely ignored. In 1990, the Rumbold
Committee had noted:

*We welcome the work of NCVQ towards establishing agreed standards for childcare
workers, including those in education settings. We believe that, given adequate resourcing,
it could bring about significant rationalization of patterns of training. It should also
improve the status of early years workers through recognition of the complex range and
high level of the skills involved and by opening up prospects for further training.*

(DES 1990: 24)

But not everybody agreed that a 'complex range and high level of . . . skills' were
involved in caring for children and, at the beginning of the 1990s, workforce development barely figured as a priority on any political agenda. As Hevey and Curtis
pointed out:

*One is forced to conclude that this lack of concern over training and qualifications for
what are in reality highly responsible roles is underpinned by something more
fundamental than free market philosophy. Rather it reflects confused and outmoded
public attitudes that commonly regard the care of young children as an extension of the
mothering role and assume it all comes naturally to women. Such attitudes in turn
reinforce the low status of early years work, helping to keep pay low and turnover high.*

(Hevey and Curtis 1996: 213)

Although the 1989 Children Act had set out to improve quality in early years and
childcare settings, its new minimum standards for training and qualifications were

very low. At the time, the main providers of childcare for all age-groups were registered childminders, where 'the threshold of entry' did not include any mandatory training. However, notwithstanding the lack of national interest, the Early Childhood Unit at the National Children's Bureau developed the highly influential concept of a 'climbing frame' of childcare qualifications, drawing on work that had taken place in 1991 as part of a project to develop national occupational standards for work with young children and their families (Hevey and Curtis 1996).

As a result of this work, National Vocational Qualifications (NVQs) in Childcare and Education at Levels 2 and 3 were launched in 1992. However, three years later, only 856 candidates had achieved Level 2; and 243 Level 3 (Hevey and Curtis 1996). Fifteen years on, over 83,000 NVQ certificates in Early Years and Childcare had been awarded (Local Government Analysis and Research 2007), together with tens of thousands of other related awards and qualifications.

This exponential growth in the availability and uptake of early years qualifications was the result of a number of factors, including demographic changes; the growing UK evidence base, which for the first time firmly linked improved outcomes for children to the higher qualification levels of people who work with them; and effective lobbying by the early years sector. Most important, however, was the incremental realisation by government that the wide spectrum of its policy goals could only be achieved through investment in raising the qualifications of the early years workforce.

The impact of demography

The National Childcare Strategy (DfEE 1998) was presented as a child-centred, educational initiative, to address the failure of the Conservative Government to implement its plans for universal nursery education. However, the strategy also reflected the changing needs of working families and the changing involvement of women with children under 5 in the workplace. In the early 1970s, less that a third of mothers with children under 5 were in paid work. By the late 1990s, this had doubled to nearly 60 per cent (Labour Market Trends 2002).

Sustained recruitment to the workforce to cater for working families was therefore a priority and it was estimated that 90,000 new recruits would be needed to deliver the strategy. But the economic changes of the 1980s, together with women's own rising educational achievements and improvements in service-sector job opportunities meant that recruitment to a career with traditionally low pay, poor training opportunities and no progression routes had very limited appeal (Cameron 2004). As a result, government became much more open to the proposition that more emphasis should be placed on developing the workforce and that new career routes should be opened up to recruit the workforce that was needed to achieve their policy goals.

Up to this date, there had been no industry training organisation for Early Years. With backing from the Department for Education and Employment, in November 1998, the first UK-wide Early Years National Training Organisation was launched to drive through these early steps to developing the workforce. These included new nationally accredited awards to meet the specific needs of parts of the sector, the development of Level 4 S/NVQs and the introduction of sector-endorsed early years foundation degrees.

The creation of the NTO was an important step because, although there had been a growing emphasis on 'quality' as a key aspiration of the government's national childcare strategy, there was very little national data about training and qualification levels to act as a lever for change. One of the NTO's first tasks was to deliver the first England-wide Children's Workforce Survey in 1998, which revealed the low levels of qualifications and training opportunities throughout the sector. However, when the national standards for childminding and day care were revised to coincide with the transfer of regulation from local authorities to Ofsted in September 2001, training and qualifications were still set at minimum levels.

This failure to use regulation as a lever to raise standards and professionalise the workforce characterised the government's approach to workforce reform in the early years for the whole of the last decade, in marked contrast to occupational models in countries like New Zealand and Denmark. Both these countries employ strategies which combine strong regulatory frameworks with public funding of *supply*, with New Zealand (in 2002) opting for a single three-year early years qualification for those working with children aged 0 to 6; and Denmark promoting a unified struc-ture for all care professions (the pedagogue) via a single full-time three-and-a-half-year degree level course, with regulation which requires that all day care facilities have fully qualified managers and deputies.

The NTO was closed down in March 2002 as part of the government's strategy to develop a network of strategic Sector Skills Councils (SSCs). This coincided with a period of intense change linked to the 2002 Comprehensive Spending Review. The various strands of the national childcare strategy were gradually being drawn together into a programme of Children's Centres, initially focused on the most dis-advantaged areas. At the same time, evidence from the Effective Provision of Pre-school Education (EPPE) project was beginning to feed through, including the finding that:

'Settings which have staff with higher qualifications, especially with good proportion of trained teachers on the staff, show higher quality and their children make more progress' (Sylva et al. 2004: 56)

However, the vacuum which had been created through the loss of the Early Years NTO meant that progress towards developing a coherent occupational model to address the fragmentation in the sector stalled. When progress resumed, it was in the context of a much broader strategy developed in response to Lord Lamming's report into the death of Victoria Climbié. From this point, developing professionalism in the early years became part of the much wider agenda of workforce reform for the *whole* of the children's workforce (DfES 2003).

Reforming the Children's Workforce

Building on ideas outlined in the Green Paper (DfES 2003) and the subsequent Ten Year Childcare Strategy (HM Treasury et al. 2004), in April 2005 the government consulted on a specific Children's Workforce Strategy to improve the skills of the workforce. At the same time, the Children's Workforce Development Council (CWDC) for England was set up to drive through the reforms. However, although the occupational groups represented by the CWDC (its 'footprint') includes all those practitioners formerly represented by the Early Years NTO, significant parts of the early years and children's workforce – teachers, teaching assistants, and play workers – were included in the footprint of other Sector Skills Councils (SSCs). To overcome these structural problems, government also set up a Children's Workforce Network (CWN) as a forum for joint working between the various sector skills councils.

The government's response to the consultation on the Children's Workforce Strategy was finally published in February 2006 (DfES 2006a). It confirmed their goal to have an 'integrated qualifications framework' in place by 2010 which would 'help with recruitment, retention and remodelling the workforce by supporting improved career pathways across [the sector] and better progression opportunities' (DfES 2006a: 22). However, it rejected the idea of a generic graduate worker for the children's workforce, based on the pedagogic approach (Boddy et al. 2005). Instead, it prioritised 'establishing a more professional workforce in the early years' in order to raise the status of working with pre-school children. Specifically, it charged the CWDC to develop a new Early Years Professional (EYP) role with graduate status for those leading practice in children's centres and full-day care settings; and allocated £250m over two years to a Transformation Fund to finance the EYP programme and to improve the qualification levels of the workforce as a whole. Arguably, an unintended consequence of these developments has been to marginalise both the long-established professional groups like nursery nurses and more recent roles and training pathways, such as Higher Level Teaching Assistants (HLTAs) and Senior Practitioners.

During 2006, the new EYP Status and training pathways were defined and developed and the first awards were made in early 2007. At the same time, work on developing an Integrated Qualifications Framework (IQF) forged ahead, based on a unit and credit framework, the Qualifications and Credit Framework (QCF), devised by the Qualifications and Curriculum Authority (QCA) in partnership with the regulatory authorities for Wales and Northern Ireland. The aim of this aspect of reform is to develop a simple and effective structure that allows for the accumulation and transfer of credit achievement over time, to meet the needs of individual learners and employers.

In early 2007, the CWDC also issued advice to government about the strategies and targets needed to raise the qualification levels in the early years workforce as a whole. It recommended that the early years career pathway should be built on Level 6 (the Early Years Professional) and Level 3; that the minimum qualification for the early years workforce should be Level 3; and that at least 70 per cent of the workforce should hold a relevant Level 3 qualification by 2010. It also recommended that the Transformation Fund should continue, and that regulation on workforce standards should be more robust. The government is due to respond to these recommendations in early 2008 in a new Children's Workforce Strategy Action Plan.

SUMMARY

Although considerable progress has been made since the Workforce Strategy response was published in 2006, the most recent Workforce Survey showed the scale of the task ahead. Only 4 per cent of early years practitioners not in schools held a qualification at Level 4 or above; and less than 60 per cent held a Level 3 qualification (DfES 2006b). Pay across the sector remains low and, although the take-up of the Early Years Professional route has proved popular (with the 1000th candidate awarded the new status in October 2007), there are concerns about how Early Years Professionals in Children's Centres will be able to achieve parity of pay and conditions with qualified teachers in schools. The early versions of the Every Child Matters workforce reform agenda talked of a strategy to:

> 'improve the skills and effectiveness of the children's workforce developed in partnership with local employers and staff. . .with the aim of moving towards a framework that fairly rewards skills and responsibilities'.

> (DfES 2003:12)

However, as noted above, references to pay and rewards are absent in later documents, and it appears that government is moving away from a commitment to review pay, conditions and rewards, at least in the short term.

Recent government changes have created two new departments to focus on improving outcomes for children, the Department for Children, Schools and Families (DCSF) and the Department for Innovation, Universities and Skills (DIUS); and from April 2008, the Children's Workforce Development Council (CWDC) will become an Executive Non-Departmental Public Body (ENDPB). Working with local authorities and its stakeholders in the statutory, private and voluntary sector, it is to these bodies that the sector will now look for delivering the next steps in professionalising the early years workforce.

Questions/points for discussion/reflection

1. What do you think is the role of graduates in the early years workforce? Do you think it should be an all graduate profession? Or should there be 'graduate *leadership*' in every setting?
2. Do you think there is a framework in the early years sector which allows skills and responsibilities to be fairly rewarded? If not, what would be needed to put one in place?
3. Discuss the pros and cons of strengthening the regulatory framework for early years practitioners (i.e. the requirements for qualifications related to job roles, sometimes known as 'license to practice').

REFERENCES

Boddy, J., Cameron, C., Moss, P., Mooney, A., Petrie, P. and Statham, J. (2005) *Introducing Pedagogy into the Children's Workforce: Children's Workforce Strategy: A Response to the Consultation Document.* London: TCRU

Cameron, C. (2004) *Building an Integrated Workforce for a Long-Term Vision of Universal Early Education and Care.* London: Daycare Trust

Department for Education and Employment (1998) *Meeting the Childcare Challenge: A Framework and Consultation Document.* London: HMSO

Department of Education and Science (1990) *Starting with Quality: Report of the Committee of Inquiry into the Educational Experiences Offered to Three-and-Four-Year-Olds* (the Rumbold report). London: HMSO

Department for Education and Skills (2003) *Every Child Matters – Summary.* London: DfES

Department for Education and Skills (2004a) *Every Child Matters: Next Steps.* London: DfES
(www.everychildmatters.gov.uk – accessed 10/10/2005)

Department for Education and Skills (2004b) *Every Child Matters: Change for Children.* London: DfES
(www.everychildmatters.gov.uk – accessed 10/10/2005)

Department for Education and Skills (2005) *Children's Workforce Strategy, Consultation Paper.* London: DfES

Department for Education and Skills (2006a) *Children's Workforce Strategy: Building a World-Class Workforce for Children, Young People and Families.* London: DfES

Department for Education and Skills (2006b) *The 2005 Childcare and Early Years Providers Surveys Brief N: RB760–764.* London: DfES

Department for Education and Skills (2007) *The Early Years Foundation Stage: Setting the Standards for Learning, Development and Care for Children from Birth to Five.* London: HMSO

Hevey, D. and Curtis, A. (1996) 'Training to work in the early years'. In G. Pugh (ed.), *Contemporary Issues in the Early Years* (2nd edition). London: Paul Chapman

HM Treasury (2003) *Every Child Matters* (Cm 5860). London: TSO

HM Treasury, DfES, DWP, DTI (2004) *Choice for Parents: The Best Start for Children* (Ten Year Strategy for Childcare). London: HMT, DfES, DWP and DTI

Jamieson, A. and Owen, S. (2000) *Ambition for Change: Partnerships, Children and Work.* London: National Children's Bureau

Labour Market Trends (2002) *Labour Market and Family Status of Women; United Kingdom, Autumn, 2001.* London: ONS

Local Government Analysis and Research (2007) *Quarterly Monitoring of Care Sector NVQs (England) Report for Second Quarter 2006.* London: LGA

McAuliffe, A., Linsey, A., and Fowler, J. (2006) *Childcare Act 2006: the Essential Guide.* London: National Children's Bureau

Nursery World (2007) 'Training today' (Summer 2007)

Ofsted (2007) *Framework For the Regulation of Childminding and Day Care.* London: Ofsted

Randall, V. and Fisher, K. (2001) 'Child day care provision: explaining local variation', *Children and Society, 15(3),* 170–80

Sylva, K., Melhuish, E., Sammons, P., Siraj-Blatchford, I., and Taggart, B. (2004) *The Effective Provision of Pre-School Education (EPPE) Project: Final report.* London: Institute of Education

Zaslow, M. and Martinez-Beck, I. (2006) *Critical Issues in Early Childhood Professional Development.* Baltimore: Paul Brookes Publishing

Further reading

www.skillsforcareanddevelopment.org.uk

www.cwdcouncil.org.uk (Children's Workforce Development Council – England)

www.childrensworkforce.org.uk (Children's Workforce Network)

www.skillsactive.com (Skills Active; the Sector Skills Council for Active Leisure and Learning, including Playwork)

www.sssc.uk.com (Scottish Social Services Council)

www.wales.org.uk (Care Council for Wales)

www.niscc.info (Northern Ireland Social Care Council)

2 DEVELOPING NEW PROFESSIONAL ROLES IN THE EARLY YEARS

Linda Miller

INTRODUCTION

As we have seen in Chapter 1, the government in England has committed to the reform of the children's workforce through 'a transformational reform agenda designed to improve life chances for all and reduce inequalities in our society' (DfES 2006: 2) to be enabled by 'Transformation' funding. This agenda acknowledges that increasing the skills and competence of the workforce is critical to its success and one outcome has been the development of a new Early Years Professional (EYP) role. The EYP role is intended to achieve graduate leadership across early years services in the private, voluntary and independent (PVI) sector which, as part of the overall process of workforce reform, will contribute to a new professional identity for the early years workforce. This chapter considers the implications of this role for the professional development of early years practitioners and explores the relationship between this role and the existing role of Senior Practitioner (DfES 2001). For both roles consultation and implementation have been carried out within relatively short and challenging timescales with little time for reflection. The chapter provides a critical review of the policy developments leading to the creation of these two roles and considers contrasting perspectives on the notion of 'professionalism'.

THE EARLY YEARS WORKFORCE: TRAINING AND QUALIFICATIONS

In England (and the whole of the UK) the range and variety of qualifications and the type and level of training required for those working with young children in care and education settings is confusing, ranging from unqualified to graduate and post-graduate. The early years workforce is under qualified, poorly paid and predominantly female; 40 per cent of the workforce are not qualified to Level 2 (a basic level of training) and just 12 per cent are qualified to Level 4 or above (related to managerial level) (DfES 2005a). Graduate leadership in 'childcare provision' ranges from childminders (2 per cent) to 13 per cent in full-day care and out-of-school provision (*The Providers Survey*, 2005, cited in DCSF 2007). We know from research studies such as *The Effective Provision of Pre-School Education (EPPE) Project* that the quality of provision in early years settings is linked to the quality of staff that work in them (Sylva et al. 2003). Reforming the workforce through a programme of training and qualifications is therefore seen by government as crucial in raising the quality of services for children and parents.

As part of this reform process, a Common Core of skills, knowledge and competence has been developed for all those who work with children, young people and families, to be taken account of in developing training and qualifications (DfES 2005b). An Integrated Qualifications Framework (IQF) for the children's workforce is under development for 2010, to promote skills acquisition and to enable career progression and work across professional boundaries. The framework will embrace four inclusion principles: qualifications will be 'fit for purpose; meet regulatory requirements where appropriate; be shared across the workforce; and will reflect the common core' (http://www.cwdcouncil.org.uk/projects/integratedqualificationsframe work.htm).

This reform agenda is intended to enable workers at all levels to increasingly work in multidisciplinary and multi-agency contexts, such as Children's Centres. However, critics of this agenda, whilst supporting a common framework of training and qualifications, also believe that early years practitioners who wish to improve their professional status will be increasingly bound by an environment regulated by central government, both in terms of qualifications and in the regulation of provision (see Chapter 11). This then raises questions about professional autonomy and what 'being a professional' means within this new agenda (Osgood 2006).

NEW PROFESSIONAL ROLES

The Senior Practitioner role

Prior to the workforce agenda outlined above and the development of the EYP role, in 2001 a Senior Practitioner status was created and defined on the Sure Start website at that time as someone who:

- understands and demonstrates high quality practice;
- integrates this with appropriate research and theoretical knowledge;
- is able to apply this to enhance her/his own personal, professional practice and the professional development of others;
- contributes to improvement and innovation within a setting; and
- can lead by example in a variety of settings.

This role was developed for practitioners working directly with young children aged birth to 8 and was to be achieved though an Early Years Sector-Endorsed Foundation Degree (EYSEFD), a vocational qualification designed to integrate academic study with work-based learning, and was endorsed by employer representatives and key stakeholders (DfES 2001). It was launched with a generous support package. This foundation degree provided a new level of professional practice and offered a progression route to graduate status or Qualified Teacher Status through employment-based and part-time routes. Students are required to meet a set of core learning outcomes based on National Occupational Standards for the sector, and to provide evidence of their work-based learning and practice. Guidance on content and delivery for providers is set out in a *Statement of Requirement* (DfES 2001) as well as knowledge and understanding and professional practice requirements. Providers of courses are allowed considerable freedom to interpret these requirements, providing they meet the conditions for sector-endorsement; reflective practice is seen as a key focus by many providers (Cable et al. 2007; O' Keefe and Tait 2004). According to Foundation Degree Forward, Early Years Foundation Degrees represent the largest number of all Foundation Degrees and by 2007 totalled over 360 (http://www.fdf.ac.uk/courses/index.php).

Since 2003 the National Centre for Social Research has undertaken a number of surveys of EYSEFDs in England. In 2007 Snape et al. reported on a sample of 566 students across 80 Institutions. A summary of some key findings is that:

- overall students have been highly satisfied with the experience and feel that they have benefited in terms of their work and increased knowledge and understanding;
- to gain increased pay, students have generally had to move to new employment;
- the most popular route through the award was the Foundation Stage route, rather than Birth to Three, Teaching Assistants or the Playwork route and students mainly wished to work in Key Stage 1 in primary schools or in reception classes;
- a third of those completing the award had already taken, or were currently enrolled on, another related course, suggesting they see the Foundation Degree as a stepping stone to further qualifications.

In England the Senior Practitioner role was largely welcomed as a sign of professional recognition. However, five years later many issues remain unresolved, including lack of pay and lack of recognition for the role in the workplace, and more recently the relationship of this role to the EYP role. Government recognises that Senior Practitioner status is now problematic:

However, having taken the course, many graduates have now reached Level 4 (Level 5 under the new National Qualifications Framework) only to find no improvement in pay and conditions because there is no requirement on providers to employ those qualified to above Level 3 but below qualified teacher status (QTS) . . ..We recognise the need to address this issue. (DfES 2005a:32)

Practitioners undertaking Foundation Degrees have expressed similar concerns (O' Keefe and Tait 2004).

Critics of this approach to training and qualifying the workforce (Dahlberg and Moss, 2005), although not discussing Foundation Degrees in particular, argue that underlying this model is a desire for consistency wherever training is delivered. This is reflected in a quote from the *Statement of Requirement* whose stated aim is to set out, 'exactly what is required, by employers, for recognition as a Senior Practitioner' (DfES 2001: 1). The *Statement of Requirement* could therefore be seen to fit Moss's (2003) description of a 'technicist' model of learning (see also Chapter 11).

Early Years Sector-Endorsed Foundation Degrees, whilst benefiting many early years practitioners by developing their skills and knowledge and in opening up routes to Higher Education and leading to promotion for some, are a strategy which has suffered from hasty development and implementation in order to meet government policy initiatives and spending targets. In 2007/8 Early Years Sector-Endorsed Foundation Degrees are under review and are most likely to become a progression route to EYP Status (personal communication with Department for Children, Schools and Families (DCSF) and Children's Workforce Development Council (CWDC) 8/6/2007). However, this leaves many Foundation Degree graduates and their employers in a state of uncertainty about the value and status of the Senior Practitioner role. There is an urgent need to clarify the relationship of this role to Early Years Professional Status as increasing numbers of practitioners complete early years foundation degrees.

The Early Years Professional role

The government's consultation on the future of the children's workforce highlighted the need for a new lead graduate professional role (DfES 2005a). In the United Kingdom teachers have typically been the lead professional in nursery schools and classes in the maintained sector, working mainly with children aged 3 to 5, despite the fact that many are not trained to work with the youngest children and early years teacher education courses have not covered the birth to 3 age range (see Chapter 4). Approximately 20,000 settings in the private and voluntary sector do not typically employ a teacher. *The Effective Provision of Pre-School Education* (EPPE) project (Sylva et al. 2003) recommended there should be a good proportion of trained teachers, or equivalent, leading in early years settings in order to achieve good outcomes. However, new research is needed to reflect new graduate leadership roles such as the EYP role and to establish what an 'equivalent role' to a qualified teacher means.

The workforce consultation document referred to above discussed two models of professional leadership, the European pedagogue and the 'new teacher' model emerging from New Zealand (see Chapter 13) and Spain. The pedagogue role, in Denmark for example, involves a holistic approach to working with children up to age 10 and beyond, while the new teacher role involves working directly with children under 5 (OECD 2006; Moss 2003). The government response to the workforce consultation was to adopt a new role 'Early Years Professional' which is more akin to the 'new teacher' than the pedagogue model, and it is proposed will have equivalence to Qualified Teacher Status. Government intends that there will be an Early Years Professional in all children's centres by 2010, and in every full-day care setting by 2015.

The Early Years Professional is intended to be a change agent who will raise standards in early years settings, in particular to lead practice in the Early Years Foundation Stage (EYFS) and support and mentor other practitioners. They are required to be graduates and to demonstrate that they can meet a set of national standards contained in a centrally derived prospectus covering the areas: knowledge and understanding; effective practice; relationships with children; communicating and working in partnership with families and carers; teamwork and collaboration and professional development. This is achieved through a choice of four pathways which are centrally funded by CWDC (CWDC 2006). For one of these pathways the candidate's degree can be unrelated to early childhood and minimal prior experience of working with young children is required. This is causing resentment amongst experienced practitioners who do not have this opportunity and who may be working in settings in which EYPs are gaining experience as part of their training (Hevey 2007).

The introduction of the EYP role raises many unresolved issues. For example, in the Statutory Framework document for the Early Years Foundation Stage (DfES 2007, Appendix 2: 50) the legal staffing requirements equate those with EYPS alongside qualified teachers (or another suitable Level 6 qualification) in terms of levels of responsibility and adult/child ratios, but there is no guidance on commensurate levels of pay to ensure parity with qualified teachers for those EYPs undertaking the same level of responsibility and leadership. Qualified teachers will lead on the EYFS in maintained settings, but without birth to 3 training, while EYPs will be restricted to the private and voluntary sector, thus leading to their being, according to Hevey (2007), ghettoised in low pay areas. This will maintain the current lack of parity in pay and conditions, which are set out and agreed for teachers but are to be left to market forces for EYPs. The Teacher Development Agency (TDA) and CWDC will need to work closely together on these issues.

Hevey (2007) has outlined other issues which she believes may prove to be a barrier to the success of the EYP programme; these include: the long-term affordability of EYPs once the initial funding is no longer available; disappointing recruitment to EYP training, linked to an under-qualified workforce that is unable to meet the graduate entry requirements (an issue currently being explored by CWDC). However, Goodliff (2007) notes that candidates report an increase in self-esteem on achieving EYPS, despite anxieties about the status and long-term future of the role.

Early Years Professional Status is an important initiative and crucial to the effective implementation of the Early Years Foundation Stage across the private and voluntary sector, the raising of standards and the establishment of a new multi-professional role. However, to ensure the success of this role increased professional recognition will be required, preferably through a system of professional registration, and linked to a pay and conditions framework. It will also be essential to determine the most enabling pathways to reaching this status to achieve the best outcomes for children and families.

DEVELOPING EARLY YEARS PROFESSIONALS WITHIN REGULATORY FRAMEWORKS

The development of a more professional workforce, through the reform process described above, has been generally welcomed by those who have been working to raise the status of early years practitioners and help them to achieve a sense of professional identity. However, critics of this agenda, such as Moss (2006) (see also Chapter 11) challenge the view in England that what matters is 'what works' and what can be measured. Moss is sceptical that teaching and learning can be reduced to measurable technical outcomes through frameworks which include standards and competencies. It can be argued that the training and assessment routes for the Senior Practitioner and Early Years Professional roles reflect this 'technician' model of training, in that they are based on achieving externally prescribed standards and outcomes. Dahlberg and Moss (2005) believe this 'technologising' of policy and practice becomes a prime means of governing the early years workforce, prescribing norms to which practitioners must conform. Osgood (2006: 7) argues that regulatory frameworks can lead practitioners to 'conform to dominant constructions of professionalism' and that the 'regulatory gaze' stemming from such an agenda threatens their empowerment. She has concerns that the 'professionalism agenda' in England, rather than leading to a strengthened position for early years practitioners and increased respect for their work, could be used as a means of external control and regulation and so inhibit their professional autonomy.

Oberheumer (2005) has explored alternative ways of conceptualising professionalism in the face of increased control and regulation through the concept of 'democratic professionalism'. This involves four levels of activity: interacting with children; centre management and leadership; partnership with parents; and professional knowledge base. Osgood (2006) also argues for an alternative construction of professionalism, which acknowledges the complexity of work that early years practitioners do, to be achieved through education and training that includes going beyond technical competence and includes opportunities for critical reflection and consciousness raising.

Reflection on practice is recognised as an important component in developing professional and pedagogical knowledge and in understanding practice (see Chapter 8). According to Oberheumer (2005) informed professional action requires a willingness to reflect on one's own taken-for-granted beliefs and an understanding that knowledge is contestable. The DfES (2001: 16) *Statement of Requirement* recognised the need to, 'develop students as reflective practitioners' and reflection on practice has been seen as central by foundation degree providers in course development (O'Keefe and Tait 2004). In a study of students undertaking an Early Years Foundation Degree through distance learning, Cable et al. (2007) argue that students and training providers do not have to see themselves as passive recipients of the workforce reform process, delivering pre-specified curricula, but as agents who have the power to enable early years practitioners to harness their own agency and thus develop a sense of professional identity.

AN ALTERNATIVE PERSPECTIVE ON DEVELOPING PROFESSIONALISM

While acknowledging the constraints imposed by regulatory frameworks and externally imposed standards, it is possible to consider an alternative perspective. The workforce agenda has brought to fruition many of the developments that those working in this field have striven for (Abbott and Pugh 1998) and is opening up new routes to training and professionalism for a diverse and under-qualified workforce. It is possible for training providers to challenge the 'regulatory gaze' (Osgood 2006) and to interpret regulatory frameworks in creative ways. As Osgood (2006) notes, practitioners (*and providers*) (my italics), need not be passive recipients of the reform process, but can be active in rising to the challenge by negotiating where they are 'positioned and defined' and thus take on the role of autonomous professionals.

Westcott (2004) argues that standards contribute to professional identity. Whilst acknowledging that the definition of 'profession' is ambiguous, she proposes that it might be applied to a 'community of practice' that:

- exhibits command of a specialist body of knowledge;
- sets standards for practitioners;
- regulates its own standards of practice.

She argues that standards are an important aspect of professionalism in that they assure a common baseline of practice and a common set of standards that can underpin professional registration, and which can then be monitored and regulated (although this formal regulation and registration of the early years workforce has yet to happen in England). Fenech and Sumsion (2007) interviewed university qualified early childhood teachers in Australia about how regulatory requirements impacted on their professional practice. Responses were mixed, but some of these teachers offered support for regulation of their practice. For example, Sarah said, 'If something goes wrong, we're protected in a way. If we're following standards and regulations then we're protected'. She went on to say, 'It can be hard to find good staff to put in long day care centres. So I think we definitely need standards these people have to work by' (117). This perspective views regulation as enabling as well as restricting.

The view that standards and regulation can be an enabling process offers possibilities in relation to the Senior Practitioner and Early Years Professional roles. The achievement of the standards that define these roles and the demonstration of a specialist body of knowledge and skills can contribute to a sense of professional identity. Wenger (1998) proposes that an individual's sense of *professional* (my italics) identity within a particular community of practice is influenced by engaging in certain experiences or practices. It is possible, therefore, to make the case that such experiences and practices might be encompassed in a set of professional standards.

The case study of Julie below offers support for the view that professionalism can be developed within a highly regulated environment, through a mix of work-based experience and relevant qualifications that enable reflection on practice.

Julie
Julie is aged 26 and has worked in the field of early years for seven years. She works as nursery manager in a privately owned day nursery from 10.00 am to 6.00 pm, where she undertakes extensive office-based management duties alongside some 'hands on' work with the children. The nursery has 154 children on role and there are 43 members of staff, including volunteers, whom Julie is responsible for managing. Full-day care is offered alongside part-time 'education' for 3 to 5-year-olds. Julie has a National Vocational Qualification (NVQ Level 3) and is currently undertaking a Foundation Degree in Early Years at the Open University. She aims to 'top up' her degree to a full honours degree and possibly achieve Early Years Professional Status. As part of a research project on professionalism Julie was filmed for a 'typical day' and subsequently interviewed (Miller et al. 2007).

Data were analysed to seek out emerging themes and dispositions. Themes included:

- the diversity, complexity, responsibilities and multiple demands of the role; leadership, management and organisational skills (including staff training and curriculum leadership);

- acting as a conduit for information;
- knowledge of the setting, children and families;
- professional knowledge base (for example, child development, curriculum); providing support and reassurance;
- being accountable for the implementation of policy and procedures;
- availability, accessibility and visibility (in relation to staff, parents and children) and trust.

Dispositions included *sensitivity, empathy, awareness and respect for others*; these are illustrated in the vignette below which draws on field note data. *Commitment* to the field of early years was also apparent in Julie's enthusiasm for her work and her commitment to the nursery philosophy, which is to create a 'home from home' environment where children are grouped with siblings. Finally, Julie's *confidence* in carrying out her role to the best of her ability was also noted.

Meeting with the pre-school teacher

Julie met with the pre-school teacher Helen and spent some time discussing plans for the implementation of the new Early Years Foundation Stage curriculum documents which had just been received (and which she introduced to other staff members throughout the day).

Julie seems to act as a *conduit* for information about important events and policy documents for the nursery staff. She showed considerable *sensitivity* and *maturity* in her conversation with Helen, who is a qualified teacher and in a school setting would have a considerably higher 'status' than someone with Julie's qualifications. She is also older and more experienced, as Julie acknowledges in the interview below. Julie showed respect for what Helen brings to her role.

> *Acting professionally could range from how I am within meetings. For example, I had a meeting with the pre-school teacher this morning and it may have been that we disagreed on something and I could have said to her 'actually, I'm not going to take your opinion into account and what I say goes', but I don't see that as a very professional approach. I see that, the way this nursery runs in particular, everyone should be able to be included and have their say.*

And in discussing other staff members:

> *I need to recognise that they are professionals too and that some of them have qualifications far above what I have and they have different experiences to me. We have to draw on that and use it to our advantage.*

I asked Julie if she saw herself as a professional:

> *Yes I do. I think that my role, especially because I am the manager here, and because I'm seen as a sort of head figure within this nursery, I do see myself as a professional. I think other people see me as a professional. I think that, in the nursery set up, what makes me a professional is the fact that I come in to do my job to the best of my abilities and I go home every day knowing that I've put 110 per cent into that day and I've done as much as I can do. I think that the*

responses I get from other people make me feel that they have trust in me and they've got confidence in me.

At the end of the day's filming and interview I was struck by the diversity, complexity and multiple demands of Julie's role and the energy that her relentless schedule must require. I had the sense of Julie being at the centre of all that was happening. She appeared to have excellent organisational skills and a detailed knowledge of what was happening and when. She had a clear sense of herself as a professional which seemed to stem from both her *experience* and the *knowledge* she was gaining from her studies. For example Julie said in the interview that both parents and staff:

are coming to you to look for answers and they want to make sure that you've got the answers and that helps them put their trust in you.

SUMMARY

Defining professionalism in the early years workforce is the subject of much debate in England and elsewhere (Oberheumer 2005). In this chapter I have argued that the diverse roles and responsibilities of early years practitioners, the variety of settings they work in, and the lack of a professional registration body and formal pay structures, make it difficult to agree what constitutes an early years professional in this context. This is particularly so when we have a centrally defined role that carries the title of Early Years Professional. This raises the question of whether those who do not have this title are not professionals. We know this is not the case as teachers are clearly regarded as such. As the OECD (2006) report notes, the opportunity is present in England to rethink workforce roles and to identify a lead Early Years Professional who would work alongside others in multidisciplinary teams. However, the key issues around which this initiative revolves – who that lead professional will be, the supply of qualified people to fill the role, and pay and incentives commensurate with such a role – remain a challenge to be resolved.

Questions/points for discussion/reflection

1 What does it mean to act as a professional in your work context?
2 Do you think you are viewed as a professional by external agencies that you come into contact with, including parents? If not, why not?
3 In what ways does having a regulatory framework that requires you to meet standards enable or inhibit your professional practice?

REFERENCES

Abbott, L. and Pugh, G. (eds) (1998) *Training to Work in the Early Years: Developing the Climbing Frame.* Buckingham: Open University Press

Cable, C., Goodliff, G. and Miller, L. (2007) 'Developing reflective early years practitioners within a regulatory framework', *Malaysian Journal of Distance Education, (9)2*, 1–19

Children's Workforce Development Council (CWDC) (2006) *Early Year Professional Prospectus.* Leeds: CWDC

Dahlberg, G. and Moss, P. (2005) *Ethics and Politics in Early Childhood Education.* London and New York: Routledge Falmer

Department for Children, Schools and Families (DCSF) (2007) 'Early Years Workforce Strategy Action Plan: Discussion Paper', Early Years Workforce Development Team, 19 July, 2007, DCSF

Department for Education and Skills (DfES) (2001) *Early Years Sector-Endorsed Foundation Degree: Statement of Requirement.* London: HMSO

Department for Education and Skills (DfES) (2005a) *Children's Workforce Strategy: A Strategy to Build a World-Class Workforce for Children and Young People.* Nottingham: DfES Publications

Department for Education and Skills (DfES) (2005b) *Common Core of Skills and Knowledge for the Children's Workforce.* Nottingham: DfES Publications

Department for Education and Skills (DfES) (2006) *Children's Workforce Strategy: Building a World-Class Workforce for Children, Young People and Families: The Government's Response to the Consultation.* Nottingham: DfES Publications

Department for Education and Skills (DfES) (2007) *The Early Years Foundation Stage: Setting the Standards for Learning, Development and Care.* Nottingham: DfES Publications

Fenech, M. and Sumsion, J. 2007 'Early childhood teachers and regulation: complicating power relations using a Foucauldian lens', *Contemporary Issues in Early Childhood, 8(2)*, 109–122

Foundation Degree Forward http://www.fdf.ac.uk/courses/index.php (accessed 15/10/2007)

Goodliff (2007) 'Achieving Early Years Professional (EYP) Status: new EYPs evaluate the process and its impact on professional identity', paper presented at 17th EECERA Conference, Prague, Czech Republic, 30th August, 2007

Hevey (2007) 'Early Years Professional Status: an initiative in search of a strategy', paper presented at 17th EECERA Conference, Prague, Czech Republic, 30th August, 2007

Integrated Qualifications Framework http://www.cwdcouncil.org.uk/projects/integratedqualificationsframework.htm (accessed 15/10/07)

Miller, L., Cable C. and Goodliff, G. (2007) 'A day in the life of an early years practitioner: perspectives on professionalism', paper presented at 17th EECERA Conference, Prague, Czech Republic, 30th August, 2007

Moss, P. (2003) 'Structures, understandings and discourses: possibilities for re-envisioning the early childhood worker', *Contemporary Issues in Early Childhood, 7(1)*, 30–41

Moss, P. (2006) 'Bringing politics into the nursery: early childhood education as a democratic practice', paper presented at 16th EECERA Conference, University of Reykjavik, 1st September, 2006

Oberheumer, P. (2005) 'Conceptualising the early childhood pedagogue: policy approaches and issues of professionalism', *European Early Childhood Education Research Journal, 13(1)*, 5–15

OECD (2006) *Starting Strong II. Early Childhood Education and Care*. Paris: Organisation for Economic Co-operation and Development

Osgood, J. (2006) 'Deconstructing professionalism in early childhood education: resisting the regulatory gaze', *Contemporary Issues in Early Childhood, 7(1)*, 5–14

O'Keefe, J. and Tait, K (2004) 'An examination of the UK Early Years Foundation Degree and the evolution of senior practitioners – enhancing work-based practice by engaging in reflective and critical thinking', *International Journal of Early Years Education, 12(1)*, 25–41

Snape, D., Parfrement, J. and Finch, S. (National Centre for Social Research) (2007) *Evaluation of the Early Years Sector Endorsed Foundation Degree: Findings from the Final Student Survey*. London: DfES Publications

Sylva, K., Melhuish, E., Sammons, P., Siraj-Blatchford, I., Taggart, B. and Elliot, K. (2003) *The Effective Provision of Pre-School Education (EPPE) Project: Findings from the Pre-School Period: Summary of Findings*. London: Institute of Education/Sure Start

Wenger, E (1998) *Communities of Practice: Learning and Meaning*. Cambridge: Cambridge University Press

Westcott, E. (2004) 'The early years workforce – towards professional status? An issues paper'. Unpublished paper presented at the Senior Practitioner Working Group, DfES, 2004

Further reading

Clark, M. and Waller, T. (eds) (2007) *Early Childhood Education and Care: Policy and Practice*. London: Sage Publications

Children's Workforce Development Council
http://www.cwdcouncil.org.uk/index.asp

Dahlberg, G. and Moss, P. (2005) *Ethics and Politics in Early Childhood Education*. London and New York: Routledge Falmer

EARLY CHILDHOOD STUDIES DEGREES: THE DEVELOPMENT OF A GRADUATE PROFESSION

3

Pamela Calder

INTRODUCTION

This chapter discusses the origins of and the issues underlying the development of Early Childhood Studies (ECS) degrees, both as a specialist subject area in universities and as a base for a new professional role. These degrees stem from a campaigning past, both from a long-standing struggle to improve provision and as part of that improvement, to enhance and change the education and training, attitudes, status, and pay of the staff working with children. Also, to change for the better the value and esteem in which such practitioners/professionals are held. The degrees originate from the view that there is a distinct body of knowledge involved when working with young children and that this deserves a place in the university, where critical understanding, research and development of the knowledge base can be at the 'cutting edge' and put into effect. Thus the development of ECS degrees has always been part of a wider context which involves how we as a society view children, the role of women, families and employment. This chapter explores both how the development of Early Childhood Studies as a distinct subject area is being taken forward and also how such degrees are a route to becoming a graduate early childhood professional.

THE BACKGROUND

From the 1970s until the end of the 1980s there were a number of issues and problems that together formed the background to the creation of ECS degrees in the early 1990s. The context of the 1970s was one of gender inequality. Women were paid less than men. The majority of women with children under 5 did not work and, in particular, did not work full time (EOC 2006). Many women wanted mothers to have the same opportunities as men who were fathers. They wanted the possibility of leaving their children, including babies, for part of the time in places where they would be happy, well cared for, stimulated and able to make continuing relationships with other children and with adults. However, at the same time there was also strong opposition to group 'out-of-home' care for young children, particularly for those under 2 or 3 years old. The ideas of John Bowlby (1953) regarding maternal deprivation were influential and were interpreted to mean that children between 6 months and 3-years-old needed the continuous care of their mothers or mother substitutes and thus should not be in 'day care'. These views stimulated much research and the questions asked changed from whether day care was harmful, to whether it was the nature of the care and education in out-of-home care that mattered, and thus whether it could also be beneficial (Andersson 1992). Research which focused on the factors involved in 'good quality' care soon led to concerns about the quality of staff. In the UK many early childhood workers had low or no qualifications. Workers in early childhood services were also in one of the most gender occupationally segregated areas of work, where the low status of the staff and the lack of esteem in which their work was held, translated into low pay.

CAMPAIGNING FOR EARLY CHILDHOOD STUDIES DEGREES

During the 1980s there were a variety of attempts to improve the training and qualifications of workers in early childhood services (Calder and Penn 1980). Local authority childcare advisors expressed concerns that many recruits entered the field not knowing what the challenges were. Nursery workers were often expected to undertake demanding jobs which required high-level skills and a flexible and critical approach to their work, for which their current training was inadequate. Many practitioners had been channelled into childcare at school because it had been seen as an 'easy' option (Penn and McQuail 1997). Many of these workers were young women and there was high staff turnover. Even those who were qualified to work at a supervisory level, usually holding a two-year post-secondary qualification, did not have the equivalent (usually graduate level) qualifications of the other professionals such as social workers, health visitors and qualified teachers, whom they were working with.

By the end of the decade it became clear that in order to influence the education and training of early childhood workers and to change attitudes, it was necessary to work for change at a national level. In 1990 leading early childhood researchers with university links, practitioners from local authorities and from the wider education and child care sector, all of whom had perspectives that spanned both care and education, came together to form the Early Years Training Group (EYTG) at the National Children's Bureau, London. The group set out the evidence citing the 'Rumbold' report, Starting with Quality (DES 1990), and research which indicated that the quality, education, training and pay of staff were linked to the quality of children's development (Whitebook et al. 1990). The group campaigned for the creation of ECS Degrees to address these needs (NCB 1992; Pugh 1996).

The Early Childhood Studies Degrees Network

By 1993 two such degrees were in existence (at Bristol University and Suffolk College) and arising from the EYTG, the ECS Degrees Network was formed to support and advance existing and future programme developments. The network shared the belief that advocating the development of a core graduate early childhood profession was the way forward to professionalising the workforce, and they wished to develop an appropriate graduate qualification. The aim was to bridge the care and education divide and develop a degree which would form the basis of a potential education and training route for an early years professional, who would combine the knowledge, skills and education necessary for the upbringing, care and education of children from birth through to later childhood.

At this time it was often a challenge to establish these degrees in universities, for reasons similar to those applying to early childhood work itself. This area of work tended not to be regarded as an appropriate area for academic study and research and was seen as 'women's work', not requiring specialist knowledge. However, in 1998 the newly elected Labour Government made a groundbreaking policy commitment to early childhood education and care (DFEE 1998) and the climate in universities rapidly changed. By 1998 15 universities had validated ECS degrees (Fawcett and Calder 1998) and by 2004 this had increased to more than 40 (ECS Degree Network 2004) and numbers have continued to grow.

Many institutions offered both full-time and part-time routes and many of the degrees were modular. Depending on their backgrounds and on the nature of the course, the accreditation of prior experience and learning (APEL) could enable students to join the second or third year of a degree course. Once Foundation Degrees in Early Years were established in 2002 (DFES 2001), many of these graduates began to join the third year of an ECS degree in order to achieve an honours degree. The majority of the ECS degrees were not specifically vocational and although in some cases students had practical experience and recognised vocational qualifications (Level 3 on the National Qualifications Framework), most entrants had taken an 'A'-level route. An ECS honours degree enabled students without any practice qualifications to undertake research or pursue professional qualifications, such as teaching and social work. However, if students wanted to work directly with children on graduation, they were not necessarily regarded as qualified to do so. Thus the network investigated ways of both introducing practice elements into degree programmes and also ways of having such programmes recognised as providing a recognised vocational qualification.

Following a period of negotiation with the DFES, Ofsted and what was then the Early Years National Training Organisation, 'Practitioner Options' were developed. Degrees with such options were recognised by the Sure Start Unit of the DFES (DFES 2004) and placed on the Children's Workforce Qualifications website, which listed the qualifications that Ofsted accepts for regulatory purposes. This database was later renamed and transferred to the Children's Workforce Development Council (CWDC) which now maintains it (CWDC 2007a). The Practitioner Options elements of an ECS degree offer practice elements and modules, through which students undertake practice in Ofsted-recognised early years settings and where student competences are matched against National Qualifications Framework (NQF) Level 3 Occupational Standards (CWDC 2007b). Students who graduate from such degrees are recognised as qualified to work in a supervisory capacity with children in full-day care settings. However, working in such a capacity can be a low-paid career option. So, although a necessary and useful development, Practitioner Options did not solve the issue of providing a recognised *professional* graduate qualification route. Also, development has been slow as degree programmes with practice elements are expensive to provide and, unlike social work and teaching, are not supported by specific funding mechanisms; thus there is no incentive for universities to offer them.

A NEW EARLY CHILDHOOD PROFESSIONAL?

The publication of the *Ten Year Childcare Strategy* (HM Treasury et al. 2004) and the following consultation on the children's workforce (DFES 2005) offered the possibility of creating a new early years professional role, for working in the proposed new integrated services and Children's Centres. The consultation document (DFES 2005) offered two examples of a possible new professional, that of the 'new teacher' or pedagogue, based on the Scandinavian 'Social Pedagogue' (see Chapters 2 and 11). The outcome of the consultation (DfES 2006) was not an explicit choice between these two models but instead the introduction of an Early Years Professional (EYP), a new role and status (CWDC 2006).

A recent report on early childhood education and care (ECEC) carried out by the Organisation for Economic Co-operation and Development (OECD 2006) in 20 countries, offered ways of understanding the choices that countries have made in developing their ECEC services. It outlined three models of early childhood worker, including the 'new teacher' and 'social pedagogue' and also the pre-primary teacher (OECD 2006; see Chapter 7). The report suggested that the type of early years worker that countries had developed was associated with their organisational model of service provision, into either 'integrated services' (0 to 6) or 'split services' (0 to 3 and pre-primary) (see Chapters 11 and 12 for a fuller discussion). Both the 'new teacher' and 'social pedagogue' model share the same pedagogical approach of integrating care, upbringing and learning, but the social pedagogue model aims to provide social support to families, as well as educational work with children. The social pedagogue also spans a lifelong age range, working in youth work and with the elderly. The training of a 'new teacher' as exemplified by Sweden, for instance, has integrated early years teaching with that of primary school teacher, so that there are now three branches of training. There is a common core training of 18 months followed by a further two years specialising in one of three branches: early years, primary or 'free-time' teaching. The training provides intensive study in child development and pedagogical work.

The OECD report argues that this training in child development and pedagogical approach is one that pre-primary teachers in many countries, including the United Kingdom (UK), often lack.

The ECS Degrees Network's response to the workforce consultation argued that either the 'new teacher' model, or the 'social pedagogue' model could equally well be a way forward, as both shared a similar pedagogical approach to combine care, upbringing and learning; aims which had always underpinned ECS degrees. In effect, the government's development of the EYP role could be seen to be closer to the 'new teacher' model, as discussed in Chapter 2, since it has an explicit early years focus. However, unlike the 'new teacher' models in other countries (cited in the OECD report), there was no discussion of how this model would integrate with the existing pre-primary teacher role in England. Services in England and across the UK do not fit neatly into either a split system or an integrated services system, but overlap. Qualified teachers can work with children from 3-years-old in maintained schools, while those with early years qualifications at (NQF) Level 3 can work in full-day care with children from birth to compulsory school age. This has made the development of a new integrated professional role particularly complex. In England, government has supported the development of graduate leaders, with the National Professional Qualification in Integrated Centre Leadership (NPQICL) as leaders of centres, or EYPs as leaders of the Early Years Foundation Stage (EYFS) (see Chapter 7), but the only *practitioners* who work directly with children who are required to be graduates remain qualified teachers.

BENCHMARKING

The most recent opportunity to increase the salience of Early Childhood Studies, both as a subject area and a research area within universities, has occurred through its recognition by the Higher Education Quality Assurance Agency (QAA) as a subject appropriate for a benchmark statement. Such a statement outlines the defining principles, nature and extent of the discipline area, the subject knowledge and skill domains and the nature of teaching, learning and assessment. It provides a public statement of the standards that students will need to meet. In 2006 the ECS Degrees Network began the work of outlining the nature of the subject area for ECS degrees.

There has been continuity in thinking about the conceptual basis of ECS degrees since they were first described (NCB 1992). At that time it was suggested that a degree should include: the child developing in a social world and have a holistic perspective; that such development should be seen in an ecological context (including a family focus, social policy and legislation); that there should also be a focus on creating a quality environment which included both professional development, leadership skills and team working, and finally, that it should cover personal and professional development. There was to be a commitment to research and to providing a theoretical framework for understanding practice. These were still the aims and core curriculum areas found in a later survey of the developing ECS programmes (Fawcett and Calder 1998).

The process of constructing the benchmarking statement offered the opportunity of reviewing the conceptual underpinnings, knowledge, skills and scope of ECS, and of developing the resulting statement (QAA 2007). In the statement, the defining principles are confirmed as including: an 'understanding of the ecology of early childhood and children in an ecological context', the importance of considering 'theory in relation to the implications for practice' and a focus that 'fosters critical evaluation' (QAA 2007: 2). ECS is to be considered as covering development from conception onwards, with an emphasis on the earliest years. The subject is recognised as interdisciplinary since in taking 'account of the ecology of children's lives, programmes would draw on disciplines such as 'psychology, sociology, philosophy and social policy, and areas such as education, health, history and cultural studies' (QAA 2007: 3). The areas of subject knowledge and understanding include professional practice, which is understood as incorporating theoretical principles and knowledge of management, leadership and organisational structures, including 'schooling' and 'care' institutions, working with other professionals and working with families.

The subject-specific and generic skills that can be expected of an ECS graduate are outlined in terms of those necessary to meet the aims expressed in the defining principles. There are additional skills listed for those taking vocational and practice options. For example, graduates would be expected to demonstrate the ability to 'meet and promote children's health, welfare and safety needs and the conditions which enable them to flourish' (QAA 2007: 6), while those not undertaking such options would only be expected to 'demonstrate an understanding of how to plan for' doing so (QAA 2007:6). The ability to be critically evaluative, to have research and communication skills and to be able to act as an advocate for children and families are among those skills listed for all graduates. The benchmarking statement has also been drawn widely enough to incorporate those degrees that might wish to offer assessed professional practice. It makes clear that the linking of theory and practice is integral throughout the whole degree but that where institutions wish, they are able to additionally 'offer the opportunity to link theory and practice to competency and the relevant and appropriate professional standards' (QAA 2007: 2). It is recognised that these standards may change over time. Although Practitioner Options have been developed to ensure that graduates could reach Occupational Standards at Level 3, as new professional standards at graduate Level 6 become available, Practitioner Options may need to be developed to match these new standards.

CAREER PATHWAYS

ECS degrees have provided a flexible route for many in the early childhood field to enhance their knowledge, skills and qualifications. Graduates with the transferable skills of: adopting reflective practice and lifelong learning; being able to communicate clearly and effectively; managing time, resources and setting priorities; applying research principles; studying topics in depth; dealing with uncertainty; the ability to work in a changing environment; acting as a mentor to others and working effectively within a team, have skills that can be used in many occupations. Additionally, ECS graduates have a deep knowledge of early childhood and a pedagogical approach which can bring a useful dimension to many fields of work.

ECS graduates have moved into a range of careers, for example with local authorities' childcare and education services and work with children's charities. They have become community support, voluntary and family centre workers. Many have followed further professional training in teaching or social work. Others have undertaken postgraduate research and gained masters degrees and doctorates, after which some have re-entered the early childhood field as lecturers in further and higher education. Those students who entered ECS degrees through an 'A'-level route have usually followed further professional training if they wanted to work directly with children. ECS degrees with Practitioner Options are still too new to have had many graduates, since it was not until June 2004 that the first of these degrees were validated. However, at one of the first universities to offer the programme (University of East London) two of the first cohort of six students graduated with first class honours degrees.

Case studies

Case studies of students from Manchester Metropolitan University (MMU), Birmingham College of Food Technology and Creative Studies (BCFTCS) and Oxford Brookes exemplify the part that an ECS honours degree has played in their career progression. MMU and BCFTCS offer examples of students who, having successfully completed their Foundation Degrees, joined the third year of a BA ECS honours programme and, following further related experience, returned as lecturers. On completing her degree the MMU student gained EYP status and will join MMU's ECS department next year. The BCFTCS student became a manager of a community day nursery on graduation, before returning to BCFTCS as a lecturer and lead assessor in the EYP programme. She is currently undertaking a Postgraduate Certificate in Higher Education.

The student from the first cohort (2000–2003) of the three-year ECS degree at Oxford Brookes University, Glynnis, has made a similar journey. She entered the course as a qualified nursery nurse with many years' experience. On graduation she became manager of a day nursery and was then 'head-hunted' to take charge of a new Foundation Stage unit in a primary school. Starting as an unqualified teacher, she then undertook the Graduate Teacher Programme (GTP) in two terms. She is now teaching in year one of a primary school because she 'wanted to see the transition between the Foundation Stage and Key Stage 1'.

Glynnis reflected on the opportunities that had been open to her because of her practice qualifications. She felt that during her degree she had been particularly able to appreciate the theoretical knowledge on offer because her previous experience of working with children allowed her to contextualise the theory. This she believed was more difficult for students who undertook the degree without this practice background, although they 'still gained from their studies and went on to make excellent practitioners'.

She described how, 'The degree itself was fantastic' and how she discovered that, as a practitioner, she had been putting into practice the ideas of Vygotsky and Piaget but 'she had not known the theory behind it. . .and having the theory was great'. She also believed that 'The ECS degree offers a great lead in to teaching. Any teacher with an ECS degree would make a better teacher.' She believed that the theoretical knowledge of child development acquired through the degree offered valuable insights to understanding children, and that this was not something all teachers had (The Professional Standards for Qualified Teacher Status, (TDA 2007) do not require specialist knowledge of child development).

Primary school teachers often have difficulty understanding children. If they know child development and know the key cognitive developmental fields then they are able to give them the things that, for example, 5-year-olds should be doing.

I was incredibly helped by the (ECS) degree. I was given the underpinning knowledge and theory for early years. Students were 'fired up' and even though some were disappointed that it did not immediately give them a vocational qualification, they went on to other related careers such as social work or teaching.

There is a shortage of experienced graduates with relevant specialist ECS knowledge in many of the areas in which CWDC are trying to implement new developments. This is illustrated by these case studies where two of the graduates were recruited to higher education positions and the other to heading up a new Foundation Stage unit. However, for those without such experience and qualifications, career options are more limited and low pay remains an obstacle to progression.

QUALIFICATIONS, ROLES, STATUS AND PAY

Many graduates have become teachers by taking a Postgraduate Certificate in Education, following their degree. However, for many this would not have been their choice if a similarly well-recognised and remunerated career pathway had been available which recognised and made use of their specialist pedagogical knowledge and approach to integrating care, upbringing and education.

Within the field of early childhood education and care, there was initial support for the new role of Early Years Professional, as it was hoped it might provide a career solution. But there remain a number of reservations about the potentially overlapping roles and responsibilities of EYPs and qualified teachers and the non-comparability of pay and conditions (NUT 2006, Kirk and Broadhead 2007), as discussed in this book. Also, for many ECS graduates the postgraduate route to teaching remains a quicker and better-remunerated route to working directly with children.

Low pay in this field is still a major issue, but it seems that a society-wide transformation in gender relations may be required to make a substantial difference, since the pay gap between women's and men's earnings has only improved by 12 percentage points since the 1970s. Women's full-time pay remains 17 per cent lower than men's, and for women in part-time work is a massive 38 per cent lower (EOC 2006). The continuation of sector-based, occupational gender segregation also contributes to the difficulties in improving the pay, and thus the status of the predominantly female early childcare and education workforce.

SUMMARY

This chapter has described the campaigning roots behind the creation of Early Childhood Studies degrees and the role of the ECS network in developing both the academic area and in advocating an associated professional graduate role. It has argued that the degrees can provide a basis of child development, knowledge and research, recognised as being vital, but which are sometimes lacking in the training of those involved in the children's workforce. These degrees offer a body of knowledge and skills which are crucial for a number of existing professional roles such as teaching and social work, and also offer the breadth and depth of knowledge, understanding and skills to meet the requirements of the new EYP role. But, potentially ECS Degrees, which are conceptualised as having a holistic view of the child in context and which entail reflection and research skills, could offer the academic underpinnings for other degree-level integrated qualifications as work on the integrated qualifications framework progresses. ECS graduates with their knowledge of children from conception, and of family and societal context, are already carrying out many valuable roles, and are contributing to an integrated children's workforce.

Questions/points for discussion/reflection

1 What do you consider to be the key body of knowledge, skills and understanding that ECS graduates should have?
2 What can ECS degrees contribute towards the development of a graduate early childhood workforce?
3 What do you understand by the 'integration of care and education' in the early years?

REFERENCES

Andersson, B. E. (1992) 'Effects of day care on cognitive and socioemotional competence of thirteen-year-old Swedish schoolchildren', *Child Development, 63(1)*, 20–36

Bowlby, J. (1953) *Childcare and the Growth of Love*. London: Penguin

Calder, P.A. and Penn, H. (1980) *An Integrated Training for the Under Fives*. London: National Childcare Campaign and NUPE

Children's Workforce Development Council (2006) *Early Years Professional Prospectus*. Leeds: CWDC

Children's Workforce Development Council (2007a) *Early Years & Playwork Qualifications Database*, http://eypquals.cwdcouncil.org.uk/public (accessed 29/7/2007)

Children's Workforce Development Council (2007b) *National Occupational Standards for Children's Care, Learning and Development (CCLD)*, www.cwdcouncil.org.uk/projects/nos_ccld.htm (accessed 29/7/2007)

Department of Education and Science (1990) *Starting with Quality – Report of the Committee of Inquiry into the Quality of the Educational Experience Offered to 3- and 4-Year-Olds*. London: HMSO

Department for Education and Employment (1998) *Meeting the Childcare Challenge: A Framework and Consultation Document*. London: HMSO

Department for Education and Skills (2001) *Statement of Requirement for the Early Years Foundation Degree*. Nottingham: DfES Publications

Department for Education and Skills (2004) *Early Childhood Studies Degrees with 'Practitioner Options'*, Letter signed by Jeanette Pugh, Children Workforce Unit and Naomi Eisenstadt, Sure Start Unit, March 2004. London: DFES

Department for Education and Skills (2005) *The Children's Workforce Strategy, Consultation Paper*. London: DfES

Department for Education and Skills (2006) *Children's Workforce Strategy. Building a World-Class Workforce for Children, Young People and Families. The Government's Response to the Consultation*. Nottingham: DFES Publications

Early Childhood Studies Degrees Network (2004) *Universities Offering Early Childhood Studies Degrees and Numbers of Enrolled Students.* Email survey carried out by the ECS Degrees Network. Unpublished

EOC (2006) *Facts about Women and Men in Great Britain*, www.eoc.org.uk/pdf/facts_about_GB_2006.pdf (accessed 29/7/2007)

Fawcett, M. and Calder, P. (1998) 'Early childhood studies degrees'. In Abbott, L. and Pugh, G. *Training to Work in the Early Years.* Buckingham: Open University Press

HM Treasury in conjunction with Department for Education and Skills (DfES), Department for Work and Pensions (DWP), Department for Trade and Industry (DTI) (2004) *Choice for Parents, the Best Start for Children: a Ten Year Strategy for Childcare.* London: HMSO www.hm-treasury.gov.uk./media/B/E/pbr04child-care_480upd050105.pdf (accessed 29/7/2007)

Kirk, G. and Broadhead, P. (2007) *Every Child Matters and Teacher Education: A UCET Position Paper.* London: Universities Council for the Education of Teachers

National Children's Bureau (1992) *The Future of Training in the Early Years: A Discussion Paper.* London: Early Childhood Unit, National Children's Bureau

NUT (2006*) NUT Response to CWDC Early Years Professional – The Response of the National Union of Teachers to the Children's Workforce Development Council Consultation 'Early Years Professional'.* NUT www.teachers.org.uk/resources/word/EarlyYearsCampaign/NUT%20RESP%20-%20CWDC%20EYP_KDR.doc (accessed 12/10/2007)

Organisation for Economic Co-operation and Development (OECD) (2006) *Starting Strong II: Early Childhood Education and Care.* OECD Publishing

Pugh, G. (ed.) (1996) *Education and Training for Work in the Early Years.* London: National Children's Bureau (Early Childhood Unit)

Penn, H. and McQuail, S. (1997) *Childcare as a Gendered Occupation. RR23.* Nottingham: DFES publications

Quality Assurance Agency for Higher Education (QAA) (2007) 'Subject benchmark statement. Early Childhood Studies'. Draft for consultation June 2007, www.qaa.ac.uk/academicinfrastructure/benchmark/statements/drafts/earlyChildhood07.pdf (accessed 29/7/2007)

Training and Development Agency for Schools (TDA) (2007) *Professional Standards for Teachers Qualified Teacher Status*, Revised QTS standards, www.tda.gov.uk/partners/ittstandards/qtsstandards.aspx (accessed 29/9/2007)

Whitebook, M., Howes, C. and Phillips, D. A. (1990) *The National Child Care Staffing Study. Final report: Who cares? Child Care Teachers and the Quality of Care in America.* Washington, DC: Center for the Child Care Workforce

Further reading

Boddy, J., Cameron, C., Mooney, A., Moss, P., Petrie, P. and Statham, J. (2005) *Introducing Pedagogy into the Children's Workforce.* London: TCRU, University of London

Dahlberg, G., Moss, P. and Pence, A. (2006) *Beyond Quality in Early Childhood Education and Care: Languages of Evaluation.* London: Routledge

THE EARLY YEARS TEACHER

Jane Devereux and Carrie Cable

INTRODUCTION

This chapter explores the implications of the considerable changes that have taken, and continue to take place in Initial Teacher Education (ITE). It considers the implications for teacher training of recent and current developments in the early years sector, in particular the introduction of the Early Years Professional (EYP) role and multi-professional working. The new standards for teachers (TDA 2007a) and those for EYPs (CWDC 2006) include some common themes and terminology, but the way in which the two sets of standards are written, presented and elaborated suggest differences and potential tensions in the models of teaching and learning. This chapter explores these differences and their relevance to working in multi-professional teams in early years settings. Alongside these differences are tensions relating to pay, conditions of service, status and professional standing and how organisations involved in providing early years services will perceive and interpret the different roles. The avowed intention that there should be equality of status and value for the roles within the early years sector will need determination, collaboration and commitment from all those involved if the desired outcomes are to be achieved.

TEACHER EDUCATION

The introduction of a graduate teaching profession in the late 1960s and the development of professional standards and a more rigorous inspection of teaching have led to the establishment of a professional status for teachers. The drive to raise standards in primary and early years education, which began with the National Curriculum in 1988, has spawned a huge range of initiatives for schools, which have included the Literacy and Numeracy Strategies, the Primary Strategy and most recently the Early Years Foundation Stage. These national policy developments, the changes in the management of educational settings and in the roles and responsibilities of Local Education Authorities (now Local Authorities) have resulted in an increase in central government control in England over what happens in schools.

It has been argued that this increase in government intervention has decreased the autonomy of teachers to respond to the needs of individual children (Cox 1996). Gammage (2006) suggests this has resulted in a very narrow curriculum for children at a very early stage in their education – a curriculum that is subject based and focused on prescribed outcomes rather than on developing the whole child, with equal emphasis being given to their social, emotional, physical and creative development. Pollard and Trigg (2000) suggest that the National Curriculum has hindered teachers' learning and their real engagement with children's actual learning in the classroom. They comment on how the National Curriculum and the related strategies have undermined the confidence of teachers to use their own imagination and creativity in meeting the needs of each child.

The establishment of the Teacher Training Agency (now the Training and Development Agency for schools (TDA)) and the development of competency outcomes for the training of teachers, have led to similar prescription in the content and delivery of teacher education courses. This has perpetuated the concerns expressed by Pollard and Trigg (2000) above, as programmes leaders have had to modify and adapt their courses to meet not only the requirements placed on them by the TDA, but also those placed on schools. Ofsted, the inspection service for schools and teacher training institutions, adds a further element of regulation and control for both teachers in schools and training providers. This prescriptive approach to teaching and learning raises potential tensions for early years teachers who may now be working in multi-professional teams providing education and care for children from birth to 5. We return to this later in the chapter after examining the different routes trainees can take towards achieving Qualified Teacher Status (QTS) and the Early Years Professional Status (EYPS).

Routes into teaching

Over recent years a wide range of routes to QTS (see Table 4.1 for a summary of some of these) have been developed; primarily to increase the diversity amongst the teaching profession in terms of gender, ethnicity and age, as well as background. These are either based in a Higher Education Institution (HEI) or are Employment Based Teacher Training (EBTT) routes.

The main undergraduate route leading to a BA with QTS is based in HEIs and links professional courses and experience with academic study of a subject specialism (which can include Early Childhood Studies (ECS)) for those who are interested in working in this field. The Registered Teacher Programme (RTP) has been introduced in recent years to support those who do not have a degree but need to work as they develop their subject expertise and their professional skills. Those trainees work in school full time, developing their professional expertise and study either by distance learning, or day release/part-time study to upgrade their academic qualifications to honours degree level. In particular, this pathway has supported early years practitioners who have completed their Early Years Foundation Degree (EYFD) and wish to move into teaching.

For graduates wishing to teach, the usual route is the Postgraduate Certificate in Education (PGCE). This is the equivalent of one year's full-time study and focuses on the professional roles and responsibilities of being a teacher. Students must have a degree that contains a significant amount of subject study of relevance to the stage they wish to teach. Early Childhood Studies degrees are now acceptable subject study. In the past the PGCE route was only available through HEIs, but in recent years has been used as a way to increase diversity. There are now work-based PGCEs such as the Graduate Teacher Programme (GTP) and School Centred Initial Teacher Training (SCITT) that allow trainees to work in school while training, either as an individual working in one school or, in the case of a SCITT, as a group of students linked to an HEI. Some of these PGCE routes are also described as 'flexible' as they

A generic summary of Routes to Qualified Teacher Status (QTS)

	Undergraduate		Postgraduate		
	Bachelor of Arts (BA) with Qualified Teacher Status (QTS)	Registered Teacher programme (RTP)	Post Graduate Certificate of Education (PGCE)	Graduate Teacher Programme (GTP)	School Centred Initial Teacher Training (SCITT)
Duration	3 years	2 years FT	1 year to 18mths	Up to 18 months	1 year
Full/part time	FT	FT paid	FT/PT	FT/PT	FT
Requirements	'A' levels or recognised equivalents	Foundation Degree or equivalent	Degree or equivalent	Degree or equivalent	Degree or equivalent
Content	Subject study, professional courses and school experience	Subject study to honours level degree, professional courses and sustained school work	Professional course and school experience	School-based professional course as individual in school	School-based professional course with HEI links and part of group
School or HEI based	HEI	School based – individuals. Some links to HEI	HEI	School based – may be some links to HEI or Recommended Awarding Body	School based with links to HEI or other Recommended Awarding Body

Table 4.1. Routes to Qualified Teacher Status (QTS)

allow trainee teachers to work in more diverse ways – to stage their school practice to fit their own work and family commitments and by extending the time taken to achieve QTS. Many PGCE programme providers are also currently restructuring their courses and providing modules that can be accredited towards a Masters degree to encourage teachers to continue their professional development from the point of qualification.

The development of Foundation Degrees in Early Years (see Chapter 2), which combine work-based learning with academic study, has provided another pathway into teaching for early years practitioners, providing they meet the necessary QTS entry requirements, which include GCSEs at level 'C' or above in English, mathematics and science.

Teaching standards

The new professional standards for teachers (TDA 2007a) set out not only the requirements for the award of qualified teacher status via any of the routes described above but also list those for:

- core teachers (C);
- teachers on upper pay scales (post-threshold teachers) (P);
- excellent teachers (E);
- advanced skills teachers (AST).

As statements of the professional attributes, professional knowledge and understanding and professional skills that teachers are required to demonstrate, the standards define 'and clarify what progression looks like' (TDA 2007a: 2). In addition, they are intended to underpin the five key outcomes for children identified in *Every Child Matters* (DfES 2003) and the six areas of the Common Core of Skills and Knowledge for the children's workforce (DfES 2005). Teachers are required to demonstrate that they have achieved these standards at each stage of their career, in order to progress to posts of greater responsibility, either through an internal, or external process of assessment. There is an expectation that all teachers will engage in continuing and ongoing professional development throughout their teaching careers, with pathways that enable them either to stay in the classroom as a teacher, or move into leadership or management posts.

Standards for Qualified Teacher Status

There are 33 standards across the three main areas of teachers' professional work, as summarised in Table 4.2, that apply to teachers working in all phases of schooling. The interpretation of these is elaborated in the Revised ITT Requirements (TDA 2007b) and the Guidance to accompany the Standards for Qualified Teacher Status (QTS) (TDA 2007c). Each standard and its requirements are elaborated with some references to early years. The terminology used in the standards refers to all phases of education and requires early years teachers and training providers to interpret each standard in language and ways appropriate to early years practice. Although some interpretation of the terminology used in the standards is provided, there is very little that alludes to the needs of very young children from birth to 3 years.

QTS Standards		EYPS Standards	
Key themes – Those recommended for QTS should have:	Sub themes	Key themes – Those awarded Early Years Professional Status must demonstrate through their practice that they meet the following standards:	Sub themes
Professional attributes	Relationships with children and young people (Q1 & Q2) Frameworks (Q3) Communicating with others (Q4 to Q6) Personal Professional development (Q7 to Q9)	Knowledge and understanding (S1 to S6)	Knowledge of how children learn and develop Principles and content of EYFS Understanding of frameworks and legal requirements
Professional knowledge and understanding	Teaching and learning (Q10) Assessment and monitoring (Q11 to Q13) Subjects and curriculum (Q14 & Q15) Literacy, numeracy and ICT (Q16& Q17)	Effective practice and show that they can lead and support others to (S7 to S24):	Have high expectations of children and promote positive behaviour Provide a safe and stimulating environment to develop children's intellectual and physical development, health and emotional wellbeing Plan child-led/adult initiated experiences, activities and play opportunities Report on progress and recognise and support children at risk with specialist help of colleagues

Table 4.2. QTS and EYPS standards (continued overleaf)

QTS Standards		EYPS Standards	
	Achievement and diversity (Q18 to Q20)	**Relationships with children (S24 to S29)**	Communicate and listen to children and develop respectful relationships with them
	Health and wellbeing (Q21)		Establish fair, respectful relationships with parents/carers/families
Professional skills:	Planning (Q22 to Q24)	**Communicating and working in partnership with families and carers (S30 to S33)**	Work in partnership with them
	Teaching (Q25)		Provide formal/informal opportunities for sharing information both ways
	Assessing, monitoring and giving feedback (Q26 to Q28)	**Team work and collaboration (S34 to S37)**	Establish culture of collaboration and cooperative working
	Reviewing teaching and learning (Q29)		Influence and contribute to policies and practice within setting and multi-professional teams
	Learning environment (Q30 & Q31)	**Professional development (S38 to S40)**	Develop literacy, numeracy and ICT skills to support their work
	Teamwork and collaboration (Q32 & Q33)		Reflect and adapt approaches and be creative and innovative to benefit all

Table 4.2. QTS and EYPS standards (continued)

The language of the standards reflects that of the primary and secondary school sector and the strategies that have been developed to implement the National Curriculum. For example, Standard Q25 (TDA 2007a: 11) suggests that teachers should 'teach lessons and sequences of lessons across the age and ability range for which they are trained'. However, the emphasis in early years settings is on continuous provision for children that enables the child, with or without the support of practitioners and other children, to explore their world and ideas, through a diverse range of experiences and using a range of materials. The emphasis on the teacher teaching rather than the child as the starting point for planning for learning sets up a tension for trainees, settings and providers between requirements and widely acknowledged effective early years practice.

One of the major concerns for any HEI providing early years routes to QTS will be trying to extend the range of settings that can be used for practice placements, especially as the regulations emphasise school settings. Even though the standards do say that the term 'schools' is meant to include further education institutions, early years settings, or other settings, where trainee teachers can demonstrate that they meet the QTS standards, the requirements specify that trainees 'must have *taught* in at least two schools prior to recommendation for the award of QTS' (TDA 2007b: 3). This would seem to clearly suggest that the two key teaching practices must be in school settings. This puts pressure on the time available for placement experience that can only have a detrimental effect on the time and quality of experience trainees can have in these 'other' settings, including work with the birth to 3 age group.

The detailed guidance goes on to suggest:

. . . in considering the extent to which time in other settings can develop a trainee's ability to meet the QTS standards, providers will wish to ensure that trainees receive the quality of support they need in that setting and that their achievements can be reliably recorded and assessed. In an early years setting, for example, a provider might wish to ensure that a trainee would have the support of a qualified teacher.

(TDA 2007d: 43–44)

This strong emphasis on qualified teachers acting as mentors in the other early years settings will be difficult to support, at least initially, as many current early years teachers have not had experience of working with birth to 3-year-olds in non-school settings such as day care and children's centres.

Providing knowledge and understanding, guidance and appropriate experience for trainee teachers and their mentors on such issues as:

- child development from birth to 3
- planning learning experiences for very young children
- supervising and supporting trainee teachers in non-maintained settings

will put a huge strain on ITE providers and their partner schools. Selecting appropriate settings, which reflect the diversity in the early years sector, will be time-consuming and developing their own expertise will have cost implications in terms of staff and resources. Adapting already overcrowded ITE programmes will also prove a challenge. Finding quality placements will not be easy until there are more direct links across the diverse range of early years settings and until EYPS qualified staff are available to support trainees during their practice.

The development of Foundation Degrees in Early Years (see Chapter 2) have provided another route into teaching for early years practitioners. However, those who do not want to become early years teachers now have the option of following the Early Years Professional Status (EYPS) pathway provided they are graduates or complete a further period of study to gain a degree.

All candidates for EYPS have to demonstrate through their practice that they have attained the required level of competence, and it is anticipated that in future only those with EYPS will lead the delivery of the new Early Years Foundation Stage (EYFS) (DfES 2007) that comes into effect for all children from birth to 5 in September 2008. In a similar way to the QTS standards, the EYPS standards, (summarised in Table 4.2) set out the requirements for the recommendation of the award and are supported by similar guidance (DfES 2003 and CWDC 2006). These standards are divided into six professional areas covering: knowledge and understanding, effective practice, the importance of relationships with children, communicating with parents and carers, working effectively in multi-professional teams, and professional development.

The language of the EYPS standards and the underpinning model of teaching and learning suggest a more child-centred approach to teaching and learning than those for QTS. For example, within S11 (CWDC 2006: 9) there is a requirement to 'Plan and provide safe and appropriate child-led and adult-initiated experiences, activities and play opportunities in indoor, outdoor and out-of-setting contexts, which enable children to develop and learn'. The terminology reflects early years practice and supports the importance of play in the learning of young children (Moyles 2005, Woods and Attfield 2005). The standards use terminology cognisant with 'best practice' in early years, speak directly to the practitioner and encourage the holistic development of the child. A link between care and education is clearly articulated.

In the foreword to the EYPS standards, effective practice is described as involving:

- establishing and maintaining good relationships with both children and adults;
- understanding the individual and diverse ways that children develop and learn;
- knowledge and understanding to actively support and extend children's learning;
- meeting all children's needs, learning styles and interests; and
- working with parents, carers, the wider community, and other professionals within and beyond the setting (CWDC 2006: 3).

These new standards and the development of the role of the EYP are seen as key to the implementation of the new Early Years Foundation Stage (EYFS) (DfES 2007), the development of a more multi-professional workforce and an holistic approach to early years education and care. The Children's Workforce Development Council (CWDC 2006) indicate that over time they see the implementation of the EYFS being led by EYPS as a collaborative multi-professional enterprise.

IMPLICATIONS FOR FUTURE POLICY, PROVISION AND PRACTICE

Policy implications

The new standards for QTS and EYPS are set at the same level in the National Qualifications Framework (NQF), at Level 6, but CWDC maintains that holders will have complementary skills. Currently there is a great deal of debate within the sector about how these complementary roles will work in settings, how the practitioners will work together and the implications of different pay and conditions of service for working relationships. The challenge for managers, in the diverse range of early years settings, will be to fully utilise staff and their skills in environments that are overloaded with initiatives that people are still coming to terms with. Managers will need to ensure that staff are not demotivated and to relocate or reassign staff sensitively. Early years teachers will have to be sensitive to these issues but, as there is no reference to EYPS in the QTS guidance or the actual standards, knowledge of the changes is likely to be very limited and could well cause tensions. ITE programme leaders will need to take account of these tensions in designing their programme and help trainee teachers to develop their understanding of the different structures within the early years sector and the changes taking place. The promise of clear guidance from CWDC (2006) before the implementation of EYFS (DfES 2007) in September 2008 is to be welcomed and is urgently needed.

Pay and conditions in the early years sector is a long-standing cause for concern, particularly in the private, voluntary and independent (PVI) sector and contrasts sharply with the situation for teachers. In the early years sector there is a huge discrepancy across the sector in terms of pay scales and the implementation of statutory employment legislation. This highlights a real need to encourage employers to support the professional development of their staff and to remunerate them appropriately. However, this cannot be done without significant investment from both the public and private sector. This is vital if the government wishes to ensure that early years teachers are attracted to and retained in the non-maintained sector. If this is not forthcoming, the early years sector will be staffed by those who can afford to work for less, despite having the qualifications. At the moment the relationship, both financially and professionally, between the two roles needs clarification. If, as has been indicated, the CWDC intends that eventually the implementation of the EYFS will be led by EYPs, presumably teachers wishing to assume this role will have to apply for EYPS. The relationship then between those EYPs with QTS and those who only have EYPS and who may be paid differently is likely to cause further tension. Pay and conditions of service are a key way to motivate staff to undertake training, but the implications for the two roles require careful consideration now rather than later. If a national pay and career framework is not developed, the drive to improve the standard of early years services for children from birth to 5 may well falter before it has begun.

Transformation funding is available for two years for those who wish to undertake EYPS, but this is a very short timescale in which to train the required number of EYPs. The take-up of transformation funding for EYPS has been slow because of the low number of graduates in the early years workforce, the complex application and allocation procedures and the uncertainty about future funding. A further longer-term, substantial investment in the sector is needed, alongside a longer timescale to achieve and establish EYPs in the workplace.

The new standards for teachers do not build on the learning outcomes and requirements for Sector Endorsed Foundation Degrees (DfES 2001) or cover the contexts and breadth of *work-based* requirements of the EYPS. Although the QTS standards were revised at the same time as the standards for EYPS were being developed, there appears to be a considerable difference in the language used and the underpinning model of learning and teaching. It seems short sighted not to have used the opportunity to consider training for the whole early years sector (birth to 5) and to include teaching standards in the overall review.

Working with children from birth to 5

The Effective Provision of Pre-school Education (EPPE) research project found that 'settings which have staff with higher qualifications, especially with a good proportion of trained teachers on the staff, show higher quality and their children make more progress' (Sylva et al. 2003: 2). However, transferring teachers from school settings to more diverse early years settings is not straightforward. It will have to involve training or professional development in order for teachers to work effectively in these contexts. For teachers wishing to move into the early years sector, a lack of detailed knowledge of child development and experience of working with birth to 3-year-olds may well be key issues, as is illustrated in the following observations from two practitioners working in a children's centre.

> Lucy and Maria are currently undertaking the EYPS in a northern town, and expressed concerns that their part-time (0.5) 'link' teacher had received no formal training in early years education and had little or no understanding of the educational needs of birth to 3-year-olds. The teacher had previously worked in a nursery class in a school. They expressed anxiety about the teacher's lack of understanding of day care and the 'wrap-around' care provided by the setting and how to plan for these, and about her understanding of the transient nature of the groups within the setting, as children arrived and left at different times of the day. Opportunities for the teacher to gain experience of diversity and to work collaboratively were difficult because the teacher was contracted to work only within normal school hours.

The NUT (National Union of Teachers) has campaigned for more qualified teachers to be working in the early years sector, arguing that, 'The early years should have equal status with every other phase of the education system and, for that to be so, it needs to be staffed by qualified teachers.' (2006: 1). They also argue that:

'Early years teams should include qualified teachers, early years professionals, nursery officers and specialist support staff. This range of expertise is vital if all the social, emotional and learning needs of very young children are to be met. Early years education is too important to be delivered on the cheap. One type of professional cannot substitute for the other.'

(NUT 2006: 1)

There would appear to be much more work to do, in order to develop a shared understanding and respect for different roles and to ensure that both the care and educational needs of children are met by appropriately trained and qualified staff.

Models of teaching and learning

The models of teaching and learning in the QTS standards (TDA 2007) and the EYP standards (CWDC 2006) are very different and best practice in early years settings, where the child is placed at the centre of curriculum planning, receives scant mention in the standards for QTS. Although an interpretation of the terminology used in the QTS standards is provided, there is little said that alludes to the needs of very young children (TDA 2007a). The QTS model acknowledges neither the social nature of learning, nor the need to embed young children's learning in contexts that are meaningful to them. The stress on teaching, content and assessment places restraints on what teachers can do. Even the guidance for the standards does not sufficiently elaborate an approach that builds on what children know but is focused around prescribed National Curriculum outcomes which assume a linear pattern to learning.

This is in contrast to the EYPS standards. which utilise a different style and language, using terms such as 'child-led' and 'observation' to describe a practice that supports how children learn best – through building their model of the world through experience. MacNaughton (2003) describes how young children construct and co-construct their understanding of the world by interacting with it, and more able others, to extend their thinking. Although in Standard Q10 (TDA 2007a: 8) there is a reference to teachers knowing 'how to personalise learning' and in Standards Q18 and Q19 (TDA 2007a: 10) a requirement for teachers to take account of social, religious, cultural, ethnic and linguistic influences, it can be argued that the requirements of the National Curriculum and assessment and inspection processes mitigate against creative approaches to teaching and learning that are an essential aspect of work in the early years. Brooker (2005: 127) states that 'the variety of children's cultural background calls not for a one size fits all learning style but for a range of learning styles.' Understanding how to plan for individual children's learning needs, to take account of their diverse social backgrounds and interests, is paramount if children are to be 'switched on' to learning from the beginning.

Another important dimension of early years practice is observing what children are doing and are interested in, to match provision to individual learning needs, interests and styles of learning. The QTS standards require trainees to '*know* [our italics] a range of approaches to assessment' (TDA 2007a: 9 Q12) but do not use the word 'observation', whereas the EYPS standards talk about the importance of 'close, informed observation' (CWDC 2006: 9 S10) and of using various assessment techniques 'to inform, plan and improve practice and provision' (CWDC 2006: 9 S10). Trainee teachers wishing to work in multi-professional early years settings will have to rely on their training institution or organisation to interpret the QTS standards and apply them to early years practice.

One way forward might be to rewrite a version of the QTS standards specifically for early years and provide more appropriate guidance for the early years teacher that embraces the importance of play, exploration and challenge, observation and diversity in the early years and places the child at the centre.

SUMMARY

The drive to develop a graduate early years workforce in England is a welcome development and long overdue. However, a number of concerns, tensions and challenges are evident in the current proposals; this is clearly illustrated in the lack of clarity over the status of the early years teacher and the Early Years Professional, and the different standards and roles envisaged for these professionals. Some of these tensions may be addressed more easily than others, but the more fundamental tension relating to pay and conditions of service could present a major hurdle in taking forward the changes. There is a need for all parties, including the CWDC and the TDA, to work more closely together to make a graduate workforce a reality for early years services in England.

Questions/points for discussion/reflection

1 What do you see as the complementary skills of an early years teacher and those who have Early Years Professional status?
2 What are the challenges in having these two workforce roles in the early years for your work?
3 How can training provision support the successful development of the two roles?

REFERENCES

Brooker, L. (2005) 'Learning to be a Child: Cultural Diversity and Early Years Ideology'. In N. Yelland (ed.) *Critical Issues in Early Childhood Education.* Maidenhead: Open University Press

Children's Workforce Development Council (2006) Early Years Professional Standards available at http://www.cwdcouncil.org.uk/projects/earlyyears.htm (accessed 13/11/2007)

Cox, T. (1996) *National Curriculum in the Early Years: Challenges and Opportunities.* London: Routledge

Department for Education and Skills (2001) *Early Years Sector-Endorsed Foundation Degree: Statement of Requirement.* London: HMSO

Department for Education and Skills (2003) *Every Child Matters.* Nottingham: DfES Publications

Department for Education and Skills (2005) *Common Core of Skills and Knowledge for the Children's Workforce.* London: DfES

Department for Education and Skills (2007) *The Early Years Foundation Stage: Setting the Standards for Learning Development and Care for Children from Birth to Five.* Nottingham: DfES Publications

Gammage, P. (2006) 'Early childhood education and care: politics, policies and possibilities', *Early Years, 26(3)*, 235–248

MacNaughton, G. (2003) *Shaping Early Childhood.* Maidenhead: Open University Press

Moyles, J. (2005) *The Excellence of Play* (3rd edition). Maidenhead: Open University Press

NUT (2006) *Campaign Leaflet for Parents/General Use* www.teachers.org.uk/resources/word/EarlyYearsCampaign/EYC_PARENT_LEAFLET .doc (accessed 27/10/2007)

Pollard, A. and Trigg, P. (2000) *What Pupils Say.* London: Continuum

Sylva, K., Melhuish, E., Sammons, P., Siraj-Blatchford, I., Taggart, B. and Elliot, K. (2003) *Research Brief RBX15-03: The Effective Provision of Preschool Education (EPPE) Project: Findings from the Pre-School Period.* Nottingham: DfES

Training and Development Agency (2007a) Professional Standards for Teachers available at http://www.tda.gov.uk/partners/ittstandards/qtsstandards.aspx (accessed 13/11/2007)

Training and Development Agency (2007b) Revised ITT Requirements (short pdf version) available at http://www.tda.gov.uk/partners/ittstandards/ittrequirements.aspx (accessed 13/11/2007)

Training and Development Agency (2007c) Guidance to accompany the Standards for Qualified Teacher Status (QTS) available at http://www.tda.gov.uk/partners/ittstandards/guidance.aspx (accessed 13/11/2007)

Training and Development Agency (2007d) ITT Requirements Guidance (full word version) http://www.tda.gov.uk/partners/ittstandards/guidance.aspx (accessed 13/11/2007)

Woods, E. and Attfield, J. (2005) *Play, Learning and the Early Childhood Curriculum* (2nd edition). London: Paul Chapman Publishing

Further reading

Brooker, L. (2002) *Starting School: Young Children Learning Cultures.* Buckingham: Open University Press

Sylva, K., Melhuish, E., Sammons, P., Siraj-Blatchford, I., Taggart, B. and Elliot, K (2003) *Research Brief RBX15-03: The Effective Provision of Preschool Education (EPPE) Project: Findings from the Pre-School Period.* Nottingham: DfES

5 TEACHING ASSISTANTS IN THE EARLY YEARS

Carrie Cable

INTRODUCTION

The number of teaching assistants (TAs) working with teachers and supporting children's learning in the early years has risen dramatically over the last 10 years. While the notion of a number of adults working to support children's learning and development in nurseries or other early years settings is not new, this situation was much less common in schools until relatively recently. Over this period, there has been considerable development in the range of courses and training opportunities open to TAs to improve their knowledge and skills and the quality of the support they provide – their professionalism, and in their status as supporters of learning and teaching in schools, what can be seen as a professionalisation of the workforce. The first part of this chapter reviews these developments. The second part of the chapter considers what this new professionalism means for teaching assistants and the impact of training and development on practice, knowledge and understanding, values and beliefs.

HISTORY AND BACKGROUND

Additional, usually unqualified, adults have long worked in infant and primary schools in England in a supportive role. Often called auxiliaries or welfare assistants, they carried out ancillary tasks, preparing resources and setting up activities, clearing up and carrying out other 'domestic tasks' for children and teachers. Other adults came into schools on a voluntary basis to hear children read or to accompany children on school visits, or trips to the library or swimming. Many of these adults were parents of children who began their involvement when their children started at the school, and for some this continued for many years. There was no expectation that these additional adults would have any qualifications or training for the roles they carried out. Teaching assistants, therefore, (classroom assistants in Scotland and Northern Ireland, teaching aides in other parts of the world) are a relatively new group of professionals working in the early years in England. Initially, they carried out many of the same roles as welfare assistants or auxiliaries and indeed their role was summed up in the title of a book published by Moyles and Suschitzky in 1997 '*Jills of all trades?. . .*'. Training opportunities were limited and, as many of the assistants were mothers, it was tacitly assumed they could draw on their intuitive and learnt skills as mothers and through observing teachers at work carry out the tasks they were assigned to do by the teachers. The exception tended to be those who had obtained training and qualifications as nursery nurses and who usually worked in more equal partnerships with nursery and reception teachers.

The developing role: support for literacy and numeracy

In 1994 the then Department for Education and Employment (DfEE) instigated and financially supported a programme of training and a set of competences for classroom assistants in England to become 'Specialist Teacher Assistants', with a focus on developing students' ability to support young children's learning of English and mathematics at Key Stage 1 (5- to 7-year-olds). These work-based learning courses, offered in Higher and Further Education institutions in collaboration with Local Education Authorities (LEAs), were at undergraduate level and provided the first official recognition that teaching assistants should have the opportunity to develop professionally related skills and knowledge. Course providers and students relied on the commitment and support of head teachers and the provision of a school-based mentor to support students with school-based tasks and learning. The courses continued to be widely available for about 10 years and were recognised by teaching assistants and most head teachers as valuable in developing their skills and knowledge. However, they were not part of any nationally recognised pay-and-conditions structure and many teaching assistants found achieving a corresponding certificate did little to enhance their status, conditions or pay.

The role of teaching assistants evolved further in the late 1990s with the introduction of the National Literacy (DfEE 1998) and National Numeracy Strategies (DfEE 1999) in England, when the need to provide support for children and teachers in delivering these strategies and the associated structured teaching approaches was recognised by government. Teaching assistants often played a critical role in helping to maintain children's attention during the sometimes long whole-class sessions and in mediating learning, particularly for children who found the teaching approach difficult, during the group sessions, although many did so with little or no formal training initially. As additional support or intervention programmes were introduced, for example the Early Literacy Support (ELS) programme, there was a growing expectation that these would be taught by teaching assistants. Teaching assistants were usually provided with training to teach these 'catch up' programmes, but this focused on preparing them to deliver the 'scripted' materials, rather than developing underpinning knowledge and understanding of how children learn. This approach to the role of teaching assistants appears to fit well with Moss's description of 'a growing army of childcare technicians, whose competences, procedures and goals are all tightly prescribed' (see Chapter 11).

In 2000, in line with a government commitment to expand the number of teaching assistants, the DfES sought to clarify their roles and acknowledge the contribution they could make to children's learning through the publication of a number of guidance documents for schools. The roles outlined included support for pupils, teachers, the curriculum and the school (DfES 2000a: 8). The need for further training and qualification pathways was also recognised and the DfES instigated the development of National Occupational Standards (NOS) at Levels 2 and 3 for teaching assistants. The DfES also commissioned the development of induction materials to be used by LEA trainers to provide four days of training for 'new' teaching assistants with a focus on role and context, behaviour management, literacy and mathematics (DfES, 2000b). Although these induction courses were designed for the new and expanding number of teaching assistants being employed in primary schools, they were the first form of training that many teaching assistants had access to and many who followed these courses had been working in the role for a number of years.

The development of the role also led to the publication of a large and increasing number of books written to help teaching assistants to carry out their new roles. It is interesting to note how often the titles contain the word 'guide' or 'handbook', sometimes prefixed by the words 'practical' or 'essential'. For some teaching assistants these books have provided the only form of training open to them and many provide useful suggestions and strategies. However, few provide underpinning knowledge and understanding of children's learning and development and, as a result, locate teaching assistants firmly in the role of technicians.

New opportunities for professional development

The introduction of Foundation Degrees in 2000 provided a new opportunity for teaching assistants to follow courses of study in Further Education (FE) and Higher Education (HE) while continuing to work. Specific Foundation Degrees for Teaching Assistants were introduced in many institutions alongside the introduction of Early Years Foundation Degrees. Unlike the Early Years Foundation Degrees, these were not 'sector endorsed' and therefore did not need to adhere to or meet externally imposed criteria or sets of standards. In addition, as there are no NOS for teaching assistants at Level 4 (certificate level) or Level 5 (intermediate level) of the QCA framework, Foundation Degree providers had no specific benchmarks to relate their course design and outcomes to, and inevitably this resulted in a wide variation in terms of course content and teaching and assessment strategies. While the gaining of a Foundation Degree often provides a sense of personal achievement for students, it is not linked to a qualification for teaching assistants and rarely results in any change in pay or conditions. Many teaching assistants with Early Years Foundation Degrees, including those with 'Senior Practitioner' status, have found that their schools did not recognise or know about this status and that it counted for little when they applied for jobs. The status of Higher Level Teaching Assistant (HLTA), which is discussed below, appears to carry more weight.

Higher Level Teaching Assistants

In 2003 the DfES and the Teacher Training Agency (TTA) introduced the new status of Higher Level Teaching Assistants (HLTA) for those supporting children's learning in schools. The status arose from government proposals to reform the school workforce and the signing of a national agreement on raising standards and tackling workload (see www.tda.gov.uk/remodelling/nationalagreement.aspx), with the aim of reducing or eliminating some of the routine, administrative tasks that teachers carried out and encouraging the development of 'professional' teams which would include teachers and support staff. HLTAs were perceived as having an extended and complementary, but not interchangeable, role with that of teachers in supporting children's learning. A series of standards were developed (TTA 2003) around professional values and practice, knowledge and understanding and teaching and learning activities, which teaching assistants were required to demonstrate through a portfolio of evidence. The standards drew on the standards for qualified teachers and included a requirement that candidates possessed GCSE grades A to C in English and mathematics. However, the standards are not linked to any qualification, which means that those with HLTA status include assistants who may not have engaged in any formal study since leaving school at age 16, in addition to those who may hold a Foundation Degree or an Honours Degree.

With the support of their head teachers and local authority funding, teaching assistants can submit themselves for assessment against the HLTA standards, either through a three-day assessment-only route (for those who consider they are already able to meet the standards), or through a 50-day training-and-assessment route (a dedicated training programme to enable candidates to meet the standards). Candidates have to complete four tasks involving work with an individual, a group of children, a whole class and one additional task. Assessment is through a school visit from an accredited assessor, who has an initial meeting with the candidate, scrutinises the portfolio of evidence, meets with the head teacher and a nominated class teacher, and has a final interview with the candidate. Interestingly, no observation of the candidate's teaching or work with children is carried out as part of this assessment – as is the case for those submitting themselves for assessment as an Early Years Professional (EYP). The government set ambitious targets for the training of HLTAs and by March 2007 15,000 candidates had gained this status (www.tda.gov.uk/about/mediarelations/2007/20070326.aspx).

As with previous initiatives, the status is not linked directly to national pay and conditions and the role has been widely interpreted by schools. While the Training and Development Agency for Schools (TDA) (previously the TTA) emphasises HLTAs' roles in supporting children's learning, many are being used to provide preparation, planning and assessment time (PPA) (another element of workforce reform) for teachers and cover for absent staff at least on a short-term basis. HLTAs' working days and weeks can vary considerably, with some being based in one reception class for the whole year and others covering PPA time across the school. Some plan with teachers, others 'deliver' lessons based on teacher planning and yet others do their own planning. Some HLTAs, especially in small schools, assume leadership roles for curriculum areas such as Physical Education, ICT or Art. Many undertake a mixture of supporting children's learning and PPA time and are paid different rates of pay for the different activities, the implication being that the higher status is not perceived as linked to an enhanced professional role, but simply to their ability to take charge of a whole class on their own. A number of HLTAs are also assuming leadership and management roles for other TAs, some as members of the senior management team. Because schools are able to establish their own employment and deployment arrangements and rates of pay and many heads to do want any government prescription in this area (Townsend and Parker 2006), many HLTAs are unaware of circumstances in other schools.

Recent developments

The establishment of the Children's Workforce Development Council (CWDC) in 2005 to carry forward the Every Child Matters agenda (DfES 2003) and provide coordination in terms of training, qualifications, support and advice for those working with children and young people, added a further dimension for those working in schools. The TDA, with responsibility for the schools workforce, is a member of the Children's Workforce Network and an observer on the board of CWDC. However, there appears to be a lack of synergy between the organisations in terms of those working with young children in the private, voluntary and independent sector (PVI) and schools exemplified by the introduction of the EYP status which, while originally designed for all those working with children in the Early Years Foundation Stage (EYFS), now only applies to those working in the PVI sector.

In September 2005 the TDA took over responsibility for the training of all support staff in schools, including teaching assistants, and it now acts as the sector skills council for the NOS for teaching assistants. Both the National Occupational Standards for teaching assistants – now called 'NOS Supporting teaching and learning in schools' (available at www.ukstandards.org/Find_Occupational_Standards. aspx) – and the Higher Level Teaching Assistants Standards (available at www.tda.gov.uk/support/hlta/professstandards.aspx) have undergone revision in 2007. The NOS have been considerably expanded to take account of the diverse roles undertaken by teaching assistants in schools as a result of the remodelling of the workforce. The new standards reflect the development and revision of standards in other areas of the children and young people's workforce, including those for children's care, learning and development. The HLTA standards have been redrafted to reflect changes in the standards for Qualified Teacher Status (QTS) (available at www.tda.gov.uk/teachers/professionalstandards.aspx) and cover similar areas – professional attributes, professional knowledge and understanding and professional skills.

Government figures suggest that the number of teaching assistants in schools more than doubled in the period from 1997 to 2007: from 61,300 to 162,900 with over 105,000 currently working in primary schools (DfES 2007). In most schools, teaching assistants now have access to a range of in-house and local authority courses to support their professional development, as well as courses in FE and HE. The second part of this chapter explores the impact this professionalisation of the workforce has had on professional practice and the views of practitioners about their own professionalism.

TEACHING ASSISTANTS AND PROFESSIONALISM

Developing professionalism

Defining what 'professionalism' looks like in the early years is the subject of much debate in the UK and elsewhere. The diverse profile of early years practitioners, the variety of workplace settings, roles, resources and regulation that cover the age range has made it difficult for agreement to be reached on what should constitute a corpus of professional knowledge. It can also be argued that 'a profession' encompasses more than just professional knowledge; it also includes skills and competencies, dispositions, values and beliefs, the 'tools' of a profession and notions of professional expertise. For many teaching assistants, these attributes are developed as part of their working practice, through their 'apprenticeship' to teachers and involvement in a specific 'community of practice' – their school. Most teaching assistants, at least for a period of time, can be viewed as apprentices, their learning as situated and derived through observation and imitation of the approaches and techniques teachers use to support children's learning, while not aspiring (in the majority of cases) to become teachers themselves. They are engaged in a community (their school) where the notion of 'legitimate peripheral participation' (Lave and Wenger 1991) is central to their effective working and development.

However, teaching assistants' access to knowledge, experience of participation and professional development is highly dependent on how their school community is constituted and interpreted and the opportunities that are provided by its members, especially those in more powerful positions. Teaching assistants are often members of the local community served by the school in which they work. Many began work in their current schools as volunteers and progressed to paid employment and training as a teaching assistant and then, in some cases, as a HLTA. A feature of teaching assistant employment is the length of time they have often served in one school, their lack of willingness to apply for positions in other schools and their lack of knowledge of differences in practice in other schools and settings. Their long-standing relationships with their schools means they often know children and their families well, but this can make it difficult for them to position themselves as professionals in their school contexts and for other members of staff to view them in this way. Being a professional (as opposed to being professional) can be as much about how others perceive you as about how you see yourself and the status that you have in the school as a teaching assistant. A number of teaching assistants mention their feelings of relative powerlessness:

> I am working in an environment which is constantly evolving, and sometimes I feel powerless because my role in the school often doesn't allow me to be involved in decision making.

> (A teaching assistant working in a reception class)

If relationship boundaries are well defined and rigid there will be fewer opportunities for teaching assistants to benefit from their 'apprenticeship' or to cross boundaries and work in the professional teams that are seen as an element of workforce reform. Lave and Wenger see the concept of community as crucial in understanding how what counts as knowledge is established and located, and see this as much more than technical skills:

> A community of practice is a set of relations among persons, activity, and world, over time and in relation with other tangential and overlapping communities of practice.

> (Lave and Wenger 1991: 98)

The ability of TAs to demonstrate their professional knowledge and skills can therefore be dependent on their relationships with, or on the dispositions and attitudes of, the teachers and head teachers they work with. This can also mean that teaching assistants need to adopt different roles or identities with different teachers. This is particularly the case for those working as HLTAs in schools where they move from a 'support role' in one classroom to a more 'collaborative' role in another, and to a situation where they are planning and teaching a lesson on their own at another point in the day or week. Thus the situation teaching assistants find themselves in may, to a greater or lesser extent, determine how they can apply their knowledge and skills to their practice and whether or not they assume a role which focuses on helping children to complete a set task, whether they 'deliver' the curriculum plans and learning outcomes of teachers, or whether they engage with teaching and learning in a way that will help children to develop as learners.

For many teaching assistants, training courses situated away from their schools or further study provides the first opportunity for them to engage with other practitioners working in different situations and to begin to question knowledge that they had previously seen as given and to engage in professional dialogue and debate and reflect:

The view that development is a transformation of participation of people engaged in shared endeavours [and] avoids the idea that the social world is external to the individual and that development consists of acquiring knowledge and skills.

(Rogoff 1998: 690)

Student reflections

The Open University (OU) offers an Early Years Sector Endorsed Foundation Degree which, like other Foundation Degrees for early years practitioners, 'enables students to learn by examining attitudes, perceptions and realities relating to their own practice in the workplace' (O'Keefe and Tait 2004: 28). The study materials and the computer-mediated conferencing (CMC) (see Chapter 9) aim to support students in developing and sharing their knowledge and understanding in a new community of practice.

A number of students who have followed the Foundation Degree in Early Years (FDEY) at the Open University are teaching assistants and some have also achieved HLTA status. As part of an ongoing research study (Cable, Goodliff and Miller 2007a, 2007b; Cable and Goodliff 2007) students completing the FDEY were asked to reflect on their learning and the impact on their thinking and practice. The majority cite an increase in confidence as an outcome of their studies and relate this to their increased knowledge and understanding of theoretical perspectives. Some also mention increased respect from colleagues, indicating that their roles and relationships have changed through the process of study linked to work-based practice and reflection:

I am able to go out quite confidently amongst other foundation stage practitioners in different forums, for example last week I was at a moderation meeting over the foundation stage curriculum and I am confident enough now to be able to go in with those sort of people and know that the knowledge, that the things that I am saying are backed up by practice and theory.

(HLTA working in a reception class)

I certainly get a lot of respect from colleagues because of my course and the sort of extra knowledge and theory that that has brought with it. I am able to plan and assess alongside class teachers and I have managed to gain a big insight into the foundation stage curriculum because of my work through the course.

(HLTA working in a reception class)

Reflection on practice is generally recognised as an important component in developing professional and pedagogical knowledge, understanding and practice (see Menmuir and Hughes 2004; Dahlberg, Moss and Pence, 1999) (see also Chapter 8). Moyles (2001: 89) suggests that '"professionalism" is related to thinking about facets of one's role' and that: 'it requires high levels of professional knowledge coupled with self-esteem and self-confidence'.

Many teaching assistants locate themselves (or find themselves located) in subordinate roles to teachers and position themselves as mediators of learning, interpreting the teacher's actions for children and the children's learning for teachers. The mediation of learning in this way requires great skill and flexibility. For teaching assistants who may feel relatively powerless in terms of decision making in some schools, their work in classrooms may be the main area in which they can develop their professional practice and demonstrate their professional competence in supporting children's learning

In the following example from an interview transcript, another OU student reflects on changes in her practice, which indicate changes in her professional thinking about her role in facilitating learning and the importance of artefacts in mediating learning:

There are certain activities that I have changed, certainly I have brought in more literacy and numeracy to the role play area and I have been more conscious of . . .the use of ICT in the role play area as well. I set up a travel agent role play in which I created luggage labels and information pads, airline tickets. I had signs that prompted discussion, communication. I also ensured that there were things like telephones, calculators, tills, a computer screen and keyboard so they could use ICT within that environment.

(HLTA working in a reception class)

In the next example a student reflects on changes in the way she positions herself with respect to activities the child is engaged with, suggesting a move from 'direct guidance' to practice that is more akin to scaffolding (Wood 1998) or guided participation (Rogoff 1998), where the adult enters into the activity and mediates learning by supporting the child in problem solving:

Again that will probably come down to the way I challenge and question them, for example a couple of weeks ago a young boy had made a helicopter in the construction area, but the propellers did not go round so I sort of said, 'Oh, I wonder how we can make the propellers go round, do you think you could have a look?' and he went off and came back having made – fixed in a new piece that made the propellers go round. So it is challenging them and encouraging them to extend their learning without specific question and answering.

(HLTA working in a reception class)

And in the last interview extract below, another student shows how reflection has become a powerful part of her learning and how this process brought about changes in her professional practice. She repositions herself as an active rather than passive participant in children's learning, recognising her own agency in determining how she will mediate learning for children rather than viewing learning as a task to be carried out.

Before my study . . . I probably would have just carried out things as a sort of routine thing, I would have just done it under the direction of the class teacher, but since my study I now – because I have a better understanding of child development and through my study I have been able to develop my own thinking and why I do things, the things that I do in the way that I do them – I now think more about what I am doing and I am more open in my thoughts about what I am doing. Say for instance a numeracy session where I would have just undertaken the basics of that group work from the teacher's plan, I now – I observe the children in a different way and I think about why I am doing what I am doing in a different way. I don't just approach it as this is the task that I have to do, but I approach it as thinking of how the children are developing and what concepts they are developing and why and what sort of stage they may be at, perhaps thinking about theories behind their learning.

(HLTA working in Year 1)

These extracts suggest that many teaching assistants want to be more than technicians carrying out tasks under the direction of teachers. They wish to understand not only the purpose of activities but how they will support children's learning, and they want to engage in professional dialogue from a well-informed knowledge base. In order to do this, they need to gain access to the knowledge of their communities through study and dialogue with others, as well as through practical experience and through recognition of their complementary role in professional teams.

SUMMARY

This chapter has examined the development and professionalisation of the teaching assistant role in primary schools over the last 15 years. It has also explored the developing professional role of teaching assistants in supporting the learning of children in the early years. Some of the barriers and constraints teaching assistants encounter have been discussed, together with the potential impact of further study on professional roles and practice. Teaching assistants have much to contribute to the development and learning of young children in schools, but their role and status needs to be seen in the context of the whole early years workforce to enable them to make an effective contribution in the future.

Questions/points for discussion/reflection

1 What do you think are the particular contributions that teaching assistants can and should make to young children's learning?
2 Do you think that professional status should be linked to professional qualifications and if so, why?
3 How has involvement in 'communities of practice' supported your professional development?

REFERENCES

Cable, C., Goodliff, G. and Miller, L. (2007a) 'Developing reflective early years practitioners within a regulatory framework', *Malaysian Journal of Distance Education, 9(2)*, 1–19

Cable, C., Goodliff, G. and Miller, L. (2007b) 'How adults perceive their role in facilitating children's learning'. Paper presented at the EECERA Conference, Prague, 30th August 2007

Cable, C. and Goodliff, G. (2007) 'Work-based learning and transitions in professional identity: women in the early years workforce'. Paper presented at the Women in Lifelong Learning Conference, Birkbeck College, University of London, May 2007

Dahlberg, G., Moss, P. and Pence, A. (1999) *Beyond Quality in Early Childhood Education and Care.* London: Falmer Press

Department for Education and Employment (1998) *The National Literacy Strategy: Framework for England.* London: DfEE

Department for Education and Employment (1999) *The National Numeracy Strategy: Framework for England.* London: DfEE

Department for Education and Skills (2000a) *Working with Teaching Assistants: A Good Practice Guide. London:* DfES

Department for Education and Skills (2000b) *Teaching Assistant File Induction Training for Teaching Assista*nts. London: DfES

Department for Education and Skills (2003) *Every Child Matters.* London: DfES

Department for Education and Skills SFR/2007 *School Workforce in England* online www.dcsf.gov.uk/rsgateway/DB/SFR/s000725/index.shtml (accessed 7/9/2007)

Lave, J. and Wenger, E. (1991) *Situated Learning: Legitimate Peripheral Participation.* Cambridge: Cambridge University Press

Menmuir, J. and Hughes, A. (2004) 'Early education and childcare: the developing professional', *European Early Childhood Education Research Journal, 12(2)*, 33–41

Moyles, J. (2001) 'Passion, paradox and professionalism in early years education', *Early Years, 21(2)*, 81–95

Moyles, J. with Suschitzky, W. (1997) *'Jills of all Trades?. . .'.* London: Leicester University/Association of Teachers and Lecturers

O'Keefe, J. and Tait, K. (2004) 'An examination of the UK Early Years Foundation Degree and the evolution of Senior Practitioners – enhancing work-based learning by engaging in reflective and critical thinking', *International Journal of Early Years Education, 12(1)*, 25–41

Rogoff, B. (1998) 'Cognition as a collaborative process'. In Damon, E. et al. (eds) *Handbook of Child Psychology* (5th edition), Vol 2. New York: John Wiley and Son Inc.

Teacher Training Agency (2003) *Professional Standards for Higher Level Teaching Assistants.* London: TTA

www.tda.gov.uk/about/mediarelations/2007/20070326.aspx (accessed 6/9/2007)

www.tda.gov.uk/remodelling/nationalagreement.aspx (accessed 7/9/2007)

Townsend, M. and Parker, M. (2006) 'Changing times, changing roles: evaluating the impact of higher level teaching assistants on learning and teaching in the classroom' (unpublished paper)

Wood, D. (1998) *How Children Think and Learn: The Social Contexts of Cognitive Development* (2nd edition). Oxford: Blackwell

Further reading

Cable, C. and Eyres, I. (eds) (2005) *Primary Teaching Assistants: Curriculum in Context*. London: David Fulton Publishers

Hancock, R. and Collins, J. (eds) (2005) *Primary Teaching Assistants: Learners and Learning*. London: David Fulton Publishers

www.ukstandards.org/Find_Occupational_Standards.aspx (accessed 25/10/2007)

www.tda.gov.uk/support/hlta/professstandards.aspx (accessed 25/10/2007)

THE 'P' WORD AND HOME-BASED CHILD CARERS

6

Sue Griffin

INTRODUCTION

Some childminders (or family day carers) choose to promote themselves as 'professional' but some seem to be inhibited from using the word; others, practitioners in other parts of the childcare sector, parents and those outside the sector have often expressed scepticism about being able to regard childminders as professionals. However, as the twenty-first century started, milestones in the history of childminding in extending training and qualification opportunities for childminders and the emergence of quality assurance schemes have enabled childminders to develop their professionalism, and so to make stronger claims to be regarded as professionals.

CHILDMINDERS' CLAIMS TO PROFESSIONALISM

In the late-1980s, the then Health Minister, Virginia Bottomley, addressed a conference of the National Childminding Association (NCMA); in justifying the government's decision to permit childminders to be the only practitioners caring for other people's children who would be able to smack them, she proffered the argument that childminders were not like professionals but 'like aunties and grannies'. The audience at the conference showed very clearly what they thought of this description of their role and status. For these childminders, committed enough to their work to travel from all parts of England and Wales to a weekend gathering, this was a slur. They did regard themselves as 'professional', even if a satisfactory definition of the word was yet to emerge.

Some childminders have long sought to promote themselves as offering a professional service/being professional/taking a professional approach to their work, and NCMA has encouraged childminders to have a sense of pride in the value of the work they do and the significance of the skills they use in that work. Owen (2006) describes the persistent opposition to characterising childminding as a profession. She sees the change in attitude as coming about through childminders' own engagement in the debate.

Childminders enter childminding from many backgrounds and some already have professional status in another role, either in the children's workforce, or in some other sector. An NCMA spokesperson quoted to me examples not only of former nurses and teachers but also a motorway services manager, a police officer and a legal secretary. Not surprisingly, these are usually the childminders most likely to want to claim professional status and develop their skills in their childminding role.

CHILDMINDERS' PERCEPTIONS OF THEIR PROFESSIONALISM

Through my work for NCMA and as a writer, I have listened to childminders for over 20 years and I have heard many expressions of understanding of what it means to be a professional in the role of childminder. Often usage of the term centres on how they present themselves to the outside world and, for many childminders, this is initially about demonstrating their business-like and organised approach to the job. The advent of easy access to information technology (IT), which can enable the production of attractive written materials, has led to growing numbers of childminders producing leaflets to promote their 'childminding services', and some have their own websites. They write policies documents for parents and want to show that they are offering families something which is on a par with nurseries that have prospectuses. They use printed contracts and record-keeping documents to show that they are business-oriented.

Of course, being business-like is not enough to win the status of professionalism, and there has to be stronger evidence than this of childminders' attitudes and behaviour in their work if they are to make a legitimate claim to that status.

I found that when probing behind childminders' desire to project an image perceived to be professional, some more practice-related concepts emerged. These range from taking proper measures to keep children safe, and providing them with healthy food, to identifying and planning experiences and activities suited to the developmental needs of particular children. The argument for rejecting the need to have smacking as part of their practice was explicitly made by childminders as being unnecessary for those who had professional skills and a calm approach to handling children's behaviour. For some childminders, communicating with parents in confident, open and honest ways, achieving a balance between friendliness and a business relationship, is a signifier of professionalism, whilst others emphasise commitment to a family by being reliable. Some will focus on generally recognised professional values, such as confidentiality and meeting the individual needs of each child within an equality and anti-discrimination agenda. Childminders who have been able to take advantage of training opportunities and participate in quality assurance schemes are more likely to emphasise the importance of the professional habit of reflecting on practice and continuing to improve that practice, including through on-going training. One strand of the meaning of professional for childminders relates to the regard that others have for their work and the status it is accorded. They express considerable frustration with the low value they feel that society at large, and even their colleagues in the sector, place on their role and work.

From time to time, the debate re-surfaces that the word 'childminder' should be abandoned in favour of some other term which would sound more professional, help to raise the status of the role, and represent more closely its value to society. A title has been sought that would carry greater connotations of a high quality service for children and families, offered by practitioners with ethical values in their work and commitment to developing their knowledge and skills, in other words, professionalism. The last time an NCMA conference debated this issue a resolution emerged to seek to develop a more positive image for the word 'childminder', rather than try to change to a term which had connotations that might command more respect.

RELUCTANCE TO CLAIM THE STATUS OF PROFESSIONALISM

Of course, not all childminders have wanted to present themselves as professionals. There are still some who want to be known as 'Auntie' and lay no claims to a status which would put them in the same category as practitioners who provide childcare services in other settings. Some childminders struggle with the idea of being in business and taking money for looking after other people's children. Mooney (2003: 123) describes 'tensions between being committed to childcare and wanting to earn a reasonable income', and identifies 'suggesting that one is motivated by financial gain rather than by caring about children appears to suggest that one cannot care enough'. For others, moving towards the idea of professionalism could undermine their self-image of providing a warmly affectionate level of care for children. Karlsson (1995: 61) reports, 'In many countries there is discussion about whether a family day carer should see herself as a professional or not . . .. [some] argue that a professional family day carer might lose her "genuine motherly feeling"'.

One of the key features in claiming professional status is training and qualifications, but some childminders cannot see the need to train for the role. A survey carried out by the Thomas Coram Research Unit (TCRU) and published as the report '*Who Cares?*' (Mooney et al. 2001) found childminders who felt that a childcare qualification was less important than the experience of being a parent, and quoted a new childminder: 'childminding is like – it just needs me to be a mother. And I don't really know what sort of qualification you really need' (Mooney et al. 2001: 23). Ferri's (1992) study of 30 childminders, attending two courses in the early 1990s, led her to generalise that childminders were strongly resistant to the idea that they had anything to learn about how to provide for children, since they were mothers.

The childminders who do want to see themselves, and be seen by others, as professionals find these views frustrating. The way some childminders attempt to define professionalism is by distancing themselves from those childminders who they consider do not take a professional approach to their work. Those with poor practice or unprofessional attitudes are seen as letting the image of childminding down. The reluctance of these childminders to claim professional status should not overshadow the efforts of others to do so. A more helpful focus is on whether the role is capable of being defined in terms of professionalism.

CAN CHILDMINDERS BE REGARDED AS PROFESSIONALS?

There is still a view, both within and without childminding, that childminders are not and cannot be regarded as professionals. The reasons for this arise from the distinct features which make childminding different from other forms of childcare and are both its strength and its perceived weakness. The nature of childminders' work is at the end of the childcare spectrum which has the appearance of being closest to parents' own care for their children. Owen (2006) makes the point that the professional status of home-based child care has always been affected by the fact that it is work done by women, within a setting in which women mother. Mooney (2003: 112) refers to the way 'the roles of mother and childcare provider are closely intertwined', especially because childminders often look after their own children at the same time as they provide care for other people's children. In addition, childminders work alone and in the domestic surroundings of their own home and this has not been seen as a professional context for work. Possibly, that perception may be changing now that more workers in a wide range of employment sectors work from home. However, Owen comments that most of such workers are engaged in activities which are different from those normally carried out in a domestic setting. Childminders' work has been seen as too close to that of a housewife and mother to be accorded the status of professional activity. Karlsson (2004) identifies the uncertainty displayed by researchers and commentators on childminding which arises from the way childminding is on the border between the private sphere of mothering and the public sphere of childcare. This 'uncertainty' has led several commentators to dwell on what Mooney (2003: 111) calls the 'close relationship with the task of mothering'. However, Dalli (2003) points out that this connection applies across all early childhood work. The tendency to see this close relationship as a negative aspect of childminding, holding it back from professionalism, can and should be challenged.

The language childminders use to describe their work can lead to an assumption that they do not (perhaps cannot) 'differentiate between the care provided as a mother and the care provided as a childminder' (Mooney 2003: 117). The TCRU report (Mooney et al. 2001: 45) quotes a childminder saying: 'I just treat them as part of a family', and reaches the conclusion that 'childminders describe their role as being very similar to that of a mother' (Mooney et al. 2001: 50). Yet this report also notes that this partly arises from the 'difficulty in expressing the difference between childminder and mother' and quotes the childminder who says, 'you're like mum, but you're not mum'. Mooney (2003: 119) acknowledges that childminders 'recognise that what they are doing is not the same as mothering'. This indicates that childminders do have an understanding of a subtle differentiation between the two roles. When Folke-Fichtelius and Vännman (1990: 10) gathered perceptions at an international conference of family day carers (childminders), asking, 'Is [the childminder] supposed to be an extra mother when the child's parents are at work?', they recorded expressions such as: 'While I enjoy each child and love them, I do not pretend to be their mother', and 'We go to great lengths to establish a definite role from that of the parent'.

The role of childminding may indeed be, according to Mooney et al. (2001), very much akin to mothering, but when childminders claim to treat childminded children *like* their own, I have found them to mean that they make the positive claim of caring for the childminded children *as well as* they care for their own children. A childminder may say, 'I'm his second Mum' but that doesn't mean that she has any intention of usurping the parents' role, or is unable to distinguish between her full-time, life-long role as a parent and her part-time, temporary role as a childminder.

Although childminding happens in a home setting and is closely linked to providing parental care, this does not mean that childminders cannot offer a professional service, defined in its own terms. Rather than being preoccupied with a negative view of childminding as close to mothering (perhaps with connotations of 'merely' mothering), it is more helpful to focus on the unique way childminding combines the personal and the intimate with the professional.

Childminders often refer with pride to how they provide loving care, and this may not fit into a definition of professionalism, which emphasises a distance between practitioner and client, but it must surely be seen in a positive light. Our growing understanding of the significance of continuity of care, from an adult prepared to make an emotional commitment, for children's emotional well-being points to the advantages childminding can offer in providing stability of emotional attachment. Instead of seeing the claim to be a loving carer as denying the right to professionalism, it could be argued that childminders are demonstrating professionalism by fulfilling this most pressing need of children, especially the youngest. Equally, taking a professional approach to work does not have to undermine the highly prized features of childminding of homeliness and loving care. Childminders and parents often describe childminding as a 'home away from home', emphasising that the reason many parents choose childminding for their children is because they want them to be in a relaxed, informal, home-like atmosphere. Karlsson (2004) comments on the discomfort of some parents at leaving children in care outside the family, which leads them to choose the form of care which involves spending time in a family home and so feels closest to the care they provide for their children themselves.

IS CHILDMINDING BECOMING A PROFESSIONAL ROLE?

There are many definitions of what it means to 'be professional'. Those that occur consistently in discussing childminding include:

- a meaningful threshold of entry;
- expectations about training and qualifications;
- a set of professional standards, which those claiming professional status are required to show they can meet;
- membership of a professional body.

As Karlsson (2004) argues, what has worked against childminders being seen as professional is that there has been the lack of requirements for training or standards of quality. But this has changed and is changing, and provides an optimistic future for the growth of professionalism in childminding.

Threshold for entry

Although regulation of childminding was introduced in the UK in 1949, the entry threshold was not set at a high level. It was the responsibility of the registering authorities to demonstrate that an applicant wishing to become a childminder was not 'a fit person'; the onus was not on the applicant to show their suitability or that they could offer a high quality service. Whilst the transfer of regulation from local authorities to Ofsted (the regulatory authority in England) did bring national consistency of standards to be met and introduced requirements for attendance at a basic introductory course and first aid training, the threshold remains low. Owen (2006) points out that self-regulation is one of the basic features of a profession, and for an occupation to be closely regulated by the state suggests that it is not capable of regulating itself. To take a path towards self-regulation would be a huge challenge for childminding.

Training and qualifications

If participation in an occupation requires a body of knowledge and skills, then the occupation may be regarded as 'professional' (see Chapter 3). To acquire this knowledge and these skills is likely to require training to enhance and develop any pre-existing experience. If a course of training has attached to it a form of assessment which enables the knowledge and skills to be confirmed, it has the added recognition as a qualification. In the mid-1980s, NCMA cooperated with the Open University (OU) to devise a pack of materials (OU/NCMA 1986) to be used in flexible ways for training childminders. For the first time, it was acknowledged that training aimed at other childcare practitioners was not likely to meet childminders' training needs accurately; there was a specific body of knowledge required to be effective as a childminder. The difference lies in a range of aspects of childminding practice. The children cared for may cover a wide age range, from birth to teenage; the home-based environment is rich in potential for flexible and individualised learning experiences and activities for children, but they must be organised in a very different way from centre-based provision; the relationship with parents is a challenging one – friendly in nature, with people coming into the childminder's home each day, but based on a written business contract; childminders are self-employed and need to know how to run their small business; because they do not work with colleagues, they do not have support and advice immediately at hand when dealing with potentially difficult matters such as a child protection issue.

In the 1990s, NCMA built on the 'OU pack' by developing *The Key to Quality*, more extensive training materials and model programmes for courses (NCMA 1991). Even for those aspects of practice which were closer to that of other practitioners', childminders (like all adult learners) find that learning materials which are based on situations they recognise and understand from their childminding work enable them to grasp concepts and explore ideas more effectively. Training which sets out to value the knowledge and skills the childminders bring to their role from their previous experience, and then shows ways of building on and developing that knowledge and skills, has done much to build up childminders' confidence and self-respect for the work they do. These are important steps on the road to professionalism.

In 1999 NCMA worked with CACHE (Council for Awards in Children's Care and Education) to launch the first national qualification for childminders, the Level 3 Certificate in Childminding Practice (revised in 2005 into the Diploma in Home-based Childcare). The students who joined the first courses were reported in NCMA's magazine, *Who Minds?*, (Griffin 1998) as saying that they saw it as raising the profile of childminding and helping their work to be taken more seriously. They saw themselves as embarking on a career in childminding in a professional way, not as a sideline. By 2005, the *Childcare and Early Years Workforce Survey* (DfES 2005) reported that 88 per cent of childminders had undertaken training, and 65 per cent held a 'relevant' qualification, 43 per cent at Level 3. This represented an increase from 2003 from 61 per cent undertaking training, 34 per cent holding a relevant qualification with 16 per cent at Level 3. This has been a highly significant step forward for the professionalisation of childminding, particularly in the light of a growing body of research linking training to higher quality provision for children.

Childminders' apparent reluctance in the past to engage in training has been shown to be more linked to time constraints than an assumption that they 'have nothing left to learn'. Childminders cannot join daytime courses and it is difficult for them to take time out on weekdays as working parents rely on them. It is a tribute to their professional commitment that so many childminders do manage to fit their training into evenings and weekends, thus encroaching on their free time.

Standards

For a work role to be regarded as professional, it could be argued that there is need for clear standards that indicate what constitutes high quality operation of that work role. Such standards have emerged for childminding through the development of quality assurance schemes, primarily as a result of the development of childminding networks. Since the early days of NCMA, childminders have met together in local groups. However, childminding networks are more formal and structured. The key role is that of an employed coordinator who has time dedicated to recruiting, supporting and monitoring childminders in the network. Network childminders have to meet defined standards for their practice, significantly higher than the low base-line required for registration. Owen (2005) has shown that networks which are quality assured by NCMA's Children Come First scheme, established in 1998, raise childminders' self-esteem and self-confidence and encourage childminders to think of themselves as professionals and to work in more professional ways, by belonging to a professional group striving together for higher standards. NCMA has also developed a quality assurance scheme for individual childminders, Quality First (NCMA 2007), which offers opportunities for self-assessment and develops understanding and skills for reflective practice, a pivot of professionalism.

A professional organisation

The importance of the National Childminding Association in developing the quality and status of childminding since its foundation in 1977 cannot be underestimated. NCMA has become a powerful voice for childminders in policy development and must be credited with the key role that childminding has been given in government plans in recent years, such as *Choice for Parents, the Best Start for Children: a Ten Year Strategy for Childcare* (HM Treasury 2004). It is a provider-led organisation, so is always closely attuned to what childminders want and need. It does not 'do unto' childminders, but responds to their strongly held and expressed views. NCMA provides childminders across England and Wales with opportunities to engage with other childminders, enabling them to exchange and share experiences of what it means to be a childminder, and to have discussions about the future development of professionalism. It provides what Owen describes as a context in which professional development is seen as an acceptable and recommended activity (2006 unpublished dissertation).

NEW ROLES, RISING STATUS

Perceptions of childminders' professionalism have also been enhanced by the emergence of new roles in childminding. From the 1980s, social services departments were using childminders in an ad hoc way to support vulnerable families. There was often an expectation that the childminders would do this for very little financial return, which could be viewed as exploitation of childminders' caring attitudes and a denial of their professional status. In the 1990s, NCMA actively promoted the development of 'community childminding', with childminders who did this demanding work being carefully selected and properly supported through networks, so they 'felt more professional' and were given 'more status . . . and recognition' (Statham 2003: 184). This moved this work forward significantly, especially in opening up access to training, for example, in working with disabled children.

When nursery education vouchers were introduced in the 1990s, childminders were specifically excluded from receiving them, reflecting the view that they were not and could not be 'educators'. However, the advent of the Curriculum Guidance for the Foundation Stage (QCA, 2000) introduced a more open approach and the role of 'accredited childminder' was created. Childminders who were members of an approved childminding network and were able to meet additional standards of practice became eligible to receive nursery education funding. This has given a boost to the professional status of these childminders, as they have been included in training alongside other Foundation Stage providers.

The development of training and networks has in itself produced new opportunities for some childminders to build on their childminding experiences and move into roles of tutor on courses for childminders and network co-ordinator, as well as development worker. Others who wish to stay in childminding but who seek new challenges have become 'support childminders', providing advice and help to new childminders who are going through the processes of registration and in their early months in the job. The opening up of roles like this is offering childminders new opportunities for professional development and leadership roles, building a professional pathway for childminding.

SUMMARY

Gelder (1998) noted that childminders like to be their own boss and see themselves as a childcare professional but, as Karlsson (2004) states, becoming recognised as a professional is a long process. That process seems to be well under way for childminders, but is not yet complete. The key elements in professionalism, training and qualifications and standards for good practice have seen major developments in recent years, which are having a positive effect in engendering professionalism in more childminders. There can be no doubt that the growth of relevant training opportunities for childminders has developed their perception of themselves as professionals, a more positive attitude to what training can offer, and an understanding of the need for continuing professional development.

Quality assurance schemes define what 'good' or 'professional' childminding might look like and help childminders to embark on the journey of reflecting on and improving their practice. Approved childminding networks have the potential to confirm professionalism for childminders, but only if the current rigorous standards are maintained. Any watering down of the networks' systems for supporting childminders' practice is likely to hinder future prospects of continuing to define and develop professional standards.

A sign that childminders have not yet won the battle for parity with others in the sector is provided by the experience of one of the earliest candidates for Early Years Professional status (see Chapter 2), who felt that there was little in the pathway she followed that related to home-based childcarers, which made her feel disadvantaged. An example she gave was that most of the scenarios used in the pathway training and assessment materials were placed in a day nursery (Faux 2006). There is still much left to achieve to convince the wider world that childminders can be professionals, offering the highest standards of care and education to children.

Questions/points for discussion/reflection

1 Why do you think working with children in a home-based environment has had lower status and less respect than working with children in centre-based provision?
2 With moves towards a common core of training and an integrated framework of qualifications, what are the imperatives for retaining a degree of specialism for home-based working?
3 Children's centres are expected to include childminding networks in their range of services. How far is this happening, and are less rigorous models of networking being used?

REFERENCES

Dalli, C. (2003) 'Mothering, caring and professionalism in family day care', Paper presented to the Third International Family Day Care Conference, Wellington, New Zealand

Department for Education and Skills (DfES) (2005) *Childcare and Early Years Providers Survey: Childminding Research Report* RR763 http://www.dfes.gov.uk/research/data/uploadfiles/RR763.pdf

Faux, K. (2006) 'In the lead', *Nursery World*, Spring

Ferri, E. (1992) *What Makes Childminding Work?* London: National Children's Bureau

Folke-Fichtelius, M. and Vännman, M. (1990) *Family Day Care Provider – Teacher or Substitute Mother?* Uppsala: Folke-Fichtelius Ab

Gelder, U. (1998) 'Childminding: does it work for women?' Paper presented at the Social Policy Association Annual Conference, July 1998

Griffin, S. (1998) 'Developing childminding practice – the story so far', *Who Minds?* Summer, 12–13

HM Treasury (2004) in conjunction with Department for Education and Skills (DfES), Department for Work and Pensions (DWP), Department for Trade and Industry (DTI) *Choice for Parents, the Best Start for Children: a Ten Year Strategy for Childcare.* London: H.M.S.O. (http://www.hm-treasury.gov.uk./media/B/E/pbr04childcare_480upd050105.pdf (accessed 29/7/2007)

Karlsson, M. (1995) *Family Day Care in Europe: a Report for the EC Childcare Network.* Brussels: European Commission (Equal Opportunities Unit)

Karlsson, M. (2004): 'Kunskap om familjedaghem' (Knowledge of family day care), *Forskning i fokus (Research in focus)* nr. 20. Stockholm: Myndigheten för skolutveckling (The Authority for School Development)

Mooney, A. (2003) 'What it means to be a childminder: work or love?' In *Family Day Care: International Perspectives on Policy, Practice and Quality.* London and Philadelphia: Jessica Kingsley Publishers

Mooney, A., Knight, A., Moss, P. and Owen, C. (2001) *Who Cares? Childminding in the 1990s.* Bristol: The Policy Press

National Childminding Association (NCMA) (1991) *The Key to Quality.* London: National Childminding Association

National Childminding Association (NCMA) (2007) *Quality First* http://www.ncmaqualityfirst.co.uk/ (accessed 11/10/2007)

The Open University (OU) and National Childminding Association (NCMA) (1986) *Childminding: Materials for Learning and Discussion.* Milton Keynes: The Open University and National Childminding Association

Owen, S. (2005) *Children Come First: the Role of Approved Childminding Networks in Changing Practice.* London: The National Children's Bureau and the National Childminding Association

Owen, S. (2006) 'Organised systems of childminding in Britain: a sociological examination of changing social policies, a profession and the operation of a service'. Unpublished doctoral dissertation, University of California, Santa Cruz (UMI number 3219644)

Qualifications and Curriculum Authority/Department for Education and Skills (2000) *Curriculum Guidance for the Foundation Stage.* London: QCA/DfES

Statham, J. (2003) 'Provider and parent perspectives on family day care for "children in need"'. In *Family Day Care: International Perspectives on Policy, Practice and Quality.* London and Philadelphia: Jessica Kingsley Publishers

Further reading

National Childminding Association Website www.ncma.org.uk

Owen, S. (2005) *Children Come First: the Role of Approved Childminding Networks in Changing Practice.* London: The National Children's Bureau and the National Childminding Association

LEADERSHIP IN THE EARLY YEARS

7

Linda Pound

Everyone who works with young children has to undertake a vast range of tasks and roles and assume responsibilities and make judgements, which require them to demonstrate the characteristics of leaders throughout their working day. Other tasks undertaken by early years practitioners may not seem to be directly related to the leadership role, as it is perceived by the outside world, and may not be readily associated with being a professional. Professionalism is popularly thought of as something which lawyers, doctors or bankers have but is not readily associated with those who change nappies and wipe noses. However, this view is changing and there is a growing acceptance that something as important to the future of society as the care and education of young children should only be undertaken with a high degree of professionalism. This chapter explores what those professional and leadership qualities are and considers how they can be developed though practice, reflection and formal study.

EVERYONE A LEADER

There are many definitions of leadership – both in the field of early childhood and beyond. Leaders may be defined by the roles they adopt, or by the styles of leadership they choose, or their characteristics. Despite the common features of leadership there are some features that are specific to leadership in the early years. Rodd (2006) highlights the fact that all early years professionals have to make vital decisions throughout a long working day. This level of responsibility means that they must reflect on what they do; treat all with whom they work with respect and empathy (Pound and Joshi 2005) and take responsibility for developing good relationships with team members, parents and other professionals.

Another important difference between leadership in this field and in many other areas of employment has to do with the fact that staff often move between roles. Most practitioners in early years settings have sometimes to act as leaders and sometimes as team members. In playgroups, for example, leadership is often in the hands of different people, depending on work patterns. Practitioners may work within a team in a children's centre but lead a team of outreach workers, or assume overall responsibility for provision during school holidays.

As deputy head of a children's centre, for example, Edward's main role is leading on children up to the age of 3. As such, he has a number of regular tasks that have to be completed – but he maintains a sense of responsibility towards children, parents and team which goes beyond his designated role. He may, for example, work with a child on a simple clearing-up task because she is becoming frustrated and is on the verge of a tantrum. His help will prevent her from giving up, enabling her to feel good about completing a task. In his role as an educator he wants to promote a child's self-esteem and acknowledge his responsibility for supporting all-round development. Similarly, on seeing water spilt in a corridor he will complete the task of mopping it up – a task undertaken in his role as a member of the team, with a sense of responsibility for the smooth running of the centre as a whole. He may also be acting in his role as a carer, with a sense of responsibility for the children's safety. The image of the centre may also be in his mind and he may be anxious to make a good impression on parents and visitors as they enter the building. Throughout the day, his role will be multi-layered and he will need to switch from task to task, reflecting as he does on his current role and his overall responsibilities.

Most leaders in the care and education of young children are women. Many writers (see for example Rodd, 2006; Coleman, 2002) suggest that although women tend to have a distinctive style of leadership, this does not mean that all women leaders are, for example, collaborative. Nor does it mean that men are not. Coleman (2002) suggests that when men lead in fields that are dominated by women, they tend to adopt approaches that are stereotypically attributed to women. This is a highly complex area but may perhaps mean that women leaders are more likely to pay attention to affective or emotional aspects of their interactions with others and less likely to adopt dictatorial approaches.

The growth of integrated centres, policies arising from *Every Child Matters* (DfES 2003) and the requirements of legislation associated with meeting the needs of children with special educational needs, has led to an increase in multi-professional work. Wigfall and Moss (2001) identify the many benefits arising from multi-agency networks but note that avoiding the costs and realising the benefits requires positive leadership at all levels.

Overall, practitioners working in the area of the care and education of young children have complex responsibilities, which include work with parents and community and complex multi-professional work that is required in multifunction or integrated centres. All of these require skills additional to those normally associated with child care and education, many of which are the very abilities which effective leaders need to develop.

Leadership roles

Leaders are often seen as being responsible for creating the vision for an organisation or institution. It is they who identify priorities and develop strategies to achieve them. Kagan and Neuman (1997) define five types of leadership, namely: pedagogical, administrative, advocacy, community and conceptual leadership. Pedagogical leadership is concerned with learning and development, administrative leadership with business, services and organisation and community leadership with the involvement of parents and community. These are not unfamiliar concepts within the field of early childhood care and education. Conceptual leadership may be a less familiar idea, although many practitioners will have sympathy with Kagan and Neuman's definition (1997: 59):

> In the early childhood field, conceptual leadership means getting beyond thinking about individual programs and having a sense of the field as a whole. As a colleague in New Mexico says, 'We are sick and tired of being funded, governed, and treated like "projects".' We want to be a profession!'

Advocacy leadership may be a similarly unfamiliar role – but a vitally important one. Since to those outside the profession, looking after babies or young children may seem a simple affair, practitioners often feel that their needs are overlooked or trivialised. There is a constant need to remind politicians, policy makers and the general public (and sometimes even colleagues) that 'investing in children- our most viable resource – is truly cost effective and productive for the society as a whole' (Blank 1997: 39).

Leadership styles

Leadership can be defined in terms of styles and these may not be fixed or mutually exclusive. Goleman et al. (2002: 55), for example, identify six different styles, namely: visionary, coaching, affiliative, democratic, pacesetting and commanding. They suggest that in some circumstances one may be more effective than another. The visionary leader, for example, is unsurprisingly said to 'move(s) people toward shared dreams' and is particularly helpful in a climate of change when a new vision is needed. It may be helpful if the leadership style can be changed to suit circumstances. Rodd (2006) suggests that a young or inexperienced team may benefit from a directive style of leadership, while teams where there is a high degree of conflict might be improved by a more democratic style of leadership. Similarly, while we may not always think of *commanding leadership* (or being very direct in telling people what to do) as an empowering style, it may help in situations where, for example, change is proving difficult. However, effective organisations generally adopt empowering leadership styles at every level of responsibility.

Characteristics of leaders

Rodd (2006) identifies five essential characteristics of effective leaders. To these I have added confidence and communication.

Curiosity

Effective leaders demonstrate a desire to know – seeking improvement and change or, as some writers term it, 'transformation' (see, for example, Whalley 2005). Many writers refer to this as promoting a learning community.

Candour

Honesty simply involves a willingness to speak the truth. But, of course, there are many situations where there is no easily discernible truth, since it is often subjective, dependent on the perspectives of the people involved. This means keeping an open mind – reading, debating and reflecting in order to arrive at some clear and well-articulated beliefs.

Courtesy

Work on anger management and personal safety shows us the power of the way in which we speak to people. Being greeted warmly in the mornings or being thanked for effort makes a difference to teams and individuals.

Courage

Risk-taking is an essential component of creativity. Good leaders have good ideas – but their commitment to change and improvement means that they reflect on things that go wrong and attempt to develop and refine their ideas.

Compassion

Rodd (2006) includes in this characteristic professional and pastoral concerns, empathy and professional development. Raelin (2003) also writes of the importance of compassionate leadership. He suggests that it has five components, namely: strong listening skill, sincerity, inner peace, a joyful spirit, and harmony (2003: 230–231).

Confidence

Many early years professionals demonstrate self-confidence in their dealings with children but often express their lack of confidence in their interactions with adults. Self-confidence leads others to have confidence in a leader and in their decisions.

Communication

Leaders and early years professionals need to be expert communicators – able to communicate effectively with children, colleagues and other professionals, parents, politicians and, increasingly, with members of the public.

Distributed leadership

Theories of leadership often overlook the fact that *distributed leadership* (Gronn 2003) is now increasingly important. Many organisations (including schools, children's centres and many other settings involved in the care and education of young children) are too complex to be in the hands of a single leader and many people, often in small and apparently insignificant ways, provide leadership of different kinds – and perhaps different styles. Raelin (2003) has developed the concept of 'leaderful' teams. By this he means that effective organisations enable team members to recognise their power and influence in the success of the work or field in which they are working. He suggests that successful leaderful teams have a style of working which includes collaboration and compassion and that 'leaderful' practice is both concurrent and collective.

The goals of successful teams cannot be achieved by leaders alone. Leaderful teams have to take joint responsibility for effective team work. While a leader strives to ensure group cohesion, team members have a responsibility to make use of their own strengths and develop other areas. This is why leadership is said to be relational – that is, resting on the relationship between leader and team or other people. It has also been suggested that leadership (Rodd 2006), in addition to being concerned with interaction, is about taking a reflective approach to practice, which is shaped by a clear set of values, regularly debated and reviewed.

BECOMING A LEADER

Distributed leadership and the importance of leaderful teams, are characteristics of early years settings. Development as a leader assumes that 'everyone can be a leader' and that 'you can learn to be a leader' (Owen 2005: xiii). Owen suggests that 'emerging leaders', or developing professionals, need to focus on people. Since work in early childhood care and education involves close work with children, parents, colleagues and other professionals, it is safe to assume that a focus on people is inevitable. He also suggests that leaders need to be positive, finding solutions rather than problems. Reflection is at the heart of this process since it enables practitioners to stand back from day-to-day concerns.

Being reflective is perhaps a key element in becoming a professional (see Chapter 8). The more advanced levels of professionalism include professional insight, perspective, making choices, predicting and explaining. All of these skills or abilities require practitioners to stand back from practice and to review what has happened; to identify common themes and to identify ways of generalising the insights gained from their analysis of events and their outcomes.

Learning from experience

Effective practitioners evaluate their daily practice in order to learn from their experience. For example, at the end of team meetings, parent interviews, sessions with groups of children – whether these have been difficult or have gone very smoothly – reflecting on what has happened supports the process of learning from experiences. In this way, what has gone well and what has not can be identified and we can learn to choose the approaches and responses that are likely to be the most effective. This insight can be unconscious, what Furlong (2000, citing Schön 1983) calls 'knowing-in-action', but reflection enables practitioners to learn to articulate their ideas and to move to a more professional level. Professionals may reach a second level that is referred to as 'reflection-in-action' – which Furlong suggests occurs when there is a problem or issue to deal with. Practitioners at this level of reflection attempt to interpret or analyse what is happening as it occurs. Finally, at Furlong's third level practitioners 'reflect-on-action', usually after the event. Efforts are made to identify and evaluate some of the processes that were going on in the actions (see also Chapter 8).

Similarly, Moyles (2006) identifies four levels of effective leadership. These begin with 'the intuitive' – in which the practitioner is able to operate effectively but without being able to clearly identify what makes practice effective. With experience and self-examination, practitioners may move through stages described by Moyles as 'reasoned and articulate', an increasingly thoughtful stage, and 'involved and collaborative'. Moyles describes as 'a different level of operation altogether where (the leader) seeks expert advice from others within and beyond the setting' (2006: 16). This advice is subsequently discussed and considered carefully. By the fourth stage or level, which Moyles terms 'reflective and philosophic', the leader is able to critically scrutinise beliefs and values. Reflection may be aided by specific tools. Johns (2004), for example, identifies a number of what he terms reflective cues. He encourages practitioners to reflect on significant events, identifying particular issues and considering the feelings (and causes of those feelings) of themselves and others involved in the focus event. The focus of reflection at this level should be the leadership – the extent to which the event under consideration demonstrated effective leadership; what other strategies might have worked and what has been learned from the event or situation (Powell and Ross 2003).

Learning to be a leader may also involve learning from experience by transferring the skills developed as a practitioner to the leadership role. The understanding of children's learning and development, which early years practitioners have acquired through their years of experience, provides an excellent foundation for developing effective leadership (Whalley 2005). Whalley draws some interesting parallels between pedagogy and leadership, focusing on good communication, sensitive intervention, building on experience, as well as support for risk-taking and decision-making.

Developing future leaders

Government plans for the Children's Workforce include the development of leaders through formal programmes of training and study routes. This is very much in line with Gardner's view (2006: 41). He suggests that leaders of the future must continue to learn because they know that knowledge is changing all the time and that therefore the only way to keep up to date is to become 'a lifelong student' who is 'passionate' about learning. He further suggests that in order to be considered a professional of any sort, practitioners must become reflective or be 'counselled out of the profession' since 'thinking and action are more closely allied than ever before' (2006: 39).

The Early Years Professional Status (EYPS) programme was introduced in 2006 and aims to enable students to achieve the equivalent of Qualified Teacher Status (QTS) (see www.cwdcouncil.org.uk). The Children's Workforce Development Council (CWDC) has highlighted the need for both graduate level managers and early years professionals who take responsibility for leading and managing the play, care and learning environment (www.cwdcouncil.org.uk). Candidates embarking upon the EYP programme are required to verify that they have graduate level qualifications, are involved in leading and managing the curriculum for children aged birth to 5 and work with other professionals.

The National Professional Qualification in Integrated Centre Leadership (NPQICL) is offered at Masters level. Those undertaking this qualification need to demonstrate 'graduateness' or be supported to achieve this. They also need to be working as a leader in an integrated centre. A major strength of the course is the diverse range of students undertaking it, and many participants go on to complete a Masters degree, using the credit gained while undertaking NPQICL.

In one cohort at one of the regional training centres the students included:

- the head of a local authority day nursery which was to become a children's centre. This student had a professional qualification equivalent to NVQ3 but no additional qualifications, although she had worked in the sector for 25 years and attended many non-accredited courses.
- the head of a children's centre which had formerly been a nursery school and a local authority day nursery. She had qualified teacher status and a Masters degree.
- a Sure Start manager who had a first degree in a subject unrelated to early childhood and another who had not undertaken any study since leaving school at age 16.
- the head of a large designated children's centre who had an MSc. Prior to working for Sure Start she had been a community health professional and had published widely on the subject of child health.

All of these participants successfully achieved the qualification and found it both demanding and rewarding. They explored research as a leadership tool, were engaged in continuous learning, developing professional expertise and all were clear that they left the course with a more open mind than they had when embarking on the course. Two participants found themselves engaged in a conversation, each complaining about the difficulties of inter-professional collaboration in their own work situation. Only gradually as they commiserated with each other did they realise that their roles, and the roles of the people they were complaining about, were reversed. The head teacher was complaining about her local Sure Start manager; while the course participant, who was a local Sure Start manager, was complaining about the difficulties of working with a head teacher in her area. This was a vital step for both of them in their learning.

Practitioner research

Practitioner research has much in common with learning from experience but it is a more conscious or deliberate process. It is also closely related to action research but is often the preferred term for less formal processes of enquiry. Practitioners identify a problem or an area needing improvement, collect data related to that area and then, in analysing data, identify future action. It can be applied to interactions with children, staff or parents and is closely linked to the process of reflection, since any data collected will require critical analysis in order to determine implications for change or action.

While practitioner research may be undertaken as part of a formal course, or informally by agreement amongst a group of staff, its importance to leadership is underlined by the fact that it is an integral and assessed element of NPQICL training.

As part of the NPQICL course, Sian was required to undertake some practitioner research in which she had to develop some multi-professional work. Sian found this challenging because in her role as the head of a newly designated children's centre, she had been finding it difficult to make contact with other agencies. She felt uncertain about her leadership abilities and was not sure how other agencies would react to her overtures. She decided that she would set up a lunchtime meeting for as many of the professionals with whom she worked as possible. She was pleased and surprised by the number that attended. An agenda for action arose from the meeting. Everyone there was aware of the need for closer professional collaboration but had not felt able to take a lead. Without being on the course, Sian felt pretty sure that she would not have been confident enough to step into that role. So confident did she feel that she was determined to make a renewed approach to those who had not attended or responded. The reflective process which was required as part of her assignment led Sian to analyse how her successes had been achieved, as well as think about what she needed to do in order to maintain and develop her achievements.

Developing as a leader

Formal study enables practitioners to benefit from the experience and reflections, problem-solving and theorising of others – both professionals and academics. Glover et al. (2002) have suggested that those successfully completing degree courses will have developed competences, which include research skills, a desire to continue learning, increased professional expertise and a more open mind. In developing as a leader, the need to inspire or motivate others requires good communication, vision, knowledge and planning. Owen (2005) suggests that experienced leaders need to be decisive but able to 'embrace ambiguity'. Groups or teams working in a democratic climate are more likely to abide by the decisions of the group and to tolerate ambiguity. This climate is best fostered through reflection and experience.

Leaders undoubtedly make an enormous difference to the effectiveness of teams and settings, but in the 'leaderful' settings which represent the best early years practice, early years professionals have many opportunities to develop as leaders and professionals through study, reflection and the intuition or 'knowing-in-action' which comes from experience. In this way they become the leaders of the future, in a professional sector which deserves only the best practitioners and leaders.

SUMMARY

The tasks, roles and responsibilities that leaders in the early years have to assume are diverse, complex and demanding. Forms of leadership are also being influenced by new professional roles and ways of working. Distributed leadership and the development of 'leaderful' teams would appear to fit well with these new approaches and models. In addition to a sound knowledge base and flexibility, the 7Cs – confidence, communication, curiosity, candour, courtesy, courage and compassion can be seen as vital elements that the effective leader needs to develop. The development of leadership skills and dispositions is vitally supported by critical reflection on experience, practitioner or action research and by formal study which leads to changes that bring benefits for children, parents and communities.

Questions/points for discussion/reflection

1 As you reflect on the tasks, roles and responsibilities that you assume in your work, what leadership qualities do you feel you are developing?
2 What skills do you have to exercise in order to ensure that everyone in your team recognises their own leadership qualities and values yours?
3 To what extent do you think your leadership reflects the 7Cs (curiosity, candour, courtesy, courage, compassion, confidence and communication)?

REFERENCES

Blank, H. (1997) 'Advocacy leadership'. In S. Kagan and B. Bowman (eds) *Leadership in Early Care and Education*. Washington DC: National Association for the Education of Young Children

Coleman, M. (2002) *Women as Headteachers: striking the Balance*. Stoke-on-Trent: Trentham Books

Department for Education and Skills (2003) *Every Child Matters*. London: DfES

Furlong, J. (2000) 'Intuition and the crisis in teacher professionalism'. In T. Atkinson and G. Claxton (eds), *The Intuitive Practitioner*. Buckingham: Open University Press

Gardner, H. (2006) *Five Minds for the Future*. Boston, Mass.: Harvard Business School Press

Glover, D., Law, S. and Youngman, A. (2002) 'Graduateness and employability: student perceptions of personal outcomes of university education', *Research in Post-compulsory Education*, *7(3)*, 293–306

Goleman, D., Boyatzis, R. and McKee, A. (2002) *The New Leaders*. London: Little, Brown

Gronn, P. (2003) *The New Work of Educational Leaders*. London: Sage

Johns, C. (2004) *Becoming a Reflective Practitioner* (2nd edition). Malden, Surrey: Blackwell Publishing

Kagan, S. and Neuman, M. (1997) 'Conceptual leadership'. In S. Kagan and B. Bowman (eds) *Leadership in Early Care and Education*. Washington DC: National Association for the Education of Young Children

Moyles, J. (2006) *Effective Leadership and Management in the Early Years*. Maidenhead: Open University Press

Owen, J. (2005) *How to Lead*. Harlow: Pearson Education Ltd

Pound, L. and Joshi, U. (2005) 'Management, teamwork and leadership'. In L. Dryden, R. Forbes, P. Mukherji and L. Pound, *Essential Early Years*. London: Hodder Arnold

Powell, S. and Ross, M. (2003) 'Building capacity from within: changing the adult working environment in our schools'. In M. Elias, H. Arnold and C.S. Hussey (eds) *EQ+IQ = Best Leadership Practices for Caring and Successful Schools*. Thousand Oaks, California: Corwin Press In

Raelin, J. (2003) *Creating Leaderful Organizations*. San Francisco: Berrett-Koehler

Rodd, J. (2006) *Leadership in Early Education* (3rd edition). Maidenhead: Open University Press

Whalley, M. for the National College for School Leadership (NCSL) (2005) *Programme Leaders' Guide: National Professional Qualification in Integrated Centre Leadership*. Nottingham: NCSL

Wigfall, V. and Moss, P. (2001) *More than the Sum of its Parts*. London: National Children's Bureau

Further reading

Moyles, J. (2006) *Effective Leadership and Management in the Early Years*. Maidenhead: Open University Press

Raelin, J. (2003) *Creating Leaderful Organizations*. San Francisco: Berrett-Koehler

For more information about Early Years Professional Status, see www.cwd-council.org.uk (accessed 27/7/2007)

For more information about NPQICL, see www.ncsl.org.uk/npqicl (accessed 27/7/2007)

2

DEVELOPING PROFESSIONAL PRACTICE

REFLECTIVE PRACTICE

8

Anna Craft and Alice Paige-Smith

This chapter is adapted from two chapters in Paige-Smith, A. & Craft, A. (Eds), *Developing Reflective Practice in the Early Years*. Buckingham: Open University Press, as follows: Craft, A., Paige-Smith, A. (2008), 'What does it mean to reflect on and document our practice?' And Paige-Smith, A., Craft, A. (2008), 'Reflection and developing a community of practice'.

INTRODUCTION

The new graduate professional status of Early Years Professional (CWDC 2006), which has been proposed should have equivalent status to Qualified Teacher Status (QTS), brings with it an expansion of roles in settings for children from 0 to 5 years, and means that early years settings such as nurseries and children's centres are likely to be led by senior staff with high sensitivity to the need to recognise others' perspectives – from within and beyond one's own sector. This capacity to co-construct understanding and ideas may be considered to be an essential part of the early years practitioner's role, constructing meaning alongside the children, and trying to understand their experiences in order to support and encourage learning. This chapter explores the growing place of reflection in, and on, professional practice in the work of the early years practitioner.

> *'Forget what you are being taught at the College. This is the real world.'*

These words were said to an early childhood student by the practitioner whose setting she had been placed in. Discussed in turn by her tutor in a journal article (Callaghan 2002), the clash of culture between 'practice' and 'thinking about practice' is starkly drawn. Whilst the context is Canadian, it is perhaps a tension experienced in common elsewhere, too.

As a newly qualified teacher practitioner working with 4- and 5-year-olds in the 1980s in London, one of this chapter's authors, Anna, certainly experienced disconnection between her professional practice and reflecting on this. She was saved by discovering Stenhouse (1985) who described teaching as an art. Highlighting complexities in developing nurturing and stimulating environments in which children might grow and learn, she explored the delicate balance between responsiveness and providing a clear, defined framework for children. Stenhouse wrote persuasively about teachers-as-researchers (1980a, 1980b, 1985), proposing reflection as a vital element to improving practice.

At the start of the twenty-first century, with increased emphasis on 'professionalism', unprecedented reflection is now expected of early years practitioners. The idea that 'practice' and 'thinking about it' are somehow completely contrasting sits uneasily with emerging practices in early years settings, whether home-based, such as childminding or nannying; or institutionally based, such as day care or pre-school nursery or primary school classroom; or something part-way between the two, such as a voluntary toy library, or a playgroup operating in a local church hall.

WHY IS REFLECTION IMPORTANT IN EARLY YEARS PRACTICE?

Recently, researchers found pre-school children thrive most successfully when engaging in activities that prompt deep thinking (Siraj-Blatchford et al. 2002a). The project, Researching Effective Pedagogy in the Early Years (REPEY) noted that environments which encouraged what researchers called 'sustained shared thinking' between adults and children, fostered the greatest linguistic, social, behavioural and cognitive progress in children (Siraj-Blatchford and Sylva 2002b). Their work demonstrated that such engagement between adults and children relies on adults observing sensitively what children are engaging with and how they are exploring their world, so that conversations with children are based on these. They showed that such discussions develop depth and meaning for all involved, much in the way that conversations in the home sometimes do, because parents and carers understand the context of children's engagement, as earlier work showed (Tizard and Hughes 1984). Adults responding in a sensitive fashion and engaging in the development of an ongoing learning experience, nurture children's learning and development to honour the child's interests and perspectives, allowing space for ideas and possibilities to emerge from dialogue.

Wegerif (2002) suggests successful engagement between adults and children can both provide and develop a powerful learning context, where children's thinking is developed explicitly alongside their interests. This was taken further by Littleton et al. (2005) showing the importance of adults listening to children, and of children hearing one another. Their work emphasises how children develop knowledge and understanding within a social environment, and that understanding is 'distributed' within a group.

Taking this into early years settings and contexts, means recognising how important our interactions are in children's development. Reflecting on how children interact with each other, and how we interact with them, is a vital part of this. Thinking together could be seen as another way of talking about sustained shared thinking, itself involving a reflective approach as integral to effective early years provision.

It has been argued that we should take note of the consequences of living and working at a time of rapid change such as we are experiencing in the early twenty-first century. So much is unknown about how conceptualisations and experiences of childhood itself are shifting, as family, social and community structures are altered by developments in technology, and changes in the global and globalised economy, and changes in the broader physical and environmental context. Perhaps, as Yelland and Kilderry suggest, we need to shift from accepting a historical wisdom about what is right, or 'good practice', to a more inquisitive approach where, as they put it, we ask ourselves 'In what ways can we create effective learning environments?' (Yelland and Kilderry 2005: 7). Their argument is that rapid change and uncertainty in wider society affects decisions about issues in our practice including ethics, equity and culture. In other words, as practitioners we need to:

- ask ourselves about how we develop practices to offer accessible and equitable care and education;
- deepen our understanding of how children learn and develop, at this time of rapid change; and
- develop practices alongside other services so as to appropriately support life-long learning and lifetime citizenship.

WHAT DOES REFLECTIVE PRACTICE INVOLVE?

At around the time that Stenhouse was writing, Donald Schön was also publishing work about reflective practice. His ideas, which develop a notion of 'professional artistry' (Schön 1987: 22), provide helpful ways for us to think about reflective practice in early years settings. Schön emphasises the complexity of the professional's role, in contrast to earlier work by Dewey (1933), who had drawn a distinction between 'routine action' and 'reflective action'. Schön, in contrast, half a century later, emphasised that professionals continually face unique situations which they frame in light of previous experience, and he recognises therefore the ongoing complexity, and embedded reflection, in practice. In particular, he distinguished 'reflection on action' from 'reflection in action' (Schön 1987), as follows:

> **Reflection-in-action: thinking on your feet.**
> **Reflection-on-action: retrospective thinking – or thinking 'after the event'.**

Schön suggested reflection is used by practitioners in encountering unique situations, where they cannot apply known theories or techniques previously learnt. As his terms suggest, reflective practice was very much embedded in the action of the setting itself.

His ideas ignited the imaginations of many working in public services including health, social care and education, and have influenced practices around the world in seeking to improve these. But as Loughran (2002) writes, in Australia, although reflective practice can offer genuine improvement-orientated feedback on practice, it is important we really develop reflection in such a way that it is shared and enables us to question assumptions we might otherwise take for granted. As he puts it, reflection on practice should enable us to see our practice through the eyes of others.

But it is more than seeing and thinking about practice. It is about exploring both how we feel about it, as well as how we understand it. Questioning what we do and how we might develop our practice builds bridges from our professional to our personal lives, and vice-versa. As Williams (2002) suggests, reflective practice 'helps to integrate the technical expertise of the professional with the personal and emotional qualities of the individual. . . Reflective practice allows our natural instincts to interact with a professional approach. Actions are so much more powerful if they arise from both feelings and thoughts' (Williams 2002: 55).

Clough and Corbett (2000) suggest that practitioners working with young learners meld personal with professional, drawing on personal histories. They suggest that by tracing our origins we come to understand better how we experience the present. They refer to the concept of the 'lived relationship'; personal and professional 'journeys'. They argue that our professional identities and our 'distinctive and influential perspectives' (Clough and Corbett 2000: 38) are determined by what we learn both professionally and personally, over time.

Such learning is drawn on experience; practitioners therefore engage in 'linking analytical thinking to their own experience of practice' (Clough and Corbett 2000: 38). This occurs in many ways: through evaluating or researching experience; through a range of means including documenting the experiences of professionals, parents and children; through observations, images, interviews, questionnaire surveys, a reflective diary, listening to children (Clarke 2004); and through policy analysis, or analysis of documents. In becoming who we are as practitioners, we build on layer upon layer of experience – our own, and that of others, generated by working within multiple communities.

In early years settings, there are good opportunities to share perspectives on the same activity, and to compare professional perspectives. This may be particularly helpful where, for example, a care professional is working alongside a health, education or welfare professional, i.e. someone bringing a different but overlapping set of sensitivities, knowledge, experience and responsibilities to the work of supporting children. The mix of cultural practices in adjacent and collaborating professional areas providing children's services means that sharing documentation of practice is both fertile and complex.

By reflecting in and on our practice we open the possibility, alongside others, of what Engestrom (1993) calls a 'problem space', at which we direct our engagement and a commitment to development and change. Pollard (2002) identified seven characteristics of reflective practice in teaching, which Warwick and Swaffield (2006) suggest are equally applicable to teaching assistants. They may be useful to early years practitioners also, some of whom are indeed teaching assistants. For Pollard, reflective practice in teaching involves:

- *active focus on goals, on how these are addressed, and the consequences of both,* alongside a concern with 'technical efficiency' (Pollard 2002: 12)
- *commitment to a continuous cycle* of monitoring practice, evaluating and revising it;
- *focus on informed judgements* about practice, based on evidence;
- *open-minded, responsible and inclusive attitudes,* with what Zeichner and Liston (1996) call 'an active desire to listen to more ideas than one. . . and to recognise the possibility of error' (Zeichner and Liston 1996: 10);
- *capacity to reframe own practice* in light of evidence-based reflection and also insights based on other research

- *dialogue with other colleagues*, both individuals and across groups (what MacGilchrist et al. 2004 suggest is integral to the 'intelligent school'), and cooperation with colleagues beyond the school – individuals, agencies, organisations;
- *capacity to mediate and adapt externally developed frameworks* for practice, making reflective, appreciative judgements about when to innovate, and when to defend existing practices, both individually and collaboratively.

Pollard's reflective practice principles emphasise the vital mix of evidence and reflection, which implies a need to collect evidence, or to *document* practice, and the formation of a community.

DEVELOPING A COMMUNITY OF PRACTICE

The notion of the community of practice has been developed from work by Lave and Wenger (1991), focusing on socially situated aspects of learning. It signifies social learning processes which occur when people have a common interest or area of collaboration over an extended time period, where they can problem-find, share ideas, seek solutions, and build innovative practices.

Wenger (1998) has taken the notion of community of practice further than its initial usage, seeing it in terms of the interplay in negotiation of meaning and the brokering of shared understanding of change. Effective change or development depends on shared understandings. He discusses a number of tensions. Of these, it is the tension between participation (involvement/shared flux) and reification (congealment of ideas), which has had the greatest influence in the workplace. These tendencies are, Wenger suggests, in continual tension between one another; reification, the process of abstracting and congealing ideas (as, for example, represented in symbols, written documents etc.), is necessary in providing structure and a common reference point for understanding. At the other extreme, and in tension with reification, is participation, demanding active social engagement in brokering meaning.

The notion of the community of practice has fired the imagination of professionals and workers in many different contexts. It is suggested (Hildreth and Kimble 2004) that this may reflect the capacity of the concept of community of practice to provide those working in rapidly and continuously changing environments with a strong sense of uncertainty within them, with a means to develop some sense of shared meaning, ownership and even control, over what is valued and recognised as 'appropriate practice'. Organisations are moving rapidly away from structure, routine, hierarchies and teams, towards much more fluid networks/communities which are reliant on shared knowledge. Communities of practice are fluid self-organising structures that may facilitate such shifts in practice. In a globalised economy where knowledge is distributed over flexible networks, often geographically dispersed, the community of practice has gained huge interest from business in offering a means for knowledge management. It has also begun to influence and inform the work of many professionals, including those in the early years sector.

The community of practice, according to Wenger (1998), is a collective endeavour and is understood and continuously renegotiated by its members. Membership emerges through shared practices; participants are linked through engagement in activities in common. It is such mutually focused engagement which creates the social entity of the community of practice. The community of practice, which is established on some kind of common ground, endeavour or interest, builds up, collectively, an agreed set of approaches, understandings, values and actual communal repertoire of resources, over time. These may include written and other documentation but also include ethos, agreed procedures, policies, rituals and specific approaches. Communities of practice share and write an ongoing narrative, evolving and reflecting collaboratively on shared issues and developing a story and collaborative approach, together. They often depend on informal relationships and ways of working.

The multi-professional early years team as a community of practice

Communities of practice can provide a means for complicated, multidisciplinary professional teams, to function together to achieve common goals. This is especially the case in the development of practice in the early years, which involves brokering across perspectives – what Wenger calls the 'boundary encounter', which helps each community to define its own particular identity and approach to practice. This depends on exchange of perspectives from one professional community of practice to another and its success depends on skilful 'boundary straddlers', who are able to facilitate reflection on, and exchange of, perspectives.

As Wenger acknowledges, this role is a complicated one; it means professionals recognising and surfacing their own boundary experiences. For example, many early years practitioners are also parents themselves; their dual roles as parent and professional in a setting may, at times, complement or contradict each other.

Professionals who work with young children in England are required to fulfil a range of policy-based expectations within their provision, relating to curriculum, assessment and access to learning opportunities. Policy frameworks offer a focus which bring colleagues and others (including parents) together as a 'community of practitioners' to develop shared approaches, requiring a commitment to shared reflection on practice over time. As Wenger (2005) notes:

> Sustained engagement in practice yields an ability to interpret and make use of the repertoire of that practice. We recognise the history of a practice in the artefacts, actions, and language of the community. We can make use of that history because we have been part of it and it is now part of us; we do this through a personal history of participation. As an identity, this translates into a personal set of events, references, memories, and experiences that create individual relations of negotiability with respect to the repertoire of a practice.
>
> (Wenger 2005: 152)

Wenger argues that when practitioners are in a community of practice, they can handle themselves competently and can understand how to engage with others. By drawing on shared experiences, and reflecting together on these, practitioners evolve collaborative/shared perspectives.

REFLECTION AND ENQUIRY IN BUILDING PROFESSIONAL COMMUNITIES OF PRACTICE

Within any setting, there will be varied perspectives rooted in each professional's sense of identity. Born of each person's interpretation of their role in the setting, practitioner identity manifests itself in tendencies to 'certain interpretations, to engage in certain actions, to make certain choices, to value certain experiences – all by virtue of participating in certain enterprises' (Wenger 2005: 153). Developing a professional community of practice involves the explicit reflection on practice, and sharing of, and debate around, differences *and* commonalities.

Documenting professional practice

In developing a professional community of reflective practice, whether we are thinking about reflection in action (on our feet) or reflection on action (afterwards), we need to consider how we capture what it is we are reflecting on – or how we *document* it. When we document action, we are providing what Loughran (2002) has described as an 'anchor', which helps us to access – often at a later point, if we are reflecting *on* action – all the different thoughts and feelings that we have about the event itself. Much documentation is held, or built up informally, and consists of memories, anecdotes shared with others, children's constructions and other artefacts such as drawings and writing. Other documentation is more intentional, or formal. Commonly used means of more formalised documentation include:

- the journal, for observations and reflections on these;
- images (digital; still or moving), collected by adults and also by children; a focus of reflection with children and adults, a source of visual narratives in which children's engagement and their voices are brought to the fore;
- sound recordings, collected by adults and also by children, enabling us to listen to children's involvement in specific episodes;
- transcriptions of what children say in conversation with one another and with practitioners.

Sometimes documentation will be gathered into a particular place; a special wall in the setting, a log for each child, a portfolio focused around specific children.

Documenting our professional practice and children's learning enables us to explore with others what has engaged and focused children; it helps us to make predictions about what they know and are confident with, and what they are grappling with. It helps us to plan our work with them appropriately, for both individual and group learning. In some early years settings, building on the practices of the Reggio Emilia pre-schools in Northern Italy, practitioners share the annotations of their documentation for all involved in children's care and learning to see. The audiences may include the child, their parent/s and/or carer/s, other staff, consultants and others.

The Reggio approach places an emphasis on the arts as a means to document and make sense of learning. Perhaps the most significant element, though, about documentation, whether the Reggio approach or one's own, is that it not only makes learning visible, but it also encourages participation in the holistic support of children's learning which takes full account of the emotional dimension. It is a focus of dialogue and interaction; it is not simply a means of 'reporting'. Thus, incorporating space in documentation for comments from parents, practitioners, children and others is a vital part of the process of undertaking it. Katz and Chard (1997) suggest that such documentation contributes to the quality of early childhood practice in signalling how seriously children's ideas and work are taken, and fostering continuous planning and evaluation.

CHALLENGES IN REFLECTIVE PRACTICE

There are numerous challenges involved in fostering professional reflective practice. At a very basic level, simply making time and space to do it may be one, so reflection and consequent learning is not accidental. One of the authors found that by making space to document a child's learning moments in relation to literacy for a period of a morning, she noticed the significance of the child's 'mark making' during play. Through her close documentation, Alice realised the child was linking her attempts to write her name in the play office area with her name on her coat peg in the corridor, by 'mark making' on a notepad in the play area, then running to her peg to read the letters in her name and to try sounding out the letters. She would then run back to the office play area to sound out the letters in attempting to write her name. Alice witnessed the journey back and forth, and it offered insights into how to support this child's developing literacy (Miller and Paige-Smith 2003). But the challenge is not purely in making time; it is the double act of capturing moments such as these, as well as managing children's learning experiences. The reflective practitioner simultaneously works with questions formed around children's learning experiences so as to capture them, for instance, 'How does Jacob participate in circle time?' or, 'How does Priya participate during the school trip?' yet simultaneously has an eye on the need to offer a framework to the children's learning.

Another challenge surrounds sharing of documentation; with whom and how. Sharing perspectives is an essential part of the development of the role of the early years professional within a variety of settings, including children's centres and schools; such communication also encompasses children's transitions both into, and onward from, the setting.

Fostering reflective practice is not easy or, necessarily, straightforward. One practical challenge, as Loughran (2002) argues, is finding the balance between expectations of learning through reflection, and time and experience involved in it. The tensions pointed up at the start of the chapter are still live (Edwards 2000). Essentially, in reflective practice we become researchers looking at our own work, to develop and improve it. As Kennedy (1997) argues, discussing the relationship between research and educational practice in the United States, we must recognise that practice and research are both situated in shifting social and political contexts. We must be realistic about how self-study can influence our practice. Edwards (2000) talks of early years practitioners 'using practical knowledge of their professions to anticipate events and maintain control of them'(185) and sees this as 'part of the constant cycle of interpretation and response that is at the core of informed professional action in complex settings' (185). Reflective practice, then, according to Edwards, is 'embedded in the practical knowledge of the community of practitioners . . . [informing] practitioners' ways of seeing and being' (185). This is challenging, since, as Edwards notes, it means positioning one's work and practices within the complex relationships with children, their families, other services and wider policies. As Kennedy (1997) points out, shifts in policy mean that some of what is changing and evolving is externally imposed.

Another challenge is how to remain open. Huberman (1995) notes, we can nurture fresh perspectives and evolve new understandings of, and approaches to, our practice when we remain open to insights from others, through what he calls 'open networks'. A weakness in reflective practice, however, can come from the closed network, where ways of doing things are not open to scrutiny, re-interpretation or development. Reflective practice demands that we create opportunities to bounce our ideas off others and to co-construct understandings and ideas. In this sense having a critical friend, a mentor or a reflective practice learning setting is helpful. Bringing more than one perspective to documentation of reflective practice can help to overcome subjectivity in our reflections. And, of course, in documenting and reflecting on practice, we must take due care of ethics, manifesting sensitivity to children's rights and privacy issues, minimising risks.

SUMMARY

In this chapter, we have traced the expanding role of reflection in – and on – practice, noting that documenting, interpreting and sharing perspectives on practice is increasingly vital for professionals working with young children. In working alongside and with other professionals, the notion of the community of practice, proposed by Wenger, was put forward as a way of establishing common approaches and agreeing 'boundaries'. Means of documenting children's learning, and challenges in developing reflective practice, have been explored.

Questions/points for discussion/reflection

1 What opportunities and challenges are offered, in your own experience, by inter-professional reflective practice?
2 How can children and parents be involved in the reflective practice of professionals in the early years?
3 What does the idea of the professional community of practice offer you in extending your own work role?

REFERENCES

Callaghan, K. (2002), 'Nurturing the enthusiasm and ideals of new teachers through reflective practice', *Canadian Children, 27(1)*, 38–41

Children's Workforce Development Council (CWDC) (2006) *Early Years Professional National Standards* http://www.cwdcouncil.co.uk/pdf/Early%20 Years/Draft_EYP_Standards_Aug_2006.pdf (accessed 26/9/2007)

Clark, A. (2004) 'The Mosaic approach and research with young children'. In V.

Lewis, M. Kellett, C. Robinson, S. Fraser and S. Ding (eds), *The Reality of Research with Children and Young People.* London: Sage

Clough, P. and Corbett, J. (2000) *Theories of Inclusive Education.* London: Paul Chapman

Dewey, J. (1933) *How We Think: a Re-statement of the Relation of Reflective Thinking in the Educative Process.* Chicago: Henry Regnery

Edwards, A. (2000) 'Research and practice: is there a dialogue?' In H. Penn (ed.), *Early Childhood Services: Theory, Policy and Practice.* Buckingham, Philadelphia: Open University Press

Engestrom, Y. (1993) 'Developmental studies of work as a testbench of activity theory: the case of primary care medical practice'. In S. Chaiklin and J. Lave (eds) *Understanding Practice. Perspectives on Activity and Context.* Cambridge, England: Cambridge University Press

Hildreth, P. and Kimble, C. (eds) (2004) *Knowledge Networks: Innovation Through Communities of Practice.* Hershey, PA: IGI Publishing

Huberman, M. (1995) 'Networks that alter teaching', *Teachers and Teaching: Theory and Practice, 1(2),* 193–211

Katz, L.G. and Chard, S.C. (1997) 'Documentation: The Reggio Emilia Approach', *Principal, 76(5),* 16–17

Kennedy, M. (1997), 'The connection between research and practice', *Educational Researcher, 26(7),* 4–12

Lave, J. and Wenger, E. (1991) *Situated Learning: Legitimate Peripheral Participation.* Cambridge, England: Cambridge University Press

Littleton, K., Mercer, N., Dawes, L., Wegerif, R., Rowe, D. and Sams, C. (2005) 'Talking and thinking together at Key Stage 1', *Early Years: An International Journal of Research and Development, 25(2),* 167–182.

Loughran, J.J. (2002) 'Effective reflective practice. In search of meaning in learning about teaching', *Journal of Teacher Education, 53(1),* 33–43

MacGilchrist, B., Myers, K. and Reed, J. (2004) *The Intelligent School.* London: Sage

Miller, L. and Paige-Smith, A. (2003) 'Literacy in four early years settings'. In *Supporting Children's Learning in the Early Years.* London: Fulton.

Pollard, A. with Collins, J., Simco, N., Swaffield, S., Warin, J. and Warwick, P. (2002) *Reflective Teaching: Effective and Evidence-informed Professional Practice.* London: Continuum

Schön, D. (1987) *Educating the Reflective Practitioner.* San Francisco: Jossey Bass

Siraj-Blatchford, I., Sylva, K., Muttock, S., Gilden, R. and Ball, D. (2002a) *Researching Effective Pedagogy in the Early Years'*, DfES Research Brief, No. 356.

Siraj-Blatchford, I. and Sylva, K. (2002b); http://ioewebserver.ioe.ac.uk/ioe/cms/get. asp?cid=1397and1397_1=5876 (accessed 26/9/2007)

Stenhouse, L. (1980a) 'Curriculum research and the art of the teacher', *Curriculum, 1,* 40–44

Stenhouse, L. (1980b) 'Artistry and teaching: the teacher as the focus of research and development'. In D. Hopkins and M. Wideen (eds) (1984) *Alternative Perspectives on School Improvement.* Lewes: Falmer Press

Stenhouse, L. (1985) 'Curriculum research, artistry and teaching'. In J. Ruddock and D. Hopkins (eds) *Research as a Basis for Teaching: Readings from the Work of Lawrence Stenhouse.* London: Heinemann Educational

Tizard, B. and Hughes, M. (1984) *Young Children Learning.* London: Fontana

Warwick, P. and Swaffield, S. (2006) 'Articulating and connecting frameworks of reflective practice and leadership: perspectives from "fast track" trainee teachers', *Reflective Practice, 7(2)*, 247–263

Wegerif, R. (2002) 'Walking or dancing? Images of thinking and learning to think in the classroom', *Journal of Interactive Learning Research, 13*, 51–70

Wenger, E. (1998) *Communities of Practice: Learning, Meaning and Identity.* Cambridge, UK, and New York: Cambridge University Press

Wenger, E. (2005) *Communities of Practice – Learning, Meaning, and Identity,* New York: Cambridge University Press

Williams, D. (2002) 'Book review of Bolton, G. (2001) *Reflective Practice: Writing and Professional Development.* Paul Chapman Publishing Ltd, *Journal of Medical Ethics: Medical Humanities 28*, 55–56

Yelland, N. and Kilderry, A. (2005) 'Against the tide: new ways in early childhood education'. In Yelland, N. (ed.) (2005), *Critical Issues in Early Childhood Education.* Maidenhead and New York: Open University Press/McGraw-Hill Education

Zeichner, K. and Liston, D. (1996) *Reflective Teaching: An Introduction.* Mahwah, NJ: Lawrence Erlbaum Associates

Further reading

Paige-Smith, A. and Craft, A. (eds) (2008) *Developing Reflective Practice in the Early Years.* Buckingham: Open University Press

Siraj-Blatchford, I., Sylva, K., Muttock, S., Gilden, R. and Ball, D. (2002) *Researching Effective Pedagogy in the Early Years',* DfES Research Brief, No. 356.

Siraj-Blatchford, I. and Sylva, K. (2002); http://ioewebserver.ioe.ac.uk/ioe/cms/get.asp?cid=1397and1397_1=5876

9

COMPUTER MEDIATED COMMUNICATION: USING E-LEARNING TO SUPPORT PROFESSIONAL DEVELOPMENT

Gill Goodliff and Peter Twining

INTRODUCTION

Elements of e-learning will now be encountered by all early years practitioners who embark on degree-level study towards professional qualifications or status, in higher or further education institutions (HEFCE 2005). In this chapter we explore the potential role and significance of information and communications technology (ICT) within early years professional practice. We then focus on computer mediated communication (CMC) and its potential to enhance the role of the early years practitioner through creating professional development opportunities and overcoming isolation. This chapter draws on evidence from the Open University's (OU) Sector-Endorsed Foundation Degree in Early Years (FDEY). The OU FDEY commenced in 2003 and is offered part-time by supported distance learning. Students are practitioners working in a range of early years settings within the maintained and private, voluntary and independent (PVI) sectors of the workforce, and include home-based (self-employed) childminders, nursery and preschool staff, teaching assistants in primary schools and practitioners working in multidisciplinary Children's Centres. Throughout the chapter we draw on the voices of early years practitioners who have studied the OU FDEY to exemplify student perceptions of how CMC enhanced and/or challenged their learning and professional development.

IMPERATIVES TO USE ICT

We are now in 'The Information Age' (Trilling and Hood 2001), and children are growing up surrounded by technology. As with other aspects of learning, early years practitioners need to build on children's prior experiences and prepare them for living in a world in which technology plays a fundamental part. They will be much better placed to do that if they have engaged with the technology themselves and feel confident and competent in using it. In order to do this, early years practitioners need to develop their own personal ICT competence to enable them to use it to support children's learning and development.

ICT has the potential to assist early years practitioners in their professional role, for example by providing them with access to up-to-date materials via the web, and helping them with administrative aspects (such as producing letters, maintaining records and analysing data). ICT skills can also facilitate the development of resources for use in their setting such as labels, posters and displays. Evidence from a survey of the first cohort to complete the OU FDEY, which explored students' perceptions of the impact of their study on their professional role, showed that the development of competence in using ICT skills had been particularly beneficial (Cable and Goodliff 2007). The ability to produce leaflets and newsletters for parents – and for practitioners in the PVI sector to improve policy documents – contributed to an enhanced sense of their identity as a professional.

There is also substantial practical and theoretical evidence to show that using ICT can significantly enhance one's own learning and professional development (for example, Twining 1999, 2001). As we shall see in the following sections, perhaps the most important aspect of this is the ability ICT gives early years practitioners to 'talk' with other early years practitioners across settings.

Thus there are three core aspects of ICT use that are relevant to the early years practitioner:

- to support children's development and learning (i.e. use with children);
- to support their professional role (e.g. use for record keeping, planning, etc.);
- to support their own professional development (DfES 2001; CWDC 2007).

WHAT IS CMC?

Computer mediated communication is one aspect of ICT. Its key defining element is that it is about communication, rather than dissemination. In other words, it provides a means for dialogue between two or more people. CMC can encompass email, instant messaging (for example MSN), online forums, computer conferencing and a host of other tools to support interaction between two or more people. With the development of Web 2.0, which is all about the deployment of tools for collaboration over the Internet, the boundaries between dissemination and dialogue are becoming blurred. Thus, whilst a traditional webpage that you browse and extract information from is not included within the definition of CMC, something like a wiki, which allows the reader to edit the page, falls into a grey area as in one sense you could view this as providing a vehicle for discussion. For the sake of simplicity, within this chapter we are using CMC to specifically refer to text-based communication systems that support both group discussions (forums) and individual 'email' communication, but are excluding Web 2.0 technologies such as wikis and other social networking tools (for example, Facebook, YouTube).

CMC could fit into all three of the ways outlined above for which an early years practitioner might use ICT. For example, they might use email with young children to support and promote the development of electronic literacy (Waller 2006), or to communicate with parents or colleagues to organise a meeting. They might also log on to their local Early Years and Childcare Partnership (EYDCP) website to identify details of training opportunities, or locate and download a recommended article about the benefits of music to children's development and learning.

Students on the OU FDEY, who are practitioners in early years settings throughout the UK, are supported by a tutor who is responsible for a group of up to 20 people. Whilst tutor groups may meet occasionally, much of the support is provided 'at a distance' through email and on-line discussion in a tutor group conference.

In this context, CMC provides the opportunity to exchange ideas with other early years practitioners, through which they can develop shared understandings. 'Talking' with other practitioners allows students to clarify their thinking, enhance their knowledge, and extend their understanding of other people's values and beliefs. Within our work with early years practitioners studying the FDEY, it has become clear that many of them find that using CMC to communicate with other colleagues reduces their feeling of isolation and provides them with reassurance and a feeling of community. These points are reflected in the following quotation from an OU student:

Using the conferences meant I did not feel isolated. Getting answers to my questions from other students, and helping them with their queries when I could, helped me to understand the course materials better. Sharing our experiences at work, and relating them to the course materials, helped me work out what was needed to write the assignments. Bouncing ideas around often helped me see new ways to approach things at work.

These benefits appear very clear for students on the OU FDEY, who are studying at a distance. The benefits for students who are studying face to face may be less obvious. However, on any course where students are studying part-time, or are on work placements for periods of time, they are in effect studying at a distance, and CMC has the potential to help them maintain communication and minimise feelings of isolation. As a result, CMC is becoming a significant feature of academic study and professional development provision for many early years practitioners.

Of course, learning to use computer conferencing effectively does take time and effort. However, evidence from the FDEY indicates that most people find that the benefits far outweigh the costs once they have overcome the initial learning curve. As another FDEY student said:

I thought that the CMC [activities] were excellent and although very time-consuming and demanding, they provided an excellent support network for our tutor group. I feel that other courses should have compulsory CMC as it really helped with the study focus.

WHY IS USING CMC FOR PROFESSIONAL DEVELOPMENT IMPORTANT?

We have already alluded to the fact that using CMC can help break down isolation and allow practitioners to develop their professional knowledge, understanding and practice through sharing views and experiences with other colleagues. This, in part, explains a second important reason for engaging with CMC for professional development – the implicit expectation, within a range of relevant government policies, that all practitioners involved in the delivery of services to children (including early years practitioners) will be able to make effective use of ICT (for example Children's Workforce Strategy (DfES 2006); Every Child Matters – Integrated Children's System (DfES 2007); The e-learning strategy 'Harnessing Technology' (DfES 2005)).

Using CMC as part of a formal course of study has also been found to offer pedagogical advantages (for example, Twining 2001), and the importance of developing 'communities of practitioners', particularly for lone practitioners or those who are 'isolated' for other reasons, provides a means of building and sharing expertise (Wenger 1998).

A further important reason is that developing understanding of how CMC (and ICT more generally) can support early years practitioners' own learning will, in turn, help them to understand more about how ICT can be used to promote children's learning and development. One of the core learning outcomes specified in the Statement of Requirement for the Early Years Sector Endorsed Foundation Degree (DfES 2001) explicitly focuses on the development of knowledge, understanding and skills to 'Evaluate and use ICT to support children's learning and development' (DfES 2001: 74). In addition to being required to develop skills such as planning, development, implementation and evaluation of ICT within the curriculum for children, students must also demonstrate that whilst working as an advanced skills practitioner they can:

- identify and develop their own ICT skills and competences;
- access and use ICT to improve their teaching and to enhance their professional role.

To achieve the new Early Years Professional Status (EYPS), candidates are required for Standard 37, within the 'Professional Development' group of Standards, to demonstrate that they can use ICT in their own practice and can lead and support others to, 'Develop and use skills in literacy, numeracy and information and communication technology to support their work with children and wider professional activities' (CWDC 2007:77).

USING CMC TO SUPPORT LEARNING

As already indicated, using CMC effectively involves an initial learning curve. Salmon (2003) proposed a five-stage model of teaching and learning through CMC, based on her research of CMC use within OU courses. This model identifies five levels that learners go through as they become more competent at using CMC. The model also provides a 'pyramid of needs', which suggests the types of activities that learners are likely to need to focus on as they progress through the different levels. A modified version of this model is presented in Figure 9.1. The higher up the pyramid students progress, the more beneficial their engagement with CMC is likely to be to their learning.

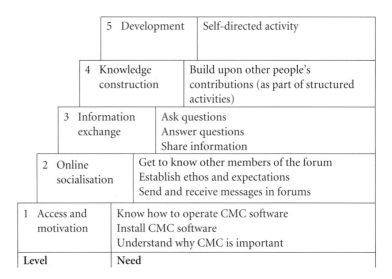

Level	Need
1 Access and motivation	Know how to operate CMC software Install CMC software Understand why CMC is important
2 Online socialisation	Get to know other members of the forum Establish ethos and expectations Send and receive messages in forums
3 Information exchange	Ask questions Answer questions Share information
4 Knowledge construction	Build upon other people's contributions (as part of structured activities)
5 Development	Self-directed activity

Figure 9.1 The five-stage model (adapted from Salmon 2003: 29)

Every course within the OU FDEY offers an on-line forum for students to communicate with each other. Participation in these is voluntary. However, the work-based learning courses have mandatory CMC elements and students are required to have regular and frequent access to a computer with Internet access.

In the first work-based learning course students are closely supported to develop and/or consolidate their knowledge, understanding and skills in relation to ICT. In the early stages they use CMC to communicate with their tutor and with other students in their tutor group. They are also encouraged to use the voluntary course discussion conference to talk with other students about course requirements and wider early years issues. Students start to access elements of CMC in very early course activities. They are also introduced to a structured four-stage Reflective Practice Cycle that scaffolds the teaching and learning as students think about, explore and begin to articulate the 'hidden' values and beliefs that underpin their practice within three early years themes:

- working with parents and other professionals;
- promoting children's learning and development;
- promoting children's rights and child protection.

Tracey, a nursery nurse, working in a foundation stage classroom, reflected on her initial thoughts about the CMC requirements within the first work-based learning course. The following account clearly shows her moving through the lower levels within Salmon's model.

When I originally received the course materials, I turned to the ICT guide because I knew that this area is not my strength. I began to read about what to do if things go wrong and saw this quote, 'look for the humour'. I somehow knew this quote would stay with me throughout the course. For example, I didn't think I would get beyond the welcome messages. . .

Like other students, Tracey felt 'alone' in her anxieties about technology. She doubted her ability to complete the early CMC activities within Levels 1 and 2 of Salmon's model. However, with the support of her tutor Tracey mastered the skills to operate the conferencing system. With renewed confidence she began to participate in the conferences and to exchange information (Level 3) with the other practitioners in her tutor group.

Here's what she wrote:

As I moved into Part 2 [Working with parents and other professionals] . . . I began to use the conferencing in a more pro-active way. I was able to send and receive messages via my mailbox and felt more confident about posting messages generally. As we progressed to Part 3 'Sharing Experiences', I began to get to know other members of my tutor group conference by reading and replying to messages. This became a very valuable tool for me in that I realised I was no longer alone in all of this and other people shared the same fears about ICT. I became so single-track-minded about what I couldn't do that I had forgotten what I could do.

Tracey concludes her account:

I have gained a better understanding of ICT as a result of this course because I now feel more confident to try things out. I am not so afraid of technical hitches because I realise that they are half the battle when using ICT. . . . I have learned that I need to assess whether ICT will enhance the learning of the children.

As students move through the first work-based learning course, the activities within it help to move them through the levels within Salmon's five-stage model. In Part 4 of the course, which focuses on understanding the implications of different theories of learning and cognitive development to early years practice, the activities are designed to engage the students in 'Knowledge construction' (i.e. Level 4).

In this part of the course students are asked to consider and contrast three influential theories – behaviourism, constructivism and socio-cultural theory – each of which is underpinned by different perspectives on how children learn, views of knowledge and the role of 'the other' in learning. The students think about, and explore, their own understanding, values and beliefs about children as learners. To further examine the different theories and to analyse the implications of different perspectives on practice, the students are required over a period of a few weeks to engage in, and contribute to, on-line asynchronous discussions. This is a compulsory activity, in as much as students know that the written reflective report submitted for assessment requires them not only to draw on these discussions in reflecting on and analysing their practice, but also explicitly to refer to their own and other people's contributions. Within this activity each student is allocated a different role or 'hat' to wear (see Table 9.1 for a summary of the different roles/hats). One of the intentions behind allocating the students to different roles is to force them to engage with and challenge each other's contributions to the discussions, thus requiring them to operate at Level 4 within Salmon's model.

Chairperson	Coordinates the discussion, ensures everyone stays in role and that the discussion stays focused on the questions that they have been asked to explore, makes links between postings, summarises, re-focuses, encourages people to respond to other people's postings, encourages people to make explicit links to course materials (and other relevant sources), etc.
Behaviourist	Believes that behaviourism explains how people learn. Sees and explains everything from a purely behaviourist perspective.
Constructivist	Believes that constructivism explains how people develop. Sees and explains everything from a purely constructivist perspective.
Socio-cultural theorist	Believes that socio-cultural theory explains how people learn. Sees and explains everything from a purely socio-cultural perspective.
Inquisitor	Challenges what people say – asks for evidence and explanation. Refuses to take anything at face value – always wants more information and/or justification.
Pragmatist	Doesn't really understand the three theories or how they underpin practice. Needs some convincing that theory is really relevant to practice – but is open to being persuaded. Asks lots of questions.

Table 9.1 Summary of the different 'hats' students in each group adopted

A bi-lingual specialist supporting children learning English as an additional language in nursery classes reflected in her assignment:

> *As I was wearing the socio-cultural theory hat within the [discussion], I was looking at this theory in depth and I could see the advantages of its approaches, in particular, with language. This challenged my thinking as originally I had seen parallels between the constructivist theory and my role but now I was leaning towards the socio-cultural theory. . . . Reading and discussing other people's points of view on the [forum] gave me a good opportunity to reflect on my practice and gave me some ideas as to how I could approach different situations or issues in my setting.*

As students proceed through the FDEY the expectation is that they will develop increasing levels of confidence and competence in using CMC and therefore progressively take greater responsibility for their own discussions. Thus, for example, in the second work-based learning course, which is the final course in the FDEY, students are expected to participate in and contribute to on-line, tutor group and wider 'route' discussions for their chosen specialism. The aim of this course is to encourage greater critical reflection about children's care and education and to extend students' personal and professional development. Engagement with CMC is consequently expected to create opportunities for learning experiences within the upper levels of Salmon's five-stage model. The tutor group conference is facilitated by the students themselves, whilst the 'route' conferences are moderated by tutors with expertise in the relevant specialism. These on-line conferences offer a valuable layer to academic discussion and debate. Throughout this course students research different aspects of their practice in order to uncover and better understand a child's experience of their setting. They select and use research tools drawn from the Mosaic approach (Clark and Moss 2001) to gather data from practice on:

- environments for children's care, learning and development;
- support for children's personal, social and emotional development;
- the curriculum for children's care, learning and development; and
- participation and inclusion.

During each small-scale 'researching practice' investigation the students participate in on-line discussions exploring pertinent 'theory-to-practice' and 'practice-to-theory' issues and questions. An interview (Cable and Goodliff 2007) with Amanda, a teaching assistant in a primary school, illustrates how participating in the on-line 'route' discussion on 'inclusion', alongside the research in her setting into views of inclusive practice, impacted on her own learning. Amanda said:

> I did find that [discussion on inclusion] quite interesting to hear . . .other people's different points of view – childminders and, you know, different people working in pre-schools and different areas, how obviously there are different ways of thinking. . .It was interesting to hear all the different points of view.

Engaging in professional dialogue with students working in other types of setting provoked Amanda to examine her thinking and enabled new understanding of issues of inclusion to emerge. Her learning was further extended when she reflected on the interviews she undertook with various colleagues in her school as part of her research. These revealed that an unexpected range of views were held about inclusion. She stated:

> I naively thought, working in a school, most people would have the same sort of beliefs – I think that was one of the eye openers to me when I did the inclusion interviews and hearing how different people thought – even working in the same school. I don't know why but you know how you think . . . we are all working for the same thing because we are all working in the same school, but no, it didn't work that way.

In the next section we consider the specific benefits of CMC for supporting reflection on practice and developing communities of practitioners through engagement in professional dialogue.

CMC SUPPORTING REFLECTION AND DEVELOPING COMMUNITIES OF PRACTITIONERS

Examining the values, beliefs and attitudes that relate to the practice in practitioners' own setting is crucial to reflection on practice. Evidence from the FDEY suggests that the ability to discuss and defend ideas and viewpoints with others through CMC extends the level of reflection, but requires considerable confidence, which takes time to emerge. Students find articulating a written response to messages that convey alternative values and beliefs challenging and they need to have time to work through the different levels of Salmon's model, and to gel as a community.

As students build relationships through the early on-line socialisation activities they develop the confidence and skills to 'converse' with each other and challenge each other's opinions. They value the opportunities to encounter accounts of early years environments and practice beyond their experience and find that engaging in debate with practitioners who have different roles and responsibilities can challenge and change their thinking. Niamh, a day nursery practitioner, summarised how participating in CMC discussions challenged and affirmed her thinking:

. . . obviously the different ways that people have of looking at things makes you think – 'oh yeah, I can see where you are coming from but I am not sure I agree with that', and then you read the responses and things that everybody else puts in and everything else, it does impact on what you were thinking in the first place or whether it is to confirm elements of what you think or not – it gets you thinking more.

Leading or participating in on-line discussions about areas of early years practice enables new understandings to be negotiated and shared together. This has the potential to influence and enhance professional practice. When Christine, a child-minder, was asked about which aspects of the FDEY had had an impact on her thinking and professional practice, she emphasised the value of CMC for offering her shared learning experiences:

I think they [CMC] have changed my thinking and influenced a great deal of what I do. I think meeting so many professionals in different settings has been a wonderful benefit really, I mean we shared so many good ideas.

As students approach the conclusion of their FDEY studies, they reflect on the professional journey they have followed and decide on targets for their ongoing professional development. Christine singled out the impact that her on-line 'route' discussion about issues of inclusion had for her continuing professional development:

. . .there was a huge discussion on inclusion and participation and it really really really brought home to me how our personal experiences influence how we see inclusion and that was quite an eye opener for me, realising it is such a diverse area and it is interesting talking to so many people and reading sort of how they perceive things, it does change your thinking, it does make you more aware of still really how much knowledge we need to gain. I mean I feel particularly that I would like some more training on inclusion because it is such a diverse area.

Without participating in the on-line discussions it is likely that Christine would not have encountered such stimulating debate nor, perhaps, defined 'inclusion' as an area for her ongoing professional development. The opportunity to engage in professional dialogue, whether face to face or through CMC, is a powerful tool to extend understandings of theory and practice. For students on a distance learning course and/or those who are otherwise 'isolated' in their practice, CMC plays an important role in enabling them to belong to a community of practitioners. Sometimes, as we saw in the discussion with Amanda above, the participation in professional conversations in an on-line community and the findings from research carried out within a particular work setting can combine to challenge previously held assumptions.

SUMMARY

As professionals working with young children in the twenty-first century it is critical that early years practitioners develop the confidence and competence to use ICT effectively. CMC is one aspect of ICT, which offers early years practitioners the opportunity to develop ICT skills and to enhance their own professional development. In particular, CMC provides opportunities for early years practitioners to communicate with other professionals. This can be particularly powerful in supporting reflective practice, where a strong community develops, which enables the sharing of alternative views on early years practice. Developing such communities is challenging, and requires a steep learning curve for the participants, but the evidence from the OU FDEY suggests that the benefits far outweigh the costs.

Questions/points for discussion/reflection

1 What is the value of CMC to the professional development of early years practitioners?
2 How can early years practitioners be supported to develop competence in CMC?
3 Reflect on ways CMC might foster opportunities for the continuing enhancement of professionalism in the early years.

REFERENCES

Cable, C. and Goodliff, G. (2007) 'Work-based learning and transitions in professional identity: women in the early years workforce'. Paper presented at the Women in Lifelong Learning Conference, Birkbeck College, University of London, May 2007

Children's Workforce Development Council (2007) *Guidance to the Standards for the Award of Early Years Professional Status.* Leeds: CWDC

Clark, A. and Moss, P. (2001) *Listening to Young Children: The Mosaic Approach.* London: National Children's Bureau and Joseph Rowntree Foundation

Department for Education and Skills (DfES) (2001) *Statement of Requirement: Early Years Sector-Endorsed Foundation Degree.* Nottingham: DfES Publications

Department for Education and Skills (2005) *Harnessing Technology Transforming Learning and Children's Services.* Nottingham: DfES Publications

Department for Education and Skills (2006) *Children's Workforce Strategy: Government's Response to Consultation.* Nottingham: DfES Publications

Department for Education and Skills (2007) *Integrated Children's System Fact Sheet.* Every Child Matters available on-line at http://www.everychildmatters.gov.uk/ics (accessed 14/10/2007)

HEFCE (2005) E-learning policy, March 2005 available on-line at http://www.hefce.ac.uk/pubs/hefce/2005/05_12/ (last accessed 14/10/2007)

Salmon, G. (2003) *E-Moderating: The Key to Teaching and Learning Online* (2nd edition). London, Kogan Page

Trilling, B. and Hood, P. (2001) 'Learning, technology and educational reform in the knowledge age or "We're wired, Webbed and Windowed, Now What?"' In C. Paechter, R. Edwards, R. Harrison and P. Twining, P. (eds) *Learning, Space and Identity.* London: Paul Chapman

Twining, P. (1999) '"Learning Matters": Adjusting the media mix for academic advantage', *ALT-J, 7(1),* 4–11.

Twining, P. (2001) 'ICT and the nature of learning: implications for the design of a distance education course'. In C. Paechter, R. Edwards, R. Harrison and P. Twining (eds) *Learning, Space and Identity*, London: Paul Chapman

Waller, T. (2006) 'Literacy and ICT in the early years'. In M. Hayes and D. Whitebread (eds) *ICT in the Early Years*. Open University Press: Maidenhead, Berkshire

Wenger, E. (1998) *Communities of Practice Learning, Meaning, and Identity.* Cambridge: Cambridge University Press

Further reading

Bolstad (2004) *The Role and Potential of ICT in Early Childhood Education: A Review of New Zealand and International Literature.* Wellington: New Zealand Council for Educational Research

Siraj-Blatchford, I. and Siraj-Blatchford, J. (2003) *More than Computers: Information and Communication Technology in the Early Years.* London: The British Association for Early Childhood Education

Learning and Teaching Scotland (2003) *Early Learning Forward Thinking: The Policy Framework for ICT in Early Years,* available on-line at: http://www.ltscotland.org.uk/earlyyears/about/approachestolearning/ictinp reschool/ictstrategy/earlylearningforwardthinking.asp (accessed 21/5/2007)

STUDYING THE EARLY YEARS FOUNDATION DEGREE: STUDENT VOICES

10

Caroline Jones

The Foundation Degree aims to provide a coherent and academically rigorous programme of professionally relevant training; . . .to deepen students' theoretical and practical knowledge; . . .to enable students to reflect on their practice; . . . to ensure the adoption of anti-discriminatory practice, equality of opportunity and inclusive practice.

(University of Warwick 2006)

This chapter explores students' perspectives on studying for the Early Years Sector-Endorsed Foundation Degree (EYSEFD) at the University of Warwick. It draws directly on evidence from a number of sources including reflective journals, anonymous student evaluations, employer and link tutor feedback and learning diaries. The chapter begins by providing some contextual information concerning the changing purpose, nature and structure of the EYSEFD at Warwick, where Foundation Degrees (FDs) are viewed as a key element in 'widening participation'. It then moves on to explore students' personal and professional profiles and how they feel at the point of application. The next part of the chapter looks at the impact of studying the EYSEFD on students' professional and practical skills. Finally, it draws attention to the way in which studying EYSEFDs can profoundly influence how early years practitioners gain a deep sense of personal, as well as professional, development as they progress through the programme. The chapter concludes that the EYSEFD is a uniquely challenging route to developing professionalism in the early years. It is far more than a qualification in its own right or a pathway to further study. Ultimately, it has the power to potentially change lives, not only of the students themselves but of their professional colleagues, families and most crucially the young children with whom they work.

BACKGROUND AND CONTEXT

The working contexts and professional roles of early years practitioners are continually evolving. Policy makers are increasingly focused on the training and organisation of the workforce. As part of this process, the introduction of FDs was announced in 2000 by the then Secretary of State for Education, David Blunkett. Flexibility was a key part of the FD design, with delivery strategies including work-based learning and part-time attendance at college or University. The University of Warwick initially piloted a Foundation Degree in Learning Support, admitting the first cohort of 30 students in 2000, all of whom were teaching assistants in primary schools. During the following year, key objectives for the Early Years Sector were set out in the Green Paper 'Schools Building on Success' (DfEE 2001). There was a growing recognition of the need of the EY sector to:

- employ skilled and qualified staff;
- provide a clear pathway for professional development;
- offer a way of learning that enabled practitioners to remain in employment.

In response to that need, the Early Years Sector-Endorsed Foundation Degree was developed by a working group of representatives from HE providers, LEAs and other key stakeholders. The EYSEFD was based on a Statement of Requirement (SoR) (DfES 2001), a vehicle to promote consistent national standards, and to link under-pinning knowledge with professional practice. The SoR was hailed as an innovative development which would introduce significant change, in that it marked a new level of professional practice known as 'Senior Practitioner' and a new career and qualifications pathway for Early Years practitioners.

> This document is about change and development. Change in the sense that a new career and qualifications pathway specifically for Early Years practitioners is being put in place. Development because for the first time there will be a foundation degree which marks out a new level of professional practice in Early Years, known as Senior Practitioner. . ..This represents the first part of an important new career pathway which will help raise standards and give individuals the recognition they deserve.

> (DfES 2001: Foreword)

Warwick revalidated the original Learning Support programme in line with the SoR and was one of the first institutions to successfully gain sector endorsement, or the 'official stamp of approval' from the DfES. Modules were developed, based on the Core Learning Outcomes (CLOs) in the SoR and taking account of Pugh's (2001: 21) suggestion that early education practitioners should understand:

> . . .how young children learn and develop; who can observe children and respond appropriately, planning for children's learning, both as individuals and in groups; who can create a stimulating and well-organised learning environment; and who can work in partnership with parents.

The programme, developed in conjunction with local employers, offered a unique combination of academic rigour with professional development, with each module having overlapping outcomes framed, for ease of reference, under the following headings:

- knowledge and understanding – theories of learning, concepts such as equality of opportunity, analysing educational research;
- professional and practical – reflective practice, linking theory, policy and practice;
- key and transferable skills – ICT, presentations, study skills, time management.

The introduction of a coherent and academically stringent part-time programme (all sessions take place in the evening and at weekends) of professionally relevant training filled the need to develop professionally and academically beyond Level 3, while remaining in employment. The flexible modular design and the option to progress to study at Honours Level attracted mature, highly motivated and experienced applicants, who would not otherwise have gained access to HE. Even at the point of application, students envisaged that studying the EYFD had the potential to change lives. The following extract from a student application form illustrates the point:

I am a very loyal and able candidate. I feel that I am ready for this Foundation Degree. I understand that I will need to work hard. I have three boys aged 12, 10 and 3. I am hoping they will be proud of me and maybe I can be an inspiration for them to also go to university. Please consider this application as I know this will change my life, for the better, in so many ways.

Students went through a powerful decision-making process before applying to study the FD. They described a combined range of personal and professional reasons, including career development, wanting to go on to become teachers, being interested in how children learn, behave and develop, and having a desire to fulfil their own potential. Some applicants were already lifelong learners and were continuing on their journey. One of the attractions was that the programme design enabled students to study and earn at the same time. Many applicants were highly motivated by a desire to develop and improve their professional practice.

The reason I have chosen to apply for this degree course is because I feel that the time is right for me to broaden my own learning and gain further knowledge. I have always valued training and used it as an effective tool to promote my own professional development.

Whilst recognising that there may not be any financial reward, some applicants were primarily driven by the need for an opportunity to achieve the EYFD, not only for their own personal satisfaction, but also to set an example for their own children.

I am a highly motivated, conscientious, well-organised professional. I want this so much, for Roger, for school, family but mostly for me.

I feel that the opportunity to study for the FD is one I cannot deny myself. As well as fulfilling my own needs, I also wish to set an example to my own children that higher education is accessible and achievable.

Since the pilot programme, a number of key changes have taken place in policy and in practice. These include, for example, the publication of the *Common Core of Skills and Knowledge* (DfES 2005a) and the *Children's Workforce Strategy* (DfES 2005b). There has also been the introduction of Higher Level Teaching Assistant status (HLTA) and Early Years Professional (EYP) status, combined with substantial investment of government monies in the form of a Transformation Fund, aimed at upskilling the children's workforce in the non-maintained sector. This has resulted in a changing cohort of students, consisting of a wider range of early years practitioners from the private, voluntary and independent sector, and a reduced number of applicants from the maintained sector.

CHANGING STUDENT CHARACTERISTICS

The first report in a series of EYFD evaluations (Mowlam, Murphy and Arthur 2003: i) suggests that EYFDs were designed with a 'typical' student in mind. This student was envisaged to be 'mature, possibly with family commitments as well as a job in a low-paid sector'. A later evaluation (Snape et al. 2006) reported that students are almost exclusively female and the most common age profile is 36 to 40. It suggested that the intake is changing from the most senior and experienced early years practitioners to include more younger and less senior applicants. These findings are generally reflected in the changing nature of the Warwick cohorts. Although all students come from their own unique context the two student profiles below are representative of the majority of those on the course.

Student profile 1
Karen: start date October 2006

Karen was 40 when she applied for the Foundation Degree. She is married with a 10-year-old daughter. She has worked with children under 11 since the age of 18. She has eight Certificates in Secondary Education (CSEs) taken in 1982 and started her career working as a nanny for four years. She then studied two years full time, for a nursery nursing qualification. For the next 15 years she worked as a nursery officer in Social Services day nurseries. Karen worked her way from nursery assistant to deputy leader. For the past three years she has worked as a Childcare Development Officer in an LEA-maintained nursery class and taken charge of the school wraparound childcare service. Over the years, she attended numerous short courses ranging from 'Consulting with Children' to 'Health and Safety'. Karen was given outstanding references, stating that she has 'contributed to policy development, is hard working and willing to undertake organisational tasks. She sets a high standard in terms of preparation, teaching and displays. Her attitude and ability when working with children is insurmountable. . .'. The referee had 'no hesitation in recommending her for the course' and was 'certain' that she would be an 'asset and a credit'. Karen has also worked as a market researcher and shop assistant.

Student profile 2
Sarnjit: start date October 2004

Sarnjit was aged 35 when she applied to study the Foundation Degree. She started working with children as a voluntary helper in a school and moved on to become a teaching assistant in 1998. She took three 'O' levels while at school and a further six General Certificates in Secondary Education at Further Education College ten years later, achieving grade 'A' in all six. She then took two 'A' levels. She gained a Certificate in Learning Support and attended a broad range of professional development courses, including one on special educational needs, and showed a commitment to further study. Sarnjit runs the before-school provision and a social club for children with expressive language difficulties. Her head teacher described her as having an 'excellent understanding of the demands of the National Literacy and Numeracy Strategies' and 'particular expertise in supporting children of all abilities with literacy'. Her reference stated that she worked 'tirelessly' to support children and colleagues, showed 'enthusiasm and commitment to studies' and recommended her 'wholeheartedly' for the Foundation Degree.

CHANGING STUDENT ATTITUDES

Studying at HE level can initially be a daunting experience for students especially if, as in the majority of cases at Warwick, they have been out of formal education for a number of years. After the induction evening one student said she felt nervous and her 'tummy went funny', another was 'absolutely panic stricken'. One student, a 45-year-old teaching assistant reflected that she was:

Slightly shell shocked. . . already thinking about the course, the assignments, the record of professional development, the travelling. I can't believe I am at university. A lamb to the slaughter springs to mind.

Other new students noted:

The initial excitement of being given the opportunity to achieve my goal without having to leave the security of paid employment soon gave way to a feeling of what have I let myself in for. Having not studied seriously for many years, I was quite apprehensive about how I would cope and whether or not I was up to it, but at the same time I felt my mind being stimulated by the challenge that faced me.

To say I was scared and anxious would be an understatement. I am unexpectedly apprehensive and beginning to question my capabilities.

Nevertheless, in time these initial nerve-wracking feelings began to change and their confidence grew. Students began to recognise changes and benefits in both work-related and non-work-related contexts. There seemed to be a close connection between improved knowledge and skills and gains in confidence. The comments below show how even during the first year students were benefiting professionally and personally.

What a difference in feelings a year has made. I now feel more confident.

The Foundation Degree has worked extremely well in conjunction with my workplace.

When I first started the course, I felt there was a lot of work and I wouldn't be able to cope with work and study. I have definitely gained tremendous confidence. I have learnt a lot about how children learn through play and recognise this at work.

By the end of the course students were able to clearly articulate the changes that had taken place. A student at one of Warwick's partner Further Education Colleges stated that:

The Foundation Degree required hard work, dedication and commitment. The results however, were worth it. My confidence grew, my academic ability improved and I had the opportunity to think about and debate many issues regarding children and education with others, all in a friendly and non-judgemental environment. As a result, I've made some lifelong friends and I have a degree to enable me to move forward towards my goal to become a teacher. The degree was one of the best decisions I have ever made.

There were also a number of barriers and concerns. Juggling work, family and part-time study was not without challenges. Over the years, personal tutor records reveal a number of family crises including bereavements, illnesses in families, marital problems and financial difficulties. Every year at least one major tragedy occurred: one student's daughter contracted leukaemia, another student's brother took his own life, others lost husbands, parents, sisters and grandparents, yet they persevered with the course, determined to succeed.

I have found this term very difficult due to home conditions. My husband has been in hospital, my father died and I was unable to submit my assignments on time.

I have had a busy and stressful week, especially with my brother having his heart operation, but he's over the worst now and I have realised that time is precious and nothing's going to stop me now.

Since the arrival of my newborn son I have found time management difficult.

Other more practical barriers also faced students. One student, for example, stated that she found it 'difficult managing the evening sessions after a day in the class-room, driving a long way in the dark evenings to get to the venue.'

DEVELOPING PROFESSIONALISM

An information leaflet produced by Sure Start (2003) listed the benefits to employers of enrolling staff on the EYSEFD including:

- It gives professionally qualified staff who can translate theory into practice and raise the quality of Early Years and Childcare Provision.
- Staff put into practice what they learn, bringing new ideas and energy to work, so you and the children can gain from the start.
- Your staff can share their new knowledge in the workplace, so colleagues benefit too.

Work-based learning was a crucial aspect of the EYSEFD. The Core Learning Outcomes in the SoR (DfES 2001) not only had to be achieved academically but also demonstrated in the workplace. Therefore, employer involvement and workplace-based learning (WBL) was a key element in the design and delivery of the Warwick EYFD. The programme was designed to have an outcomes and content balance of approximately two-thirds theory and one-third professional practice. A steering group made up of local employers and university staff was established for consultative purposes. Modules varied in emphasis, but work-based learning was integral and the theory / practice relationship was ever-present both in the taught sessions and in the WBL elements. The key strategies for work-based learning were: Work-Based Tasks (WBTs), carried out in the workplace and assessed by the module tutor; a final year workplace-based research project; and a record of professional development, incorporating professional targets and learning diaries. There were also a number of ongoing directed professional tasks. Employers, mentors and link tutors (visiting settings) have a crucial role to play in supporting workplace-based learning. A robust system of mentoring and link tutoring was established to support the professional elements of the course, including training sessions and a workplace-based learning handbook. Both students and mentors were generally positive, although a small number of students were less well-supported in their settings than others. Nevertheless, in their evaluations, students commented frequently on the professional benefits of studying the EYFD. Many recognised that they had become more reflective and confident practitioners:

Throughout the year I have developed personally and professionally. I have become more confident in my approach to work and have learned how to be more reflective in my practice. The knowledge I have gained about theories of learning has helped me understand why I do the things I do now, rather than just accept that that is the way it's done.

Professionally I have moved on. I am looking at my work in a different way, using observations more. I have definitely improved my practice. I feel more confident now.

I believe I have moved on professionally after completing and submitting my module portfolios. I have gained much confidence and am more determined to succeed and achieve as much as I am capable of. I now feel I have more confidence as well as knowledge and understanding. I am moving on professionally in my career as well as academically.

I have really enjoyed the course so far. I feel so energised. I am far more reflective within my daily practice and am able to observe, monitor and extend children's learning further.

While a few teachers initially felt a bit 'threatened' by the increasing knowledge of their teaching assistants, most were overwhelmingly positive. Feedback sheets usually referred to specific modules. For example, one mentor commented on the storytelling module that her teaching assistant 'loved this module' and was 'collecting props to develop her own skills as a storyteller with all ages in the school.' Others noted the development of students' confidence and a concomitant development professionally:

She has shown increasing confidence in Foundation Stage Practice and Birth to Three. She is more reflective in her practice.

They also commented in relation to the impact on the practice of other staff in school. The workplace research project was notably influential in prompting changes, not only in the students' practice, but more widely in the setting. One student, who conducted a project in relation to role-play, stated in her presentation, for example, that her research had brought up several key issues to be addressed by the school. As a result of her findings, all staff would go on further training and would spend more time supporting children in the role-play area.

Personal development

In the non-work related sense, students repeatedly thought that studying the FDEY had improved their study skills, time management, self-esteem and confidence.

Overall I have found that studying at Warwick University has made me a more assertive and confident person.

I can honestly say that although the year has been hard work, I have enjoyed the learning process. It (the study skills module) has helped me structure my time.

CHANGING KNOWLEDGE AND SKILLS

The development of skills and knowledge is one of the five core features of Foundation Degrees (DfES 2001). Very early on in the course, students became conscious that they were beginning to develop new knowledge and skills. Even by the end of the first term, comments in the learning diaries show this to be the case:

Before applying for this course I always thought I had enough knowledge about children. Starting the module 'How Children Learn and Develop' has extended my knowledge and understanding of this subject. I have deepened my understanding of the needs and characteristics of young children. I have gained a lot of knowledge of why 'play' is an important aspect of a child's life.

'How Children Learn and Develop' was useful and made me look at my work in a different light. I have gained knowledge and understanding and am now able to use critical thinking and questioning in my setting as to why children behave in certain ways. I have been more reflective on my practice.

This change continued over time. As the same student explained, 'My knowledge and understanding seems to heighten as I continue through the course'. This knowledge was not confined to the individual students but also taken back and shared in the workplace. This raised the status of the students in their settings. One student wrote:

I have been able to take information back to my workplace which makes me feel that I am gaining knowledge and skills.

Overall, the student voices provide a unique insight into the potential impact of studying the EYSEFD. However, a number of issues remain unresolved, not least the future of Senior Practitioner Status, originally an integral part of the award. There is now a lack of funding for teaching assistants and others who cannot access transformation funding. Confusion remains between EYP status, HLTA status and Foundation Degrees. Sector-endorsement is being revised and a new system for endorsement is proposed from 2008.

SUMMARY

This chapter has used student voices to show the impact of studying the part-time EYSEFD at the Institute of Education, University of Warwick. It has demonstrated that studying has influenced students academically, professionally and personally. Even at the early stages of the course, students recognised changes which in turn were linked with increased confidence and self-esteem. This had resulted in developing professionalism as students felt empowered by their new-found knowledge and ability to take information back to the workplace. In spite of this, there is still no clear career ladder or pay structure to motivate or reward those students who are clearly improving their own professionalism and ultimately positively influencing the quality of early childhood education and care.

Questions/points for discussion/reflection

1 How has your own professional development impacted on you personally and professionally?
2 What do you see as the advantages of Foundation Degrees as a means of widening participation?
3 What are the key issues for early years practitioners in developing professionalism through studying at HE level?

REFERENCES

Department for Education and Employment (2001) *Schools Building on Success*. Norwich: The Stationery Office Ltd

Department for Education and Skills (2001) *Statement of Requirement*. Nottingham: DfES Publications

Department for Education and Skills (2005a) *Common Core of Skills and Knowledge*. Nottingham: DfES Publications

Department for Education and Skills (2005b) *The Children's Workforce Strategy*. Nottingham: DfES Publications

Mowlam, A., Murphy, J. and Arthur, S. (2003) *Evaluating the Introduction of the Early Years Foundation Degree*. London: SureStart/NatCen

Pugh, G. (2001) 'A policy for early childhood services'. In G. Pugh (ed.) *Contemporary Issues in the Early Years* (3rd edition). London: Paul Chapman Publishing

Snape, D., Tanner, E., Mackenzie H., National Centre for Social Research (2006) *Evaluation of the Early Years Sector-Endorsed Foundation Degree*. Nottingham: DfES Publications.

SureStart (2003) *Information for Employers.* Nottingham: DfES Publications.

University of Warwick (2006) *Early Years Sector-Endorsed Foundation Degree Course Handbook.* Coventry: University of Warwick.

Further reading

Department for Education and Skills (2005) *The Children's Workforce Strategy.* Nottingham: DfES Publications

Snape, D., Tanner, E., Mackenzie H., National Centre for Social Research (2006) *Evaluation of the Early Years Sector-Endorsed Foundation Degree.* Nottingham: DfES Publications

3

RETHINKING PROFESSIONALISM

THE DEMOCRATIC AND REFLECTIVE PROFESSIONAL: RETHINKING AND REFORMING THE EARLY YEARS WORKFORCE

11

Peter Moss

> [The early childhood worker needs to be] more attentive to creating possibilities than pursuing predefined goals. . . [to be] removed from the fallacy of certainties, [assuming instead] responsibility to choose, experiment, discuss, reflect and change, focusing on the organisation of opportunities rather than the anxiety of pursuing outcomes, and maintaining in her work the pleasure of amazement and wonder.
>
> (Fortunati 2006: 37)

INTRODUCTION

English policy on the early years workforce gives a central role to the 'Early Years Professional', who by 2015 is intended to provide graduate-level leadership in all nurseries. Other workers, by implication, will not be professionals, but at best will have a Level 3 qualification (equivalent to 'A' level). This chapter argues the need for professionals in early years, but as the core workers in the system, making up over half the workforce, not just leaders; in other words, making the quantum jump from a low qualified/poorly paid workforce to a workforce on a par to that in school, taking young children as seriously as we take school children. But I go further, to enquire into the image of this professional: how is this worker understood, with what values are they inscribed, and what conditions are needed to achieve the quantum jump? And in doing so, I lift the lid on a can of worms. How can we justify the current devaluation of early years work? What type of services do we want? Is the market model necessary and desirable? How should we fund early childhood education and care (ECEC)?

INTEGRATED RESPONSIBILITY, SPLIT SYSTEM

Early childhood education and care has changed a good deal in Britain over the last decade: sustained policy attention has led to more services, more funding and a more integrated approach, including the bringing together (in England and Scotland) of responsibility for all services within one education department. Yet much has not changed. Thinking – both in government and public psyches – remains split between 'childcare' and 'early education': hence, government has a 'childcare strategy', a 'childcare tax credit', a 'childcare act'; and whereas 'early education' is treated as a public good for which there is a universal entitlement, 'childcare' is viewed as a private commodity to be purchased by parent-consumers in a private market where suppliers are mainly for-profit providers.

This split thinking is reflected in a continuing split structure: different services for 'childcare' and 'early education', different systems of funding, and different workforces. 'Early education' for 3- and 4-year-olds is mainly school-based, where a large part of the workforce consists of teachers. While 'childcare' is carried out mainly in nurseries, where most of the workforce are nursery or childcare workers, the remainder being family day carers. (I shall focus in this chapter on workers in centre-based services; however, family day carers are a large part of the total early years workforce, and any quantum leap in education and conditions needs to take them into account – see Chapter 6.)

If we compare teachers and nursery workers, we find a yawning gap separates them. Analysis of the Labour Force Survey shows that, over the period 2001–2005, nursery workers are younger (average age 33), have a relatively low level of qualification (only a fifth have the equivalent of NVQ Levels 4 or 5) and are extremely poorly paid (average hourly pay over this period being £5.95). Teachers are older (42 years old, on average), predominantly graduates and earn nearly three times as much (£14.41 per hour), not to mention having access to good occupational pensions schemes, a key employment condition that childcare workers can mostly only dream of (indeed under current circumstances, childcare and other 'care' workers are at risk of forming a large part of the retired poor in the next generation). The one common theme is gender: both teachers and childcare workers are overwhelmingly female (Simon et al. 2007).

Nor is this two-tier pattern unique to Britain. *Starting Strong II*, the final report of the major cross-national OECD study of ECEC, concludes that:

> *'[The situation of staff and levels of training in ECEC across the countries covered] is mixed, with acceptable professional education standards being recorded in the Nordic countries but only in early education in most other countries. . ..Levels of in-service training vary greatly across countries and between the education and child care sectors. . .Figures from various countries reveal a wide pay gap between child care staff and teachers with child care staff in most countries being poorly trained and paid around minimum wage levels'.* (OECD 2006: 15)

WHY?

At the heart of Britain's continuing split ECEC system is this split workforce: a relatively small group of teacher professionals and a growing army of childcare technicians, whose competences, procedures and goals are all tightly prescribed. Why does this split persist? Why does British society seem to take for granted that work with young children (but also, at the other end of life, elderly people) should largely depend on poorly qualified workers earning, on average, not much above the minimum wage? I would suggest four interlocking reasons.

First, it is because young children are still widely seen as immature, uncomplicated, incomplete human beings, whose physical and developmental needs can be met through applying simple formulas. Second, it is because any paid work understood and named as 'care' – 'childcare' for example – is widely seen as essentially the commodification of what women do, unpaid and untrained, in the home; understood in this way, 'care work' requires little additional training for women workers and merits only low payment. Third, it is because successive neoliberal Conservative and Labour governments in Britain have adopted a market model for 'childcare', delivered overwhelmingly by private, for-profit providers and premised on parental fees, mediated for lower-income families by tax credits: such private market provision cannot stand the cost of a well-educated and well-paid workforce (any more than schools could do so if parents had to pay most of the costs).

Fourth, and here I am more speculative, there is the hidden hand of paradigm, the overarching system of ideas, values and beliefs by which people see and organise the world in a coherent way. In Britain, and indeed throughout the English-speaking world, ECEC is dominated by a positivistic paradigm, that values certainty and mastery, linearity and predetermined outcomes, objectivity and universality; and believes in the ability of science to reveal the true nature of a real world, giving one right answer for every question (see Dahlberg, Moss and Pence 2007 for a fuller discussion). This paradigm calls for technicians trained in right answers, not professionals trained to reflect and question (see Chapter 8).

Where do we go from here? One direction, set out for us by government, is basically more of the same, a continuing split workforce but with incremental improvement in the childcare sector, giving graduate leadership in nurseries by 2015 and gradual increases in levels of vocational qualification, with Level 3 as the main aspiration. But there are other directions that we, as a society, could choose to take. I want to map out here one of those directions, that of enhanced and rethought professionalism as part of a wider rethinking and reforming of policy that addresses the 'wicked' issues that government has shied away from confronting. My main aim is not, however, to urge this direction on you, the reader, but to stimulate or nurture critical and democratic thinking by 'opening up a new horizon of possibilities mapped out by new radical alternatives' (Santos 1995: 481): we have choices and those choices should be the subject of lively debate and critical thinking.

THE CASE FOR A DIFFERENT DIRECTION

But before explaining my choice, it is worth pausing a moment to consider the case for not following the current route but instead risking a new direction. The case has three legs. First, equality: why should young children require or get less than school children? Why should the workforce be devalued and treated so inequitably? Second, quality: OECD's *Starting Strong II* report concludes, succinctly, that 'research from many countries supports the view that quality in the early childhood field requires adequate training and fair working conditions for staff' (OECD, 2006: 158). Finally, the work demands it: new understandings require different education and structures. Let me discuss this last point in more detail.

Instead of a technology for (re)producing predetermined outcomes in children and a business selling a commodity of childcare, dominant ways of thinking about ECEC services in modern Britain, these services can be understood in very different and far more complex ways. Gunilla Dahlberg, Alan Pence and I have proposed that ECECs institution may be understood (please note, 'may' – this understanding is a political choice not a necessity) as a children's space or a public forum, where children and adults meet and which are capable of many projects and many possibilities: social, cultural, economic, political, aesthetic, ethical etc., some predetermined, others not predicted at all and, therefore, capable of generating what Fortunati refers to as 'amazement and wonder' (see Dahlberg et al. 2007, but see also Moss and Petrie 2002 for elaboration of this concept of 'children's space').

In using the term 'projects', I want to invoke Carlina Rinaldi's use of the word as: 'a dynamic process, a journey that involves the uncertainty and chance that always arises in relationship with others. . .[growing] in many directions, with no predefined progression, no outcomes decided before the journey begins' (Rinaldi 2004: 19). Here are just a few of the possible projects of the ECEC centre, to give a hint of the potential of these social institutions, definitely not a complete inventory:

- construction of knowledge, values and identities;
- researching children's learning processes;
- community and group support and empowerment;
- cultural (including linguistic) sustainability and renewal;
- gender equality and economic development;
- democratic and ethical practice.

Elsewhere I have explored the possibilities for both democratic and ethical practice (Dahlberg and Moss 2005; Moss 2007). For example, bringing democratic politics into the nursery (or other ECEC centre) means citizens having opportunities for participation in one or more of at least four types of activity: *decision-making* about the purposes, the practices and the environment of the nursery; *evaluation* of pedagogical work through participatory methods; *contesting dominant discourses*, by making core assumptions and values visible and contestable; and finally, opening up for *change*, through developing a critical approach to what exists and envisioning utopias and turning them into utopian action.

This possible understanding of the ECEC centre has been further elaborated. Using metaphors that capture the idea of possibility and creativity that are at the heart of this understanding, Carlina Rinaldi, from Reggio Emilia, has spoken of ECEC centres not only as places of encounter, but also as construction sites, workshops and permanent laboratories. She uses these metaphors to capture the idea that they offer possibilities for creating bases of new knowledge, new values, new identities, new solidarities. Reflecting on Reggio Emilia's 'municipal schools', Jerome Bruner emphasises their public and communal role; they are 'a special kind of place, one in which young human beings are invited to grow in mind, sensibility, and in belonging to a broader community. . .[I]t is a learning community, where mind and sensibility are shared. It is a place to learn together about the real world, and about possible worlds of the imagination' (1998).

It seems to me that if we were to go down this pathway of understanding, then we need to think of an early childhood worker who will be 'at home' in this inclusive, experimenting, creative and democratic early childhood centre. This is the early childhood worker who is a critical thinker and researcher, who works as a co-constructor of meaning, identity and values, and who values participation, diversity and dialogue: in short, a democratic and reflective professional. This understanding of the worker is embodied in the quotation from Aldo Fortunati, with which I began this chapter, and in the concept of what Oberhuemer (2005) has termed 'democratic professionalism': 'it is a concept based on participatory relationships and alliances. It foregrounds collaborative, cooperative action between professional colleagues and other stakeholders. It emphasises engaging and networking with the local community' (13).

Values for democratic professionalism

The English government's *Every Child Matters* agenda for children and children's services foregrounds the need for a common core of skills, knowledge and competence for the 'widest possible range of workers in children's services', to support the development of more effective and integrated services. I agree that a common framework for a wide range of workers in children's services (including schools) is a good idea. I would, however, go back a step or two: to a common core of understandings and values (I would also want to avoid closure by treating this core as provisional and open, therefore, to critical enquiry and contestation). The common understanding would be the worker as a democratic and reflective practitioner, while I set out below, as a basis for discussion, qualities that I believe this professional might value, as well as some hints, starting points for reflection, of what these values might mean.

- Dialogue: '[Dialogue] is of absolute importance. It is an idea of dialogue not as an exchange but as a process of transformation where you lose absolutely the possibility of controlling the final result. And it goes to infinity, it goes to the universe, you can get lost. And for human beings nowadays, and for women particularly, to get lost is a possibility and a risk' (Rinaldi 2006: 184).
- Critical thinking: '[I]ntroducing a critical attitude towards those things that are given to our present experience as if they were timeless, natural, unquestionable: to stand against the current of received wisdom. It is a matter of introducing a kind of awkwardness into the fabric of one's experience, of interrupting the fluency of the narratives that encode that experience and making them stutter' (Rose 1999: 20).
- Researching: 'Research can and should take place as much in the classroom and by teachers as in the university and by 'academics' . . . The word 'research', in this sense, leaves – or rather, demands to come out of – the scientific laboratories, thus ceasing to be a privilege of the few (in universities and other designated places) to become the stance, the attitude with which teachers approach the sense and meaning of life' (Rinaldi 2006: 148).
- Listening and openness to otherness: '[Listening requires] welcoming and being open to differences, recognising the value of the other's point of view and interpretation . . . It demands that we have clearly in mind the value of the unknown and that we are able to overcome the sense of emptiness and precariousness that we experience whenever our certainties are questioned' (Rinaldi 2006: 65).

- Uncertainty and provisionality: '[Uncertainty is a] quality that you can offer, not only a limitation . . . You have to really change your being, to recognise doubt and uncertainty, to recognise your limits as a resource, as a place of encounter, as a quality. Which means that you accept that you are unfinished, in a state of permanent change, and your identity is in the dialogue.' (Rinaldi 2006: 183-184)

- Subjectivity: 'There is no objective point of view that can make observation neutral. Point of view is always subjective, and observation is always partial. But this is a strength, not a limitation. We are sometimes frightened by subjectivity because it means assuming responsibility. So our search for objectivity is often driven by the fear of taking on responsibility' (Rinaldi 2006: 128).

- Border crossing, multiple perspectives and curiosity: 'We must think of the pre-school teacher as a person who is part of contemporary culture, who is able to question and to analyze this culture with a critical eye . . . An intellectually curious person who rejects a passive approach to knowledge and prefers to construct knowledge together with others rather than simply to "consume" it' (Rinaldi 2006: 137).

The education and continuous professional development of this reflective and democratic professional involves deepening understanding of these values and learning how to give expression to them in everyday practice. This will involve, as Fortunati puts it so well, being 'attentive to creating possibilities', assuming 'responsibility to choose, experiment, discuss, reflect and change' and maintaining 'the pleasure of amazement and wonder'.

RESTRUCTURING THE WORKFORCE

I have deliberately started from understandings and values rather than structures, because it seems to me essential to first ask the critical question: what is my/your image of the professional? Having attempted to answer the question, at least provisionally and sketchily, I can move on to how this image might be realised in practice. In my view, this democratic and reflective professional has a strong, graduate-level, initial education, followed by strong continuous professional development supported by collaborative working relations, pedagogical documentation (see Dahlberg et al. 2007; Rinaldi 2006), pedagogistas (experienced educators each working closely with a small number of centres), and opportunities for higher degrees. This professional could be designated a 'teacher' specialising in work with younger children (i.e. from birth to 6 or 8 or 10 years) or a 'pedagogue'. Both professions (unlike the 'Early Years Professional', produced out of thin air by the English government) have long traditions, strong theoretical bases and a relationship with the wider children's workforce (the Danish pedagogue, for example, works not only in ECEC services but also in a wide range of child and youth services (Cameron and Moss 2007); while the teacher is a core profession across a wide range of educational services). In a British context, 'teacher' may make more sense, but that does mean a willingness to rethink 'education' in its broadest sense, and the role of teachers as practitioners of this broad view of education.

This professional would be the 'core' worker of a fully integrated ECEC system, working in all services with children under and over 3 years, and possibly well into primary school; indeed ideally, the reform of the early years workforce would provide the opportunity to rethink and reform the workforce from birth through to (and possibly into) secondary school, based on a shared image of the child, the (pre)school, the educator, and education. What proportion of the workforce should this core worker constitute? Some years ago, the European Commission Childcare Commission (1996) proposed that professional (graduate) workers should account for 'a minimum of 60 per cent of staff working directly with children in collective services' (24), and this still seems to me a good target, as does the proposal that these staff should enjoy pay parity with school teachers.

What is proposed here is not ground breaking, indeed it could be said to be a necessary catching-up exercise. England and Scotland are part of a select group of countries that have taken the brave (and in my view correct) decision to integrate responsibility for the whole ECEC system within education: other countries that have taken the same decision include Brazil, Iceland, New Zealand, Norway, Slovenia, Spain and Sweden. Most of these countries have a core graduate professional, either an early years teacher or a pedagogue. Their proportion of the total workforce varies: for example, in Norway the pedagogue makes up a third, while in Sweden the teacher makes up a half. Most ambitiously, New Zealand has set itself the goal of a 100 per cent teacher workforce by 2012 (New Zealand Ministry of Education 2002) (see Chapter 13). Compared then to most countries that have moved ECEC fully into education, England and Scotland have still to make the quantum jump – from a split workforce with a large undervalued childcare sector to a fully integrated workforce, organised around a well-valued professional.

PUTTING THE RIGHT CONDITIONS IN PLACE

Rethinking and reforming the workforce along the lines I have suggested requires rethinking and reforming policy. It means developing a truly integrated and inclusive system of ECEC, to replace the current split system. It means new understandings of ECEC centres matched by making 'full service' children's centres – capable of many projects and possibilities – the norm for the whole country, not just in disadvantaged areas. It means moving away from the model of markets, parent consumers and competitive private providers to collaborative networks of community services for child and parent citizens, provided by a mix of public and private providers, all committed to democracy and inclusion. And it means spending more to develop a valued early years profession.

International comparison confirms the intuitively obvious, that a well-qualified workforce requires sustained public funding of services and cannot be achieved if services rely on parental fees and demand subsidies: 'demand-side funding [for example tax credits] is, in general, under-funding and the burden of costs in market-led systems falls essentially on parents, who, in the market economies pay fees ranging from 35 per cent to 100 per cent of the costs of child care, unless they belong to low-income groups' (OECD 2006: 116). Moreover, parent subsidies may not be passed on fully to providers and they make it difficult for services to plan for the longer term.

Those few countries (I am thinking here particularly of Denmark and Sweden) that have achieved an ECEC system that is available to all children as an entitlement, that offers holistic and community based services, and that has a workforce at least half of whom are well-educated professionals, spend between 1.5 and 2 per cent of GDP on supporting this system (OECD 2006: Chapter 5). England currently, and despite considerable increases in recent years, still spends only 0.5 per cent (OECD 2006: Chapter 5); the difference is made up by parental fees (English parents spend six times as much, on average, for a nursery place as their Swedish counterparts) and the poor education and employment conditions of the workforce. (The gap is also partly accounted for by the Nordic ECEC system covering children up to 6 years, while the English system stops at 5 years or earlier).

What is, of course, unknowable is the cost of *not* rethinking and reforming. As women's educational qualifications continue to rise and their employment opportunities continue to widen, it will prove increasingly hard to recruit the 'childcare' workforce, even with some modest enhancement of training and pay. As the traditional recruitment pool of young, low qualified women dries up, employers will have to find new sources of low paid labour, including migrant workers. There may be increasing differentiation in the private market, with some businesses offering higher qualified staff for higher fees (alongside the French and violin lessons). Large corporations providing nurseries will also spread, using economies of size to keep costs down, including group training programmes and monitoring systems. All this will mean a workforce increasingly governed by detailed procedures and prespecified outcome goals, standardised production methods implemented by a workforce of low-level technicians accustomed to measuring themselves and children against external norms. Whether or not this achieves a few points difference on standardised measures remains to be seen; for certain, though, it will leave no space and little will for research, experimentation or democracy.

SUMMARY

This chapter has been about the continuing weakness of the ECEC workforce in Britain today, the poverty of current policy ambition and the reasons for that poverty. I have also offered an alternative direction for the workforce, pursuing the idea of a democratic and reflective professional, inscribed with a number of core values and working in an integrated, inclusive and democratic early childhood centre, a service for which the public take responsibility and which is one of the necessary social institutions for a cohesive society. I have suggested that this professional might make up 60 per cent, or so, of the total workforce, and would need certain conditions to flourish; I have also indicated that some other countries have already achieved, or else aspire to, this goal.

But the chapter is also an expression of anger and a call for resistance. Anger at the poor education, pay and other employment conditions that we, as a wealthy society, accept for so many of our early childhood workers (but also for other women doing important work, such as the multitude caring for very elderly people); resistance to the narrow visions, the meagre ambitions, the unchallenged assumptions that constitute current policy. You may not agree with the direction I have proposed for the early years workforce: that is fine, I have little problem with that. But I hope you agree that choices exist and decisions still need to be made; we should not accept current policy as a necessity.

Questions/points for discussion/reflection

1 What is your image of the early childhood worker?
2 What do you think are the most important values for early childhood work?
3 How do you respond to the quotation by Aldo Fortunati that starts this chapter?

REFERENCES

Bruner, J. (1998) In Ceppi, G. and Zini, M. *Children, Spaces, Relations: Metaproject for an Environment for Young Children.* Milan: Reggio Children and Domus Academy Research Centre

Cameron, C. and Moss, P. (2007) *Care Work in Europe: Current Understandings and Future Directions.* London: Routledge

Dahlberg, G. and Moss, P. (2005) *Ethics and Politics in Early Childhood Education.* London: Routledge

Dahlberg, G., Moss, P. and Pence, A. (2007) *Beyond Quality in Early Childhood Education and Care; Languages of Evaluation* (2nd edition). London: Routledge

European Commission Childcare Commission (1996) *Quality Targets in Services for Young Children.* Brussels: EC Equal Opportunities Unit

Fortunati, A. (2006) *The Education of Young Children as a Community Project: The Experience of San Miniato, Azzano.* San Paolo: Edizioni Junior

Moss, P. (2007) 'Bringing politics into the nursery: early childhood education as a democratic practice', *European Early Childhood Education Research Journal, 15(1),* 5–20

Moss, P. and Petrie, P. (2002) *From Children's Services to Children's Spaces.* London: Routledge

New Zealand Ministry of Education (2002) *Pathways to the Future: a 10 Year Strategic Plan for Early Childhood Education,* http://www.minedu.govt.nz/web/downloadable/dl7648_v1/english.plan.art.pdf (accessed 18/9/2007)

Oberhuemer, P. (2005) 'Conceptualising the early childhood professional', paper given to the 15th Annual EECERA Conference, Malta, 3rd September 2005

OECD (2006) *Starting Strong II: Early Childhood Education and Care.* Paris: OECD

Rinaldi, C. (2004) 'Is a curriculum necessary?', *Children in Europe, 9,* 19

Rinaldi, C. (2006) *In Dialogue with Reggio Emilia: Listening, Researching and Learning.* London: Routledge

Rose, N. (1999) *Powers of Freedom: Reframing Political Though.* Cambridge: Cambridge University Press

Santos, B. de S. (1995) *Towards a New Common Sense: Law, Science and Politics in the Paradigmatic Transition.* London: Routledge

Simon, A., Owen, C., Moss, P., Cameron, C., Petrie, P., Potts, P. and Wigfall, V. (2007) 'Secondary analysis of the Labour Force Survey to map the numbers and characteristics of the occupations working within Social Care, Childcare, Nursing and Education', unpublished report for the DCSF

Further reading

Moss, P. (2007) 'Bringing politics into the nursery: early childhood education as a democratic practice', *European Early Childhood Education Research Journal, 15(1)*, 5–20

OECD (2006) *Starting Strong II: Early Childhood Education and Care*. Paris: OECD

Rinaldi, C. (2006) *In Dialogue with Reggio Emilia: Listening, Researching and Learning*. London: Routledge

WHO IS AN EARLY YEARS PROFESSIONAL? REFLECTIONS ON POLICY DIVERSITY IN EUROPE

12

Pamela Oberhuemer

INTRODUCTION

Looking back over the past decade, there is considerable evidence to suggest that, across Europe, early childhood education and care has been assigned a new and more visible status on the policy agenda. The recent OECD reviews in 15 European (and five non-European) countries provide excellent documentation of this trend (Neuman 2005; OECD 2001; 2006).

At the European Union level, first-time common targets for expanding early childhood provision were drawn up at the Barcelona European Council in 2002. More recently, the EU education ministers (at an informal meeting in Heidelberg in March 2007 during the German EU Council Presidency) spoke out explicitly in favour of improving not only early childhood education in general, but also the professional preparation for work in early childhood settings:

Cultural, economic and social participation by every individual must be our goal. Early childhood education is of central importance in this respect. . . . In order to achieve these goals, the governments in Europe will increase their efforts to improve the training of teachers working in early childhood education. In this connection it is important that institutions offering early childhood education are adequately equipped with both staff and funding.

(Press Release, 2/3/2007, www.eu2007.de, accessed 7/9/2007)

A joint statement on the value of early childhood education – and more specifically on proposed objectives to improve the training and work conditions of early childhood professionals – suggests that early education and professionalisation issues may now also find a new place on the policy agenda of the EU.

This chapter will look at some of the current policies on initial and continuing professional development in selected EU countries and examine implicit concepts of professionalism embedded within different approaches. It draws on previous and ongoing research at the State Institute of Early Childhood Research (IFP) in Bavaria funded by the German Federal Ministry of Family Affairs (Staatsinstitut für Frühpädagogik 2007).

132

Who is an early years professional? Reflections on policy diversity in Europe

It is now well established that our understandings of children, childhood, learning and development are anchored within specific historical, cultural, economic and geo-political contexts (see, for example: Alexander 2000; Fleer 2007; James, Jenks and Prout 1998; Penn 2005; Rogoff 2003).

The European Union currently comprises 27 countries (= EU-27) representing considerable diversity in terms of geographical location, (socio-)political history, and cultural and pedagogical traditions. These variations have generated a range of policy approaches towards the implementation and regulation of national systems of early education and care. One such area of policy diversity is the age adopted for beginning compulsory schooling. Whereas the Nordic and Baltic EU members (Denmark, Finland, Sweden, Estonia, Latvia, Lithuania) and also Bulgaria maintain a preference for late school entry at 7 years, most central and eastern European states (Austria, Belgium, France, Germany, Luxembourg; Czech Republic, Hungary, Poland, Romania, Slovak Republic, Slovenia) and southern European countries (Greece, Italy, Spain, Portugal) continue to opt for 6 years as the official age for starting school. Today, Cyprus, Malta, the Netherlands and the United Kingdom are the only countries to consider a school entry age of 5 years or younger appropriate. It is interesting to note that these are countries with a comparatively unfavourable track record in the past of providing publicly funded services for children in the years preceding compulsory schooling.

Policy diversity can also be observed in the chosen overall regulatory framework. In the Nordic and Baltic EU countries, Slovenia, and to a certain extent in Spain and the United Kingdom, public early childhood provision from birth to school entry (which in the Nordic countries also includes family day care services) comes under the auspices of a single coordinating ministerial department. In most cases this is now the Education department, a move initiated by Spain in 1990 in the then 15 EU countries (= EU-15). In Denmark it is the Ministry for Family and Consumer Affairs and in Finland the Ministry of Social Affairs that has overall responsibility. Despite this discernible trend towards an integrated and coordinated view on policies for the years preceding compulsory schooling, the majority of EU states still have systems of split ministerial responsibilities, with services for children from 3 or 4 years up to school entry coming under the auspices of the Education department and those for younger children under Social Affairs, Family Affairs, Health or Gender Equity departments. These differing regulatory measures have not been without consequence for the qualification routes of those wishing to work with young children.

I shall illustrate this by briefly outlining specific characteristics of professionalisation routes in four countries: one with a federal system (Germany); one with an integrated approach towards service regulation (Slovenia); and two with a system of split responsibilities (Luxembourg and Malta). I shall conclude by contrasting varying constructions of the professional role and looking at the notion of professionalism as a situated concept.

Early childhood workers in Germany

Early childhood centres in Germany, which may be day nurseries for children up to 3 years of age (*Kinderkrippe*), kindergartens for 3- to 6-year-olds, or mixed-aged centres from birth up to school entry, are part of the public welfare system, i.e. they are located *outside* the public education system. Responsibility is shared between the federal government and the 16 regional governments or *Länder* (see, for example, Diskowski 2007). The same applies to the system of professional training for the main type of practitioner (*Erzieherin/Erzieher*) in these centres. A framework regulation at the federal level sets down guidelines for both the content areas and structure of training, but each federal state is responsible for translating these into regional policies. In practice, entry requirements and overall length of professional training as well as the duration of the workplace component may vary from region to region.

Most countries in the EU expect staff with group responsibility in early childhood centres to have a higher-education-level specialist qualification, although in the countries with split-sector systems this only applies to those working with children in pre-primary centres for the 3- to 6-year-olds, not to those working with under 3s. Germany is one of the remaining six countries in EU-27 *without* an agreed academic study route for the main workers in early childhood centres. Only 2.6 per cent of staff with group responsibility and 19.6 per cent of centre directors has a degree-level qualification (KOMdat Jugendhilfe 2006: 11). The majority of workers have a three-year post-secondary training completed at a vocational college for social pedagogy (comprising in most cases two years' full-time study and one-year work placement). This qualification enables them to work not only in early childhood centres, but also in out-of-school services for school-age children and in centres for residential care.

Since 2004, new initiatives have mushroomed which are changing the overall picture of professional training. Within the framework of the Bologna Process, an agreement signed in 1999 by 45 European states, a growing number of higher education institutions in Germany are now starting to introduce BA-level qualifications for work in early childhood centres. At the beginning of the academic year 2007/2008 there were around 30 such study routes in operation. However, this has not come about through a major policy thrust. Instead, it is the timely response of individual higher education institutions both to a long history of academic critique of the present training and advocacy for a degree-level qualification and also to the recent, first-time introduction of official curricula for work in early childhood centres, which implicitly pre-suppose a high level of professional expertise. While the Standing Conference of the Ministers for Youth Affairs supports these developments in principle (Jugendministerkonferenz 2005), no steps have as yet been taken either at the federal or at the state level to adopt a degree-level qualification as a necessary requirement for assuming a post of responsibility in early childhood centres.

Opportunities for continuing professional development (in-service training) in Germany tend to depend on local conditions and the particular programme that practitioners' employer associations offer. As yet, there is no state-level or federal-level framework with an accredited and modular system of compatible qualifications for the early childhood field. Continuing training is in no way mandatory. Motivation for updating and in-depth enhancement of initial qualifications, i.e. for participating in lifelong learning activities on a regular basis, thus tends to remain located at the level of individual preferences and possibilities rather than at the systemic level. Some federal states (*Länder*) are currently supporting the establishment of centre-based forms of collegial support and consultation at the local level.

Professionalisation routes in Slovenia

Full-day early childhood centres in Slovenia are organised into two age bands (1 to 3 years and 3 to 6 years) and each (generally same-age) group is staffed by a university educated early childhood teacher/pedagogue and a pre-school assistant trained (since 1995) at upper secondary level. The majority of centres are state maintained and come under the auspices of the Ministry of Education, with municipalities being responsible for managing and funding the centres. Compared with most other EU countries, centres are large and may comprise up to 30 groups. This requires significant collaboration at the management level, and the centre director generally coordinates an inter-professional team of leaders, comprising one or two deputy directors, a pedagogical consultant for targeted work with children, teachers and parents, and a health adviser. This team of senior workers supports the pedagogical work of the early childhood staff. The university-level specialist training for early childhood work, a three-year course of study, has been in place since 1992. It is also possible to follow a one-year postgraduate specialist route on completion of a four-year undergraduate degree in an unrelated field.

Slovenia has an exceptionally highly structured system of credit point acquisition for continuing professional development, enabling teachers, counsellors and centre directors to acquire different levels of recognised expertise, such as a mentor or adviser. Titles gained are permanent and do not have to be renewed. They are rewarded with an increase in pay. Regular in-service training days for directors of centres and other staff takes place at municipality level. These have been criticised for their 'one off' character and it has been suggested that more practice-based and problem-linked ongoing forms of in-service support are needed (Vonta 2007). Early childhood teachers/pedagogues are granted at least five days per calendar year for continuing professional development.

Alongside the 300 or so regular early childhood centres in Slovenia, there are also 40 centres with an explicit mentoring or advisory function. The aim is to provide collegial support, impart new knowledge and demonstrate innovatory practices.

Training and professional development in Luxembourg

In Luxembourg, responsibility for education and care provision in the years preceding primary schooling is split between the Ministry for Family Affairs and the Ministry of Education. The former is responsible for childcare facilities such as *crèches* for children under 4 and *maisons relais* or *foyers de jour* for children aged 3 to 12; the latter for early learning classes (*précoce*) for 3 to 4 year olds and obligatory pre-primary provision (*spillschoul*) for 4 to 6 year olds, both of which are offered on five mornings and three afternoons a week. A clear division is thus made between pre-primary education and care/recreational provision. The professional training of early years workers also reflects this division (Oberhuemer and Ulich 1997).

Pre-primary education classes are staffed by a pre-school teacher who, up to 2003, was trained alongside primary school teachers for three years at a higher education pedagogical college. Today, the required four-year training (BA professional, requiring 240 points within the European Credit Transfer System) takes place at university. At least one semester is spent at a university abroad. Work placements are firmly integrated into this study route: three weeks during each semester for the first three years and around six weeks each semester during the last year of study (Wantz 2007). Students graduating from this programme may work either in pre-primary settings or in primary schools. There is no longer a specialist professional qualification for the pre-school years.

A 2005 regulation states that at least 80 per cent of staff working in care and recreational provision outside the education system must be qualified, and half of these are required to have a socio-pedagogical training (*éducateur*). This is a three-year, higher education training scheme for work in a variety of socio-pedagogical and special needs settings. Approximately one-third of the course is spent in work placements.

Forms of in-service training for these different professional job profiles vary significantly. Whereas teachers (pre-primary and primary) are awarded a certificate after attending 90 hours of continuing professional development seminars, which can influence pay and career chances, there are no certificated courses for *éducateurs* with significance for promotion prospects.

Professional training policies in Malta

Young children in Malta officially enter the regular school system at age 5, although they may be as young as 4 years 9 months when they start. The system of early education and care prior to school entry is split both vertically in terms of ministerial responsibility and horizontally in terms of providers. Kindergarten centres for 3 and 4 year olds may be state-maintained, church-run, or private and come under the responsibility of the Ministry of Education. They are predominantly located in school buildings. Childcare centres for the under 3s, which are almost exclusively private enterprises, are regulated by the Ministry of Family and Social Affairs.

Neither staff in kindergarten centres or practitioners in childcare centres are trained at graduate level. Staff in the independent/private sector may even have no relevant qualifications. Lead practitioners in the kindergarten centres are known as 'kindergarten assistants'. Between 1993 and 2003, their two-year initial training took place at a post-secondary vocational college (pre-school education centre) following 11 years of compulsory schooling. However, this two-year government-endorsed certificate course was phased out in 2003. Since this time a two-year post-16 vocational qualification (BTEC National Diploma in Early Years) is being offered by a further education college, but it has not yet been recognised by the government. The majority of kindergarten assistants currently employed in the state sector have been working in the field for more than 20 years. They were trained at a time when the entry requirements to the field were four GCE 'O' levels and a six-week workplace training upon taking up employment (Sollars 2007: 20). Kindergarten assistants are

136

Who is an early years professional? Reflections on policy diversity in Europe

required to attend an in-service 'refresher' course offered by the Education Division of the Ministry every two years.

WHO IS AN EARLY YEARS PROFESSIONAL?

The four case studies presented suggest that policy perceptions of an Early Years Professional – in terms of the length, level and goals of professional education/training – vary considerably from country to country. In both Slovenia and Luxembourg, it is assumed that the pedagogical staff leading groups in early childhood settings should have a graduate-level qualification. However, the professional profile to be aimed for differs in each country. In Slovenia, the professional is seen to need specialist knowledge for working with children aged 1 to 6 years, anchored in an integrated conception of education and care work. Close collaboration with other professionals in the field – particularly at the level of centre leadership – is an integral part of the professional self-image of pedagogical staff. This contrasts with the approach in Luxembourg. According to the system of split responsibilities, there are two sets of training for work with young children. Professional preparation for work in pre-primary settings is part of the same study route that primary school teachers follow, i.e. it is about working with children aged 3 to 12 in designated educational institutions. It does not include preparation for work in out-of-school settings or with children under 3, which are considered to be the domain of other professionals.

In Germany and Malta, there are as yet no policies in place for ensuring that professionals for early childhood pedagogy follow a study route at the higher education level. In Malta, in particular, the majority of those with group responsibility have a very low formal level of professional training – and a professional title which describes them as 'assistants'. This contrasts with Germany, where a growing number of graduates are entering the field. However, Malta and Germany are two of the six remaining countries in the EU-27 where a clear policy decision in this direction has still to be made. Whereas new graduate-level professional routes have been proposed and are currently being piloted in two of these six countries, in the Czech Republic and the Slovak Republic, in Austria and Romania no such plans are currently known. Also, in the Czech Republic and the Slovak Republic it seems that there will in future be two parallel routes, with initially only a minority of the workforce holding a degree-level qualification.

The four case studies also illustrate that policies for continuing professional development vary considerably from one country to another. Not all early childhood workers have the same opportunities to participate in supportive systems for ongoing professional reflection.

Early years professionals participating in the recent *Care Work in Europe* project shared the view – across countries and systems – that their work is important, not only for young children and families but also for society at large (Moss and Korintus 2004: 98). However, if we consider the examples presented regarding professional preparation for that work, this high regard is not uniformly reflected across Europe. Diverse cultural and organisational systems of services for young children have generated distinctly varying role constructions and understandings.

In countries with split or multi-sector approaches towards provision for young children from birth to school age, workers in the education sectors appear to be more highly valued than those in the so-called childcare sectors. Predominantly market models of childcare tend to generate highly differential systems of training, payment and employment conditions (Bennett 2003). Formal job requirements remain highly uneven across services for children below compulsory school age. Moreover, they are generally at a significantly lower level in care settings outside the education policy framework.

The picture in countries with an integrated system of provision is very different. Here the training requirements for lead practitioners are far more equitable across settings, although the age-range in focus may vary. Whereas professional preparation policies in, for example, Finland and the Baltic countries and, as we have seen, in Slovenia, relate to work with children from birth up to 6 or 7 years, a common feature of the approaches in Denmark and Sweden is that they conceptualise early childhood professionals within a far broader perspective.

The Danish model emphasises the social and cultural role of pedagogues (*pedagoger*) in settings across the life course outside mainstream schooling. The professional role combines educational, social and health elements with an understanding of pedagogy which prioritises relational aspects of the work (Jensen and Krogh Hansen 2003). Pedagogues working in the early childhood field are seen to play a significant role in a culture of collaboratively supporting young children in their growth and development – not only in the institutions they may find themselves in, but also in the community as a whole. The Swedish approach is a more institution-oriented model, linking pre-schools and schools within a policy framework that aims for shared understandings of childhood, knowledge, learning and care across the entire education system from 1 to 18 years (Cohen et al. 2004; Korpi 2002). The professional role is considered to be that of a teacher (*lärare*) – but with a strong socio-pedagogical knowledge base for work with young children. In both countries, high levels of public funding are earmarked for maintaining and supporting a professionalised workforce across the entire early childhood period. While the direction for the early years workforce is similar in its holistic approach, the two occupational groups, pedagogues and teachers, are quite distinct, with different traditions, identities and career possibilities (Moss 2006: 33).

These varying policy approaches reflect culturally embedded understandings of the role of early childhood institutions and the people who work in them. These in turn shape the images that early childhood professionals have of themselves. Pre-primary specialists rooted in public education systems with a prescribed curricular framework, and often with a system of external evaluation or inspection, are likely to perceive their work within these specific parameters, whereas the early childhood pedagogues and workers with a broader-based, more socio-pedagogical understanding of care, learning, education and upbringing as interrelated, are more likely to view their profession in a wider context – child oriented, but also family and community oriented.

In my view it is this latter understanding of the professional role which signifies the way forward. This type of role conceptualisation demands a high level of professionalism in the ECEC field. It requires practitioners who are able to forge strong links with the compulsory school system, while maintaining a clearly defined and more broadly understood societal role.

PROFESSIONALISM: A SITUATED CONCEPT

Professionalism is a situated concept, embedded – like our understandings of children and childhood – within specific historical, socio-cultural, organisational, economic and political contexts. Definitions of professionalism, or what it means to act professionally, are linked to value-based assumptions about what constitutes 'quality of action' in a particular occupational field.

The chosen scope and emphasis in initial and continuing professional development will depend on the prevailing cultural constructions of early childhood workers and on the visions of the purpose of early childhood services. Certainly, the impacts of ever-changing economic, social and knowledge contexts on the globalised labour market, on the migration patterns of families, and consequently on the everyday lives of children, present a continual challenge for early childhood centres. It seems to me that both centres for young children and primary schools increasingly need to construe their role as multi-purpose facilities, integrating care, learning, education and health elements for children and as resource centres for families and the community – a model currently being pursued with the concept of children's centres in England. Elsewhere I have dwelt on the concept of 'democratic professionalism' as a conceptual framework for thinking about the professional dispositions necessary for working in such contexts (Oberhuemer 2005). The term has evolved as an alternative way of conceptualising the role of teachers in the face of increased control technologies in education systems, as a counterbalance to what have been described as managerial and technical understandings of professionalism (see Day and Sachs 2004: 6). It is a notion of professionalism based on participatory relationships and alliances between professionals and other stakeholders. It emphasises engaging and networking with the local community. Within such a framework, the competencies needed for care and education work with young children could be described as relational, analytic and reflective, cultural and aesthetic, and drawing on a broad, cross-disciplinary knowledge base.

However, this is an ambitious model. It requires not only critical thinking and analytic, collaborative dispositions and skills, but also new societal understandings of professional pedagogical-educational work with young children, new approaches towards valuing that work, and new policy commitments regarding the available resources for supporting this work. In this sense, it is to be hoped that the informal declaration of the EU ministers quoted at the beginning of this chapter will be translated in the near future – where necessary – into concrete policy steps at the national level.

SUMMARY

In many countries, the early years have higher policy priority than ever before – in terms of providing places for young children while their parents work or study, and in terms of providing early education and combatting social exclusion. The professional preparation and in-service support of personnel working with young children are critical quality issues in these contexts of expansion and increasing access. This chapter looked first at some general characteristics of policy diversity in Europe, followed by a description of professionalisation routes in four countries with differently organised systems of early education and care: Germany, Slovenia, Luxembourg and Malta. The four case studies presented suggest that policy perceptions of a core early years professional – in terms of the length, level and goals of education/training for pedagogical work in early years settings – vary considerably from country to country. These policy approaches reflect culturally embedded understandings of the role of early childhood institutions, which in turn impact on the self-image and public image of being a pedagogical professional in these institutions. The chapter concluded by contrasting varying constructions of the professional role. Professionalism is seen as a situated concept, and reaching agreement on what are appropriate professional dispositions for work with young children, or what is required professional knowledge, or what are desired professional skills is viewed as an ongoing, collaborative and interpretative act informed by our current understandings of childhood, parenthood, participation, learning, and the societal and educational role of early childhood centres.

Questions/points for discussion/reflection

1 In which direction do you think the early childhood centres in your country should be moving?
2 Which professionals and other persons should be working in these centres?
3 What are key competencies needed for a leadership role in early childhood centres in your country?

REFERENCES

Alexander, R. (2000) *Culture and Pedagogy: International Comparisons in Primary Education.* Oxford: Blackwell Publishers

Bennett, J. (2003) 'Starting strong. The persistent division between care and education', *Journal of Early Childhood Research, 1(1),* 21–48

Cohen, B., Moss, P., Petrie, P. and Wallace, J. (2004) *A New Deal for Children? Reforming Education and Care in England, Scotland and Sweden.* Cambridge: The Policy Press.

Day, C. and Sachs, J. (2004) 'Professionalism, performativity and empowerment: discourses in the politics, policies and purposes of continuing professional development'. In C. Day and J. Sachs (eds), *International Handbook on the Continuing Professional Development of Teachers.* Glasgow: Bell & Bain.

Diskowski, D. (2007) 'Split responsibility, decentralisation and subsidiarity – key features of the system of child and youth welfare in Germany'. In Pestalozzi-Fröbel-Verband (ed.), *Frühe Bildung und das System der Kindertagesbetreuung in Deutschland. Early Childhood Education and Care in Germany.* Berlin: Verlag das Netz.

Fleer, M. (2007) 'The cultural construction of child development: creating institutional and cultural intersubjectivity', *International Journal of Early Years Education, 14(2)*, 127–140

James, A., Jenks, C. and Prout, A. (1998) *Theorizing Childhood*. Cambridge: Polity Press

Jensen, J.J. and Krogh Hansen, H. (2003) 'The Danish pedagogue – a worker for all ages', *Children in Europe 5*, 6–9

Jugendministerkonferenz (2005) 'Weiterentwicklung der Erzieherinnen- und Erzieherausbildung', http://www.bildungsserver.de/db/mlesen.html?Id=29780 (accessed 7/10/2007)

KOMdat Jugendhilfe 10, Heft 1 – drawing on 2006 statistics from the Federal Statistics Office

Korpi, B. Martin (2002) 'Pre-school in Sweden – the first step in lifelong learning', paper presented at the State Institute of Early Childhood Research Conference in Munich, October 8/9, 2002

Moss, P. (2006) 'Structures, understandings and discourses: possibilities for re-envisioning the early childhood worker', *Contemporary Issues in Early Childhood, 7(1)*, 30–41

Moss, P. and Korintus M. (2004) 'Work with young children. A case study of Denmark, Hungary and Spain. Consolidated report: care work in Europe – current understandings and future directions', http://144.82.31.4/carework/reports/WP7%20final%20consolidatedreport.feb04.pdf (accessed 3/9/2007)

Neuman, M. (2005) 'Governance of early childhood systems: recent developments in OECD countries', *Early Years, 25(2)*, 129–142

Oberhuemer, P. (2005) 'Conceptualising the early childhood pedagogue: policy approaches and issues of professionalism', *European Early Childhood Research Journal, 13(1)*, 5–16

Oberhuemer, P. and Ulich, M. (1997) *Working with Young Children in Europe*. London: Paul Chapman Publishing

OECD (2001) *Starting Strong. Early Childhood Education and Care*. Paris: Organisation for Economic Co-operation and Development

OECD (2006) *Starting Strong II. Early Childhood Education and Care*. Paris: Organisation for Economic Co-operation and Development

Penn, H. (2005) *Unequal Childhoods. Young Children's Lives in Poor Countries*. London, New York: Routledge

Rogoff, B. (2003) *The Cultural Nature of Human Development*. Oxford: Oxford University Press

Sollars, V. (2007) 'Early education/care and professionalisation in Malta', Commissioned Report for IFP Munich

Staatsinstitut für Frühpädagogik (IFP) (2007) *Systems of Early Education/Care and Professionalisation in Europe* – project data http://www.ifp.bayern.de/projekte/laufende/informationenseepro-english.html

Vonta, T. (2007) 'Early education/care and professionalisation in Slovenia', Commissioned Report for IFP Munich

Wantz, M. (2007) 'Personal communication', 25/3/2007

Further reading

Moss, P. (2006) 'Structures, understandings and discourses: possibilities for re-envisioning the early childhood worker', *Contemporary Issues in Early Childhood, 7(1)*, 30–41

OECD (2006) *Starting Strong II. Early Childhood Education and Care*, Paris: Organisation for Economic Co-operation and Development (overview of early childhood education and care policies in 20 OECD countries)

13 THE NEW TEACHER IN NEW ZEALAND

Carmen Dalli

INTRODUCTION

The New Zealand government's 10-year strategic plan for the early childhood education sector, *Pathways to the Future: Ngā Huarahi Arataki* (Ministry of Education 2002), envisages a fully trained early childhood workforce in teacher-led services by 2012. The strategic plan is premised on the notion that professionally trained early childhood teachers are essential to ensuring a quality early childhood education sector. This chapter backgrounds the emergence of a teacher-led early childhood workforce against the growth of a discourse of professionalism. It argues that in seeking to rethink professionalism in the early years, it is important to foreground teachers' own perspectives of their work. Insights from a recent study of early childhood teachers' views of professionalism and professional behaviour are used to support this argument and to outline key concepts for a new ground-up definition of professionalism that reflects teachers' perspectives and responds to the lived reality of early childhood work.

THE NEW ZEALAND EARLY CHILDHOOD EDUCATION CONTEXT

Most New Zealand children start school at the age of 5, though school is not compulsory till age 6. In 2006, 94.5 per cent of all children who started school had participated in some form of early childhood education (Ministry of Education 2006). A distinctive feature of the New Zealand early childhood context is that since 1986 it has had an integrated approach to policy for childcare and pre-school services. Two years later, integrated three-year training for childcare and kindergarten teachers was introduced in Colleges of Education. Together, these events established the important principle that care and education are inseparable: they abolished the *education vs care* divide that still persists in many other countries.

New Zealand parents may choose from seven main types of licensed early childhood services: kindergartens; playcentres; education and care centres (formerly known as 'childcare' centres); licensed Te Kōhanga Reo (indigenous Māori language nests); home-based (family daycare) networks; correspondence school; and casual education and care centres that operate in shoppers' malls and recreation centres. Most early childhood services accept children on a full-time or part-time basis, with kindergartens offering separate morning and afternoon sessions for different groups of children; in recent years, many kindergartens have departed from this traditional practice (Duncan, Dalli and Lawrence 2007). Education and care centres are the largest growing part of the early childhood sector and are sometimes distinguished by whether they are 'community based' or 'for profit'. Education and care centres are a very diverse group and include special character centres, such as Montessori, Rudolph Steiner and Pasifika centres (centres that operate with a pedagogical style rooted in Pacific cultural practices).

EARLY CHILDHOOD EDUCATION IN TRANSITION: TWO DECADES OF CHANGE

Crèche originally was not for us to be educators – though I know we are now. We were just childminders; but we are more than that. It was originally to give mum a break, but now we're definitely into programme planning and observing children and planning the programme on their needs.

(Sarah, early childhood teacher, interviewed 1993)

This statement by an inner-city community crèche early childhood 'educator' in a major urban area of New Zealand illustrates the emerging awareness in the mid-1990s that things were changing for the early childhood workforce. Sarah's statement was in response to a question about how she saw her professional role. Sarah was a qualified and experienced primary school teacher, who after 'parent-helping' at her children's childcare centre decided to join the early childhood workforce. When I interviewed Sarah as part of a project on starting childcare (Dalli 1999), she had worked at the community crèche for four years. Two of Sarah's colleagues had likewise entered the early childhood workforce through the parent route; one was part-way through her training and the other was untrained. Only one of the four staff at the community crèche, the supervisor and licensee of the centre, held a three-year diploma of early childhood teaching, a qualification that was rare in the early 1990s but is now the benchmark qualification for work in an early childhood setting.

Such a profile of practitioners was not uncommon a decade or two ago in many parts of the New Zealand early childhood sector. With the exception of the state kindergarten service, which from its origins in the late 1880s has applied a policy of employing only qualified teachers, the diverse range of services that make up the sector have historically operated in a minimally regulated environment with a workforce whose qualification and training background was the subject of over 30 reviews and reports in the 1980s and early 1990s (Early Childhood Group 1994). The key theme of the reports was the need for coherent policies on early childhood training and qualifications within a national framework.

As we approach the end of the first decade of the new millennium, it is fair to say that the call for coherent policies, heard so regularly in the 1980s and 1990s, has been answered. Starting with the transfer of administrative responsibility for childcare services from the Department of Social Welfare to the Department of Education in 1986, successive waves of policy changes over the last two decades have transformed the New Zealand early childhood sector from one divided along philosophical, historical, administrative and funding lines to one that is united around a common curriculum framework, *Te Whāriki* (Ministry of Education 1996a), a shared funding structure, and a 10-year strategic plan, *Pathways to the Future: Ngā Huarahi Arataki* (Ministry of Education 2002) that maps out the policy direction of the early childhood sector until 2012. A key target of the strategic plan is that all teacher-led early childhood services will be staffed by fully qualified and registered teachers by 2012.

BECOMING A TEACHER-LED PROFESSION

The implementation of the staff qualification and teacher registration policy as a key part of government's 10-year strategic plan for early childhood education (Ministry of Education 2002) effectively means that the New Zealand early childhood education sector, with the exception of parent-led services such as playcentres, playgroups and some kōhanga reo, is becoming a teacher-led profession.

The process of transformation into a teacher-led profession has not always been a smooth one. Many early childhood policy commentators have chronicled the twists and turns of policies during the 1980s and the 1990s as changing political winds threatened to derail a process of advocacy for change that had been building over many years (Dalli 1994; May 2007; Meade 1990). Nor has the desired outcome of a fully qualified early childhood teaching profession been uncontested. When the staffing goals for 2012 were announced in 2002, 56 per cent of all those working in teacher-led early childhood services were qualified to the benchmark level of a three-year diploma or its equivalent; within the early childhood education and care part of the sector, previously known as 'childcare' (May 2007), this percentage was lower, at 46 per cent (Harkess 2004). Fears were raised, mainly by groups of private providers of education and care services, that the policy would create recruitment difficulties for the sector. Some predicted that at a time when there is already a dearth of professionals the 'up-skilling plan' would be 'unworkable' (Montgomery 2002: 27), and that there would be more teachers leaving the sector than new ones coming in (Haines 2002). Others were concerned about the impact of the policy on the distinctive character of centres such as Montessori and Rudolph Steiner centres, as well as Pasifika centres. Centres of this kind have traditionally employed staff with qualifications that match the centre's philosophy. As Freeman (forthcoming) has shown in her case study of the impact on the Montessori context of the staff qualification policy in the first five years of its implementation (2002 to 2007), for centres of distinctive character, the national recruitment problems are compounded by the need to employ staff who hold specialist training on top of the regulated benchmark qualification.

Nonetheless, and despite recruitment difficulties (see Mitchell and Brooking 2007) the transformation to a teacher-led sector appears to be working. In May 2007, the Ministry of Education reported that by July 2006, 58 per cent of teacher-led services had already reached the goal of having 50 per cent of their staff holding benchmark qualifications. The 50 per cent mark had been set as the half-way target for 31 December 2007 (Ministry of Education 2007).

Moreover, the transformation into a teacher-led profession also appears to be accepted by the early childhood workforce. A Belgian colleague, Jan Peeters from the University of Ghent, remarked on this when he visited New Zealand early in 2007. He recounted his experience of attending a workshop on professionalism at a practitioner conference in which he had been a keynote speaker:

There were around 30 participants and the workshop facilitator asked how they would describe themselves as professionals in their work with children. One of those present immediately said that she thought of herself as a teacher. The workshop leader then asked how the others saw themselves, and they all said that they were teachers. For me as a continental European, the notion of 'teacher' especially for children aged 0- to 3-years-old sounded a bit strange, so I asked if the ones who worked with very young children saw themselves as teachers, and their answer was: 'yes, we are teachers'.

(Personal communication, 3 April 2007)

TEACHERS AS RESEARCHERS: TRANSFORMING PROFESSIONAL PRACTICE THROUGH COLLABORATIVE WORK

Alongside the focus on professionally qualified early childhood teachers, the 10-year strategic plan is having a strong impact on the early childhood sector's growing sense of professionalism through the Centre of Innovation (COI) policy. This policy has enabled early childhood services to apply to be nominated a 'centre of innovation' and to work with a research associate during a three-year action research project to showcase excellence in their teaching practice. In the first cycle of the implementation of this policy, initiated in 2003, six centres took on the role of 'centres of innovation' and ten others have been added in two subsequent cycles.

Meade (2006) has documented how, for those involved in the projects, the experience of researching one's practice in collaboration with colleagues and supportive researchers, has been transformative:

Teacher-researchers have become educational leaders, by making their practice-based knowledge both explicit and public. They enjoy connecting theory and practice. Academics have developed new ways of carrying out research, in collaboration with early childhood teachers, to facilitate reflection and fairly immediate change for teaching and learning.

(Meade 2006: 45)

The COI research teams themselves also have written about the benefits of involvement in the projects and have noted, in particular, their new sense of empowerment as researchers, including their increased confidence to 'reflect, dialogue, and continue to discover what is possible' (Ramsay et al. 2006: 44) .

Other common elements of the COI experience include an 'increased awareness of, and deeper empathy for, children', together with 'more effective advocacy for each child based on fuller knowledge and understanding' (Simmons et al. 2006: 69).

It could be argued that the benefits of participation in the COI programme are most immediately felt by those directly involved in the research activities of each

COI project. Nonetheless, it is reasonable to hypothesise that since the dissemination components of the projects draw in the broader early childhood community as audiences at conferences, or as users of resources produced by the COI teams, the COI programme is contributing to the construction of a new professional context for the New Zealand early childhood sector. The following statement from a paper by the research team of one of the original six COIs funded in 2003, would support this hypothesis:

Our growth as professionals has had amazing spin-offs for us as teachers, for children, for parents, and for the wider educational community; and that has to be good news for early childhood education. (Simmons et al. 2007: 69)

RETHINKING PROFESSIONALISM IN THE CONTEXT OF THE NEW PROFESSIONAL TEACHER

The testimonies of the COI teachers about the impact of their collaborative research provide an 'inside' perspective on professional practice that is still rare in early childhood scholarship even as global interest in defining, deconstructing and redefining professionalism in early childhood education continues to expand (for example: Dalli 2006; Manning-Morton 2006; Oberhuemer 2000; Osgood 2006; Urban 2005).

In New Zealand, scholarly discussions of what it means to be 'an early childhood professional' have tended to refer to traditional definitions of professionalism (e.g. Katz 1985) with their focus on training and qualifications, and notions such as distance from the client and professional autonomy, to ensure unclouded decision-making (e.g. Dinniss 1974; Cooper 1993; Dalli 1993). There have been debates about ways of continuing to value the contribution of untrained mothers (or other home carers) who work alongside their children in services like playcentres or in the indigenous Kōhanga Reo, and about how to define optimal distance in these contexts (Dalli 2003). There are also questions about what professionalism means in the family day-care context, where it is the network coordinators who are required to be qualified, not the actual caregivers (Everiss and Dalli 2003), as well as how the diversity of early childhood services generally impacts on how professionalism might be understood (Aitken and Kennedy 2007). Notions about cooperative forms of centre management that are more in line with a community of learning approach to professional practice (e.g. Oberhuemer 2000) have also been used (e.g. Aitken 2006; Scrivens and Duncan 2003), but studies of views of professionalism from the teachers' perspectives remain very few.

In 2003, when the 10-year strategic plan was just beginning to roll out, it seemed an appropriate year to fill this research gap. In undertaking a ten-year follow-up survey to investigate how early childhood teachers were using the Early Childhood Code of Ethics (Dalli and Cherrington 2006), we included three questions about teachers' perspectives on the nature of professional behaviour. Respondents were asked to list the qualities they would expect to find in a 'professional' early childhood educator; to describe how they would recognise professionalism in early childhood educators' interactions across a range of workplace relationships; and to comment in any other way about the issue of professionalism in early childhood practice. The survey was sent to 594 early childhood centres; this represented one in every six licensed centres. Since we wanted to tap into teachers' perspectives on professionalism, we requested that the survey be completed by a staff member who held a benchmark early childhood qualification (3-year diploma or its equivalent). There was a 43.7 per cent response rate (260 returns).

The answers to our questions have enabled us to start articulating a ground-up definition of professionalism that would sit comfortably across the different types of early childhood services in New Zealand (e.g. Cherrington and Dalli 2005; Dalli and Cherrington 2005; Dalli 2006). The definition is based around three major themes that emerged as key components of teachers' perspectives on the nature of professional behaviour. The components are: pedagogical strategies and style; professional knowledge and practice; and collaborative relationships.

We also identified another 14 categories relating to qualities of a 'professional teacher' nominated by the survey respondents. These were: advocacy; communication skills; confidentiality; respect for diversity/difference; emotions (for example, passion) about teaching; high ideals/seeking excellence/true to the profession; integrity/honesty/trustworthiness; leadership (providing and taking); appropriate pay/work conditions; personal qualities/style/ personality; respect for personal and professional boundaries; caring about the public image of early childhood education; self-management; and good self-presentation. A further category was used to code for qualities and behaviour considered to be unprofessional.

In the following sections, I briefly elaborate on each of the three key themes from our research as these are the starting point for our rethinking of a definition of professionalism that would reflect the lived reality of early childhood work.

Pedagogy: strategies and style

The respondents had much to say about the type of pedagogy that they associated with the professional early childhood teacher: put together, the statements produced a multi-dimensional picture of pedagogy as a set of strategies and a style of behaviour. These were constructed around an attitude of respect and a stance that is responsive to children and their interests. The teachers wrote about the professional teacher as 'friendly, courteous and sensitive to [children's] needs' and as 'being inviting to the children so they want to be with this person'.

As a set of strategies, the pedagogy of the professional teacher included 'listening to the child, not imposing their own agendas on children, not singling out children for special attention, and ensuring that children maintain[ed] control over their own play'.

'Pedagogical strategies' encompassed those statements that included behaviours such as 'planning, scaffolding, evaluating, reflecting on practice' as markers of professionalism. This is in line with Mortimore's definition of pedagogy as 'any conscious action by one person designed to enhance learning in another' (1999: 3). For one teacher these strategies went hand in hand with 'appropriate touching and affection', indicating that to be an early years professional involves an affective dimension as well as its physical demonstration, a view consistent with a pedagogy of care perspective (Noddings 1984; Goldstein 1998).

Other statements elaborated how respect would be shown through teachers' manner and tone of voice, with examples including:

Speaking to the child not <u>at</u> the child (original underlined);

Reflecting back some of the child's conversation, asking questions to extend thinking and working at the child's level, not standing over them;

Getting down to [children's] level, using calm and appropriate language with children. Showing respect by listening and planning from observations recorded. Focusing on them at all times possible, varying their [teachers'] style depending on situations, guide rather than show, learn rather than teach.

Professional knowledge and practice

Being knowledgeable about children and about the 'theory of early childhood education' was generally seen as the starting point for professional practice, with qualifications, training and ongoing professional development being the route to achieve these. One education and care teacher wrote that 'professionalism cannot happen in early childhood education until all teaching staff have qualifications', and a kindergarten respondent expressed a similar view in stating that 'professionalism is directly related to qualifications, teacher registration, and experience'. In other responses the important role of continued learning was emphasised as in the phrase from an education and care respondent: 'professional development is ongoing throughout one's life – it never stops'.

The statements about qualifications and training highlighted that there is great support within the sector for the current policy direction of achieving a fully qualified and registered early childhood profession. One teacher captured the views of many when she wrote:

I am really pleased that the sector is aiming for all teachers to be qualified with a Dip Tchg ECE and for all qualified teachers to gain their registration; it enables teachers to continue reflecting on their teaching and keeps them in touch with professional development.

There was substantial elaboration by the respondents of the specific content knowledge that they saw as essential for professional teachers. This content ranged from knowledge of the early childhood curriculum document, *Te Whāriki*, to knowledge of the Early Childhood Code of Ethics, to familiarity with other early-childhood-specific compliance documents, such as the *Statement of Desirable Objectives and Practices*, locally referred to as the 'DoPS' (Ministry of Education 1996b), and licensing regulations. Being up-to-date with current theory, knowledgeable about teaching strategies, as well as able to justify actions on the basis of educational scholarship and an informed personal philosophy, were other key features. The following statements by a home-based and a playcentre educator respectively, illustrate these views:

[Someone who is professional is] trained and qualified in the field; able to articulate a personal philosophy based on theory, and consciously competent and skilled in techniques; able to plan and able to critique one's own performance.

[A professional] understands and follows regulations, safety policies, and practises current early childhood 'thinking'. She appraises and reflects on her own practice, up-skills through professional development, passes on knowledge to others.

The ability to be a reflective practitioner, willing to critique and improve one's practice, was also highly valued, with the word 'reflective' appearing in many respondents' statements. Being reflective was seen as both an individual responsibility and a team one. As one education and care teacher said, professional teachers 'reflect openly on their teaching and share this with colleagues'. (See also Chapter 8.)

Collaborative relationships

As noted earlier in this chapter, 'promoting collaborative relationships' is one of the three main goals of the New Zealand government's 10-year strategic plan. The respondents in our survey also valued collaborative relationships highly: phrases such as 'working together', being 'supportive of colleagues', 'working in partnership' or 'as a team', 'modelling a co-operative approach', or 'consulting with other professionals' were used to describe this aspect of desirable professional behaviour across the full range of workplace relationships. Offering support and guidance, being approachable and working together were mentioned as ways of building collaborative relationships with all participants in the early childhood teachers' workplace. And, as with pedagogical style and strategies, a respectful attitude towards all involved underpinned the professional teacher's approach.

In relationships within the teaching team, the professional teacher would be seen to enhance teamwork through 'listening to other points of view, modelling good practices, using good interpersonal skills, sharing the workload, planning together [with colleagues] and sharing information'. Professional teachers would moreover be:

pleasant, positively reinforce each other's work; offer support and guidance when necessary; be team players who are approachable and consultative and work together to achieve best practice; give honest constructive 360 degree feedback; laugh together and show enjoyment of their work generally.

For collaborative relationships with parents, one education and care teacher advised that the professional would: 'listen to them at first; ask a lot of questions about their child; be able to give advice when asked/needed; treat them with respect'. Another education and care respondent wrote that professional teachers 'acknowledge parents/whānau (family) as primary teachers [of their children]. . .and want to work with them not dominate them'.

Finally, encouraging participation and being willing to contribute were also valued professional traits, as shown in the following statement:

Someone who can contribute ideas/views in a collaborative manner; someone who values others' diverse contributions; someone who has knowledge of, and contributes to policies, procedures, management plans, strategic plans and is supportive and open.

SUMMARY

The focus in this chapter has been on the new professional teacher in New Zealand. The early part of the chapter outlined the background that led up to government's

10-year strategic plan and the policies within it. These have positioned the early childhood sector at the dawn of a brave new world: the world of a fully qualified and registered teacher-led early childhood profession by 2012. It was argued that this transformation has not been a smooth one; but despite the difficulties, it appears to have been accepted by the early childhood workforce. I have suggested that as the early childhood sector takes its place alongside other parts of the education sector as a teacher-led profession, it is timely to rethink traditional notions of professionalism and develop a new ground-up definition that reflects the realities of early childhood work. Drawing on data from a national survey which investigated qualified teachers' perspectives on the nature of professionalism and professional behaviour, three key themes were presented around which it might be possible to construct such a definition: pedagogical strategies and style; professional knowledge and practice; and collaborative relationships.

Questions/points for discussion/reflection

1 How well does the term 'teacher' fit your image of what you do as an early years practitioner? What works and what doesn't?
2 What is your response to the three key themes of: pedagogical strategies and style; professional knowledge and practice; and collaborative practice being seen as starting points for a new way of thinking about professionalism?
3 Consider the list of 14 qualities discussed in this chapter (page 147) that stand alongside the three key themes in the suggested rethinking of the notion of professionalism. Would you agree that they should be considered part of the profile of the new professional teacher? If not, why not?

REFERENCES

Aitken, H. (2006) 'Too much, too soon? The multiple roles and identities of newly qualified early childhood teachers'. *New Zealand Research in Early Childhood Education Journal*, 9, 1–14

Aitken, H. and Kennedy, A. (2007) 'Critical issues for the early childhood profession'. In L. Keesing-Styles and H. Hedges (eds), *Theorising Early Childhood Practice. Emerging Dialogues.* New South Wales: Pademelon Press

Cherrington, S. and Dalli, C. (2005) 'Collaborative relationships: Exploring their place in our professional discourse'. Paper presented at the Early Childhood Symposium, University of Otago, 5 December

Cooper, D. (1993) 'Perceptions of issues in early childhood teacher education', paper presented at the NZ Association for Research in Education Conference, University of Waikato, December

Dalli, C. (1993). 'Are we a profession? The contribution of the national curriculum guidelines and the need for a code of ethics'. In *Early Childhood Education: Papers presented at the CECUA National Curriculum Conference*, October 1993. Wellington: NZEI

Dalli, C. (1994) 'Is Cinderella back among the cinders? A review of early childhood education in the early 1990s'. In H. Manson (ed.) *New Zealand Annual Review of Education 1993(3)*, 223–254. Wellington: Faculty of Education, Victoria University of Wellington.

Dalli, C. (1999) 'Starting childcare before three: narratives of experience from a tri-partite focus'. Unpublished PhD thesis, Victoria University of Wellington

Dalli, C. (2003) 'Professionalism in early childhood practice: thinking through the debates'. Paper presented at the 13th annual conference of the European Early Childhood Education Research Association, University of Strathclyde, Glasgow

Dalli, C. (2006) 'Re-visioning love and care in early childhood: constructing the future of our profession', *The First Years, 8(1)*, 5–11

Dalli, C. and Cherrington, S. (2005) 'Pedagogical style and professionalism: practitioner perspectives'. Paper presented at the Asia Pacific Conference of Organisation Mondiale pour l'Education Prescolaire (OMEP), Aotearoa, New Zealand, 3 December

Dalli, C. and Cherrington, S. (2006) 'The early childhood code of ethics: a decade later'. Paper presented at the annual conference of the New Zealand Association for Research in Education, Rotorua, 5–8 December

Dinniss, P. (1974) 'Professionalism in early childhood education: some trends'. In M. Bell, P.E. Dinniss and G. McDonald (eds), *Trends and Issues in Early Childhood Education*. Wellington: NZCER

Duncan, J., Dalli, C. and Lawrence, J. (2007) 'The changing face of kindergarten: a national picture of two-year olds within kindergartens', *New Zealand Annual Review of Education, 16(2006)*, 119–140

Early Childhood Group (1994, February) 'Early childhood qualifications and training: a summary of key developments'. Unpublished paper circulated to government and opposition officials and early childhood organisations. Archives: Institute for Early Childhood Studies, Victoria University of Wellington

Everiss, E. and Dalli, C. (2003). 'Family day care in New Zealand: training, quality and professional status'. In A. Mooney and J. Statham (eds), *Family Day Care. International Perspectives on Policy, Practice and Quality*. London: Jessica Kingsley Publishers

Freeman, S. (forthcoming) 'Unintended consequences: the Montessori story of the early childhood education qualification requirement – 2000–2007'. Unpublished MEd thesis. Victoria University of Wellington

Goldstein, L. (1998) '"More than gentle smiles and warm hugs": applying the ethic of care to early childhood education', *Journal of Research in Childhood Education, 12(2)*, 244–271

Haines, L. (2002) 'Preschool deadline', *Dominion Post*, 16 September

Harkess, C. (2004) *Qualifications and Registration in the Early Childhood Teacher-led Workforce. Sector Overview and Service Type Breakdown*. Wellington: Ministry of Education

Katz, L. (1985) 'The nature of professions: where is early childhood education?' In *Talks with Teachers of Young Children*. New Jersey: Ablex Publishing Corp

Manning-Morton, J. (2006) 'The personal is professional: professionalism and the birth to three practitioner', *Contemporary Issues in Early Childhood, 7(1)*, 42–52

May, H. (2007) 'Minding, working, teaching: childcare in Aotearoa, New Zealand, 1940s–2000s', *Contemporary Issues in Early Childhood, 8(2)*, 133–143

Meade, A. (1990) 'Women and children gain a foot in the door', *New Zealand Women's Studies Journal, 6(1/2)*, 96–111

Meade, A. (2006) (ed.) *Riding the Waves. Innovation in Early Childhood Education.* Wellington: NZCER Press

Ministry of Education (1996a) *Te Whāriki: He Whāriki matauranga: Early Childhood Curriculum.* Wellington: Learning Media Ltd

Ministry of Education (1996b) 'Revised Statement of Desirable Objectives and Practices (DOPs) for chartered early childhood services in New Zealand', *The New Zealand Gazette*, 3 October 1996

Ministry of Education (2002) *Pathways to the Future: a 10 Year Strategic Plan for Early Childhood Education.* Wellington: Ministry of Education

Ministry of Education (2006) 'Education Counts. Education Statistics of New Zealand' http://educationcounts.edcentre.govt.nz/publications/ece/ed_stats_nz/ed_stats_nz_06

Ministry of Education (2007) 'Travelling Pathways to the Future: Ngā Huarahi Arataki', Early Childhood Education Symposium proceedings, 2–3 May. http://www.minedu.govt.nz/index.cfm?layout=document&documentid=12207&indexid=10944&indexparentid=10943

Mitchell, L. and Brooking, K. (2007) *First NZCER National Survey of Early Childhood Education Services 2003–2004.* Wellington: New Zealand Council for Educational Research

Montgomery, D. (2002) 'The other teacher crisis', *Listener*, 27 April, 27–31

Mortimore, P. (Ed.) (1999) *Understanding Pedagogy and its Impact on Learning.* London: Paul Chapman Publishing

Noddings, N. (1984) *Caring: A Feminine Approach to Ethics and Moral Education.* Berkeley: University of California Press

Oberhuemer, P. (2000) 'Conceptualising the professional role in Early Childhood centers: emerging profiles in four European countries', *Early Childhood Research and Practice, 2(2)*, Fall. http://ecrp.uiuc.edu/v2n2/oberhuemer.html

Osgood, J. (2006) 'Deconstructing professionalism in early childhood education: resisting the regulatory gaze', *Contemporary Issues in Early Childhood, 7(1)*, 5–14

Ramsay, K., Breen, J., Sturm, J., Lee, W. and Carr, M. (2006) 'Roskill South Kindergarten COI team reflections'. In A. Meade (ed.) (2006) *Riding the Waves. Innovation in Early Childhood Education.* Wellington: NZCER Press

Scrivens, C. and Duncan, J. (2003) 'What decisions? Whose decisions? Issues for professional leaders in decision-making in New Zealand childcare centres', *Early Education, 33*, 29–37

Simmons, H., Schimanski, L., McGarva, P., Woodhead, E., Haworth, P. and Cullen, J. (2006) 'A reconstruction of roles at Wycliffe Nga Tamariki Kindergarten COI: teachers as researchers and researchers as teachers'. In A. Meade (ed.) (2006) *Riding the Waves. Innovation in Early Childhood Education.* Wellington: NZCER Press

Urban, M. (2005) 'Quality, autonomy and the profession'. In H. Schonfeld, S. O'Brien and T. Walsh (eds.), *Questions of Quality.* Dublin: Centre for Early Childhood Development and Education

Further reading

Dalli, C. (2006) 'Re-visioning love and care in early childhood: Constructing the future of our profession', *The First Years, 8(1)*, 5–11

May, H. (2007) 'Minding, working, teaching: childcare in Aotearoa, New Zealand, 1940s–2000s', *Contemporary Issues in Early Childhood, 8(2)*, 133–143

Osgood, J. (2006) 'Deconstructing professionalism in early childhood education: resisting the regulatory gaze', *Contemporary Issues in Early Childhood, 7(1)*, 5–14

14 PROMOTING YOUNG CHILDREN'S DEVELOPMENT: IMPLICATIONS OF THE UN CONVENTION ON THE RIGHTS OF THE CHILD

Martin Woodhead

This chapter is a revised version of 'Early Childhood Development: A Question of Rights', *International Journal of Early Childhood*, 37(3), 79–98.

INTRODUCTION

The focus of this chapter is on the implications of one of the most significant documents shaping research, policies and practices for all children, globally. The United Nations Convention on the Rights of the Child, 1989 (abbreviated as UNCRC) applies to all children, including the youngest children. I begin by briefly explaining the significance of the UNCRC, especially as it applies to professional work with young children. Next, I outline implications of the UNCRC for recent developments in policy and services in England, in the wake of the Laming Report (2003), *Every Child Matters* (2003), the Children Act (2004) and the Common Core of Skills and Knowledge for the Children's Workforce (DfES 2005). The rest of the chapter looks in some detail at one of the key principles of the UNCRC, 'the development of the child', which is also one of the six elements of the Common Core.

CHILDREN'S RIGHTS AND CHILDREN'S SERVICES

Building early childhood services on respect for the rights of the child is one of many kinds of rationale currently available to the professional. Other kinds of rationale include:

- scientific evidence about early childhood programmes improving outcomes in later stages of education;
- social welfare concerns that children's services protect children while at the same time enabling families, especially mothers, to combine working with caring;
- economic arguments that the long-term benefits to society can outweigh the costs of providing services for children and families;

▪ and political priorities for early childhood services to serve as a powerful tool for intervention in social inequalities (based on Myers 1992).

In many ways, a human rights argument for early childhood services is the most compelling case of all. It does not rest on the availability of scientific evidence, cost-benefit analyses, nor even a political context valuing social justice, even though each of these is important to implementing rights in practice. The significance of the UNCRC is that the child is placed at centre stage. Survival, health, development, education etc., are recognised as each child's entitlement, irrespective of their linkage to wider policy goals, and that feelings and views of the child must be respected in decision-making, from birth onwards.

Over the past two decades, the UNCRC has become a powerful catalyst for action on behalf of young children, with ratification virtually universal (192 countries, all except USA and Somalia). For detailed commentary on UNCRC, see Hodgkin and Newell (1998). The UNCRC requires all children to be respected as persons in their own right, including the very youngest children. National governments ('States Parties') make regular reports on progress in meeting their obligations to the UN Committee on the Rights of the Child. This committee comprises 18 independent experts elected by UN States and representing major world regions, providing a highly significant mechanism of international accountability. But the influence of the UNCRC is arguably much more pervasive, as fundamental children's rights principles gradually become embedded within the policies and practices of all who work with and on behalf of young children:

> The CRC has more signatories than any other international convention, and it is important for us to recognize the legal implications of this achievement in how we position our work. Countries are legally bound to honour children's rights, and this gives us a strong basis for initiating public dialogue and action on behalf of young children
>
> (Arnold 2004: 4)

The specific challenges surrounding implementation of young children's rights were first discussed in detail by the UN Committee on the Rights of the Child during a 'Day of General Discussion' held in Geneva, September 2004. The Committee followed this up by preparing General Comment 7 'Implementing Child Rights in Early Childhood' (http://www.ohchr.org). The General Comment was formally adopted at the Committee's session in September 2005 and now serves as authoritative guidance on interpretation of the UNCRC in relation to young children. For a guide to General Comment 7, see UNCRC/UNICEF/Bernard van Leer Foundation (2006).

For the early childhood professional, adopting a rights-based perspective can require a radical shift from some more traditional ways of working with the young children. Members of the UN Committee have emphasised a fundamental goal is 'to emphasize that the young child is not merely a fit object of benevolence, but, rather, that the young child is a right-holder as is the older child and, indeed, every human being' (Doek et al. 2006: 32). To achieve this goal, it is not sufficient to think of young children as in need of care and teaching, as developing through a pre-planned curriculum, or as objects of social intervention. Of course, these perspectives have a place in professional work, but the foundation principle is respect for each young child in their own right. Ensuring quality of life for and with young children now and in the future is valued as an end in itself, and not just as the means to achieve broader goals of protecting and promoting human potential and preventing social ills. The UN Committee summed up this shift towards a positive agenda for early childhood:

A shift away from traditional beliefs that regard early childhood mainly as a period for the socialization of the immature human being towards mature adult status is required. . .Young children should be recognized as active members of families, communities and societies, with their own concerns, interests and points of view. For the exercise of their rights, young children have particular requirements for physical nurturance, emotional care and sensitive guidance, as well as for time and space for social play, exploration and learning. These requirements can best be planned for within a framework of laws, policies and programmes for early childhood. . .

(General Comment 7, para. 5).

Note how the young child is re-positioned in the extract above, as the rights-bearer, who 'for the exercise of their rights' requires the protection, support and guidance of peers, parents, professionals etc., in order to realise their rights. In this way, a rights perspective sets new challenges for all who claim to be 'child-centred'.

Progress towards respecting young children's rights has not always been explicitly linked to international activities inspired by the UNCRC. In 1989, legislation closer to home was much more influential for professionals in England, namely the Children Act, which became law in the same year as UNCRC was ratified. The Children Act 1989 incorporated principles consistent with the UNCRC, notably redefining parental roles in terms of responsibilities, insisting that the welfare of the child must be the paramount consideration, and requiring that courts take account of children's wishes and feelings. Yet overall, references to meeting children's needs, safeguarding their welfare and achieving positive outcomes have been much more central to government agendas than promoting their fundamental rights, and this reflects the recent history of British child policies (Parton 2006). Thus, Lord Laming's 2003 report on serious failures in coordination amongst child protection services prompted the Green Paper *Every Child Matters*, with the principal recommendations implemented within the Children Act, 2004. This involves a radical restructuring of children's services in order to achieve the five key outcomes for children: be healthy; stay safe; enjoy and achieve; make a positive contribution; and achieve economic well-being. While the five outcomes are not explicitly framed in terms of children's rights, it is possible to map them onto the articles of the UNCRC (see UNICEF 2006).

The Every Child Matters agenda has also prompted radical overhaul of professional training for early years, notably through specification of a Common Core of Skills and Knowledge for the Children's Workforce (DfES 2005). Interestingly, the introduction to the guidance document does include 'the rights of children and young people' as part of the rationale for the Common Core, even if not as its central justification:

The Common Core reflects a set of common values for practitioners that promote equality, respect diversity and challenge stereotypes, helping to improve the life chances of all children and young people and to provide more effective and integrated services. It also acknowledges the rights of children and young people, and the role parents, carers and families play in helping children and young people achieve the outcomes identified in Every Child Matters

(DfES 2005: 4).

The six areas of professional expertise set out in the Common Core are: effective communication and engagement; child and young person development; safeguarding and promoting the welfare of the child; supporting transitions; multi-agency working; and sharing information. The first three of these areas most obviously connect with articles of UNCRC, and with the guidance given on implementing child rights in early childhood within General Comment 7. The rest of this chapter explores these connections, taking just one element of the Common Core as a starting point, the 'development of the child'. Numerous textbooks are available to professionals, summarising the most up-to-date knowledge about children's development. My aim is to step back from the particularities of research findings, and summarise some key debates surrounding what 'promoting development' entails within a framework of rights.

THE YOUNG CHILD'S RIGHT TO DEVELOPMENT

The UN Committee emphasises that rights to development are to be understood in a holistic way and that all rights are interrelated, interdependent and indivisible. To this end, the UN Committee has identified four articles which – when taken together – can be seen as offering general principles. These, briefly, are:

▨ Article 6 ensures to the maximum extent possible the survival and development of the child;
▨ Article 2 assures rights to every child without discrimination;
▨ Article 3 sets out that the bests interests of the child are a primary consideration:
▨ Article12 states that children have a right to express views in all matters that affect them.

The reason for highlighting these general principles is that – when taken together – they begin to point to some of the challenges in interpreting children's right to development. For example: how far should professional frameworks build on assumptions that child development is a universal process; and how far is it more appropriate to be thinking in terms of respect for a range of developmental pathways, according to children's individuality, their economic and social circumstances, and their parents' cultural beliefs and aspirations? How can a balance be achieved between respecting diversities in children's development (in terms of expectations, treatment, styles of care and approaches to education) and guaranteeing all children's entitlements, without discrimination, for example related to their gender? How should 'best interests' be applied in practice – and by whom – especially when there is dispute amongst parents, professionals and others? How far can, or should, children's voice be listened to in these circumstances? How can they be enabled to express their views, and what are the roles and responsibilities of adults in (individually and collectively) guiding children's effective participation?

As a vehicle for exploring these dilemmas in greater detail, I will concentrate on three key debates: about the universality of child development processes; about what drives and shapes development; and about the status of the child in these processes. I will pose these as a set of competing perspectives, which I call the three 'Ns' and the three 'Cs'. The three 'Ns' involve thinking about what is 'Normal' and 'Natural' as well as about children's 'Needs'. The three 'Cs' involve thinking about development in ways that are 'Contextual', 'Cultural' and based on respect for children's 'Competencies' (see Table 14.1).

Major theme	'Ns'	'Cs'
Universality and diversity	Normal development	Contexts for development
Influences on development	Natural processes	Cultural processes
Status of the child	Needs of children	Competencies of children

Table 14.1: Debating early childhood: three Ns or three Cs?

Summarising diverse views on early childhood into three Ns and three Cs is of course an oversimplification. Neither the 'Ns' nor the 'Cs' offer a complete picture, nor are they necessarily in opposition, as will become clear if we look at each in turn.

NORMAL DEVELOPMENT OR CONTEXTS FOR DEVELOPMENT?

Identifying 'normal' patterns of development – as well as the extent and causes of variations – has been a major feature of child development research. Indeed, the typical textbook title 'Child Development' conveys the traditional approach. The singular 'child' has been the starting point and a major goal has been to identify universal features of growth and change, for example through detailed accounts of stages of physical, mental, social and moral development associated with the names of Piaget, Kohlberg, Erikson and other leading theorists. While identifying universal features of development as an attractive starting point for realising rights for all children, this approach also has serious limitations. Despite claims to universality, developmental accounts are often very closely tied to quite specific cultural contexts and expectations about what makes for a normal early childhood.

Early childhood is typically understood as being about children's gradual transition from dependency to individualised autonomy, which is highly valued in economically rich Western societies that originate most research, but does not always reflect traditional child-rearing values in other contexts (Kagiticibasi 1996). Similarly, theories about parents' role in supporting development are all too often based on research carried out in laboratory playroom settings, often with middle-class mothers and children, which then become the basis for universal generalisations. Many textbook accounts of early child development give the impression that mother is the only significant care giver; that she engages in reciprocal, playful interactions with her infant; and that she frames or scaffolds her child's learning within an environment well resourced with childcare equipment, toys and books, etc. One classic, 12-country study concluded that the care-giving style observed in the USA was (in global terms) abnormal, in terms of the extent of mothers' sociability with their children, and in the number of playful interactions in which children were treated as equals (Whiting and Edwards 1988). Yet, this style of interaction has become part of child development orthodoxy as the normal, and indeed, healthy way for adults to relate to their children (Singer 1998). Accounts of 'normal' development are also weak in their capacity to accommodate the impact of major social changes on care systems. For example, the HIV/Aids pandemic has resulted in loss of parents and/or siblings becoming a 'normal' feature of child development for millions of the world's young children (Richter et al. 2006).

Dominant expectations of what is 'normal' child development are not about normality in the statistical sense; on the contrary, conventional understandings of what makes for a normal childhood are in global terms often quite unusual, highlighted, for example, by studies of children's early initiation into work, which is still 'normal' for millions of the world's children (Woodhead 2002). Normal childhoods defined by professionals in one society are similarly likely to reflect a range of features of a very particular developmental niche (Super and Harkness 1986). They risk overlooking the diversities in children's developmental contexts and experiences, even with a community or region, including differences in the ways children learn, play and communicate, develop personal identity and social understanding, as well as the diversities in the ways they are treated according to parents' cultural goals for their development. Any particular account of young children's development is always partial, and can never encompass the varieties of childhood. The risk is when specific cultural patterns of early development and care become normalised and universalised. For early childhood professionals, the practical implication is that looking beyond dominant, textbook accounts of development is essential, especially for those working in multi-ethnic settings, as illustrated in Brooker (2002). This requires recognising that a range of pathways through early childhood can be consistent with promoting children's well-being, and that the challenge is to negotiate what is in each child's best interests (Woodhead 1996).

CHILD DEVELOPMENT AS NATURAL OR CULTURAL?

Ideas about 'normal' development have been closely linked to beliefs that development is underpinned by 'natural' processes of maturation. In the same way the importance of 'context' goes hand in hand with recognising that children's development is fundamentally a social and a 'cultural' process. Respecting young children's nature has roots in Rousseau's philosophical writing and found strongest expression in Jean Piaget's account of the child's progress through sensori-motor, pre-operational, concrete-operational and formal-operational stages (Donaldson 1978). Piaget's developmental stage model was coupled with a vision of individual children's exploratory play as the process through which they construct an increasingly sophisticated understanding of the world. These theories became the underpinning rationale for child-centred curricula and play-based pedagogy, as well as being reflected in guidelines on Developmentally Appropriate Practice issued by the US National Association for the Education of Young Children (Bredekamp and Copple 1987; see also Mallory and New 1994).

Piaget's universal stages in cognitive development offers a persuasive framework for interpreting children's development which strongly resonates with Western images of young children – innocence, playfulness and learning. But the scientific evidence for the theory is much less robust than has generally been assumed (Donaldson 1978). Since the 1970s, increasing numbers of developmental psychologists turned to a different theoretical framework which seems to account much more adequately for the social and cultural dimensions of the developmental process, informed by the work of Lev Vygotsky and his followers. In this view, developmental stages are embedded in institutional and social practices and relationships as much as in processes of maturation. In fact, children's development might most accurately be described as 'naturally cultural' (Trevarthen 1998: Rogoff 2003).

There is nothing fundamentally natural about modern environments for child-care, either at home or with in a pre-school setting. The early childhood settings and practices that foster early development are culturally constructed, the product of generations of human activity and creativity, mediated by complex belief systems, including about the 'proper' way for children to develop. The most significant features of any child's environment are the humans with whom they establish close relationships, parents, siblings and peers, care workers, teachers, etc. These individuals are themselves shaped by their cultural history, circumstances and training, and in the case of professionals, by the laws and policies that guide their work. These structures, relationships and belief systems translate into the everyday interactions that give meaning and direction to the experiences of young children, as adults scaffold their acquisition of skills and ways of communicating. For example, comparing mother–child dyads in India, Guatemala, Turkey and the USA, Rogoff et al. (1993) found that 'guided participation' was a feature in all these settings, but that the goals and processes of learning and teaching varied. These in turn were linked to the extent to which children's lives were segregated from the adult world of work. For example, while US mothers were often observed to create teaching situations, the Guatemalan mothers relied on a child's engagement with activities of the community.

Acceptance of this view – that children's behaviour, thinking, social relationships and adaptation, are culturally as much as biologically constituted – has profound implications for the way children's right to development is understood. The 'developmental appropriateness' of children's experiences, the 'harmfulness' or 'benefits' of their environment cannot be separated from the social and cultural processes through which they develop, the values and goals that inform the ways they are treated and understood. Unlike frameworks that emphasise normal and natural criteria for judging the quality of children's development, as well as the appropriateness of a particular environment or professional practices, cultural approaches argue that these criteria are culturally constructed and embedded in the particularities of child development contexts. In due course, human societies may come to share beliefs about what is 'normal' and 'natural' for young children. Indeed, in some ways, the UNCRC is a step in that direction. But universal consensus about the rights of the child does not make the beliefs and principles, or the arrangements for their implementation, any less cultural. The implication of accepting that child development has to be understood as a cultural process is that benchmarks are not intrinsic to the child, fixed and prescribed by nature in a simplistic sense. They are, to a large extent, also relational, historically specific and negotiable within a framework of promoting respect for young children's rights, as understood now, and in the future.

NEEDS OR COMPETENCIES?

Making a claim for children (or any other minority, low status group – the poor, the disabled, etc.) in terms of 'meeting needs' emphasises their dependencies. While children's right to protection from neglect, ill-treatment, exploitation and abuse is an important principle within the UNCRC, the underlying image of the needy child has been criticised, as underestimating children's actual and potential agency, in terms of their capacities to contribute to their development and well-being. While children's innocence, immaturity and vulnerability is emphasised, the role of adult society is disguised, through the projection of society's judgements onto children, as 'the child's needs' (Woodhead 1997). Framing children's development and welfare in terms of safeguarding their needs continues to be influential (Thomas 2005). Most recently, van Oudenhoven and Wazir (2006) have identified what they describe as 'Newly Emerging Needs'.

Other theorists have emphasised respect for children's competencies as a more positive starting point for policy and for professional work. This is very much more in the spirit of the UNCRC and General Comment 7. It involves recognising the young child as a social actor, engaged with their social environment from the beginning of life. Moss et al. (2000) compare traditional discourses of the 'child in need' within British policies on early childhood with discourses of 'the rich child' associated with early childhood services in Reggio Emilia, inspired by the work of Loris Malaguzzi:

Our image of children no longer considers them as isolated and egocentric. . .does not belittle feelings or what is not logical. . .Instead our image of the child is rich in potential, strong, powerful, competent and most of all, connected to adults and other children

(Malaguzzi 1993:10).

While an image of the child in need can be linked to protection rights, an image of the competent child is more consistent with participatory rights, summed up in Article 12 of the UNCRC:

States parties shall assure to the child who is capable of forming his or her own views the right to express those views freely in all matters affecting the child, the views of the child being given due weight in accordance with the age and maturity of the child

(UN Convention on the Rights of the Child, 1989, Article 12)

Article 12 sets one of the strongest challenges for early childhood professionals, and is linked to Articles 13, 14, 15 and 16 on freedom of expression, thought, conscience and religion and the right to privacy and freedom of association, according to children's evolving capacity. These articles of the UNCRC demand a reappraisal of children's role in shaping their development, in influencing those with responsibilities for their care and education and being listened to in all matters that affect them. Article 12 reminds us that children have their own perspective on the issues that concern parents, teachers, psychologists and child rights' workers. To put it bluntly, respect for children's rights to participation demands that children be viewed not just as 'subjects of study and concern', but also as 'subjects with concerns' (Prout 2000). Article 12 demands that children's views be respected, not as evidence of their relative competence, but as evidence of their unique experiences of the world they inhabit (Woodhead and Faulkner 2008). 'Effective communication with children, young people and families' is of course one of the areas of expertise within the Common Core of Skills and Knowledge for the Children's Workforce (DfES 2005). This area of expertise builds strongly on respect for children's capacities, concerns and preferred ways of communicating ideas and feelings.

During the past decade, numerous initiatives have translated participatory principles into practice, including in early childhood (Alderson 2000). For example, Lancaster (2006) proposes five principles for listening to children: recognising children's many languages; allocating communication spaces; making time; providing choice; and subscribing to a reflective practice. Other initiatives have been about effective consultation with young children, and increasing opportunities for contributing meaningfully to decision-making about issues that affect them (Einarsdottir 2007; MacNaughton et al. 2007). Amongst the most influential has been the Mosaic study that has developed techniques to listen to the perspectives of 3- and 4-year-old children on their nursery provision, for example based around children's drawings, their photographs and tape recordings (Clark and Moss 2001).

Respecting children's competence is not an alternative to safeguarding their welfare, especially for very young children. It is important to emphasise the qualifier in Article 12 that the views of the child should be given 'due weight in accordance with the age and maturity of the child'. Achieving balance between respecting the competent child and acknowledging their need for guidance is crucial to the practical implementation of participatory principles. How the balance is struck, in turn, depends on which theories about developing competence are given strongest weight. In earlier sections of this chapter, I contrasted two very different views of development.

One view drawing on Piagetian theory might argue as follows:

> Stage theories of intellectual development can be used to predict when children have sufficient capacities for understanding, such that their views should be listened to and taken seriously. Stage theories can also guide judgements about when children's capacities have evolved sufficiently that they no longer require so much direction and guidance from parents. According to this line of thought, the key question would be: 'At what stage does the child become competent to participate?' The role of adults would be to monitor children's growing capacities and make judgements about whether they are ready to participate.

An alternative view drawing on Vygotskian ideas would be:

> The stage theorists are asking the wrong question! Respecting children's growing competence isn't about measuring the progress of their development, like you might measure the height of a growing tree in order to decide when it should be felled. The more useful question is, 'How do children's competencies develop through appropriate levels of participation?' This way of posing the question draws attention to principles of guided participation. It highlights the ways children's competence can be guided and supported, or 'scaffolded' by adults and more competent peers in ways that are sensitive to their 'zone of proximal development'.

Different views on developing competencies, are not exhaustive, nor necessarily in opposition. Lansdown (2005) suggests three interpretations: a developmental concept – fulfilling children's rights to the development of their optimum capacities;

an emancipatory concept – recognising and respecting the evolving capacities of children; and a protective concept – protecting children from experiences beyond their capacities. (For further discussion of theoretical perspectives that support participatory rights, see also Smith 2002; and Woodhead 2006.)

SUMMARY

This discussion began by asking about the meanings attached to the concept of development, when viewed as one of children's fundamental rights. I have offered two contrasting paradigms for understanding development, summarised as three Ns versus three Cs. Polarising these paradigms is, of course, an oversimplification designed to draw attention to the diversity of ways that a 'right to development' can be interpreted in practice. Recognising the interdependencies between children and adults sets a further challenge. Realising children's rights requires close attention, not only to children, but also to the status and role of the adults children are destined to become. Conventional images of childhood view individual, adult maturity as a developmental endpoint; of having achieved independence, autonomy, competence, etc. Against this standard, children are marked off as dependent, needy and incompetent, as 'human becomings' rather than 'human beings' (Uprichard 2008). Promotion of children's participatory rights would be better served by recognising that the process of 'growing-up' is relative, not absolute. Adults can also be dependent, albeit in more subtle and sophisticated ways, surrounded by elaborate systems of biological, social, emotional and informational support. These patterns of interdependency are prerequisites for 'mature' psychological functioning and social adjustment, enabling adults (most of the time) to convey the impression of competence and autonomy that Western societies have so much valued as a 'developed status'. Arguably, a lifespan perspective (addressing the shifting patterns of participation and dependency from birth to old age) is a more appropriate basis for addressing these issues (Hockey and James 1993; Greene 1998). In short, implementing the UNCRC does not just alter the status of children. It also alters the status of adults, professionals, parents and others. Respecting the rights of young children changes the way we think about ourselves!

Questions/points for discussion/reflection

1 In developing your understanding of child development, why is it important to look outside your own beliefs and practices, and those considered normal in your own country?
2 In what ways is respect for the rights of the young child reflected in your professional practice; for example, how far do you think of children as 'being' as well as 'becoming'?
3 How are children viewed in the policy and curriculum documents you use in your setting?

REFERENCES

Alderson, P. (2000) *Young Children's Rights: Exploring Beliefs, Principles and Practices*. London: Jessica Kingsley Publishers

Arnold, C. (2004) 'Positioning ECCD in the 21st Century', *Coordinators Notebook*, 28

Bredekamp, S. and Copple, C. (eds) (1987) *Developmentally Appropriate Practice in Early Childhood Programs*. Washington: National Association for the Education of Young Children

Brooker, L. (2002) *Starting School: Young Children Learning Cultures*. Buckingham: Open University Press

Clark, A. and Moss. P. (2001) *Listening to Young Children, the Mosaic Approach*. London: National Children's Bureau

Department for Education and Skills (2005) *Common Core of Skills and Knowledge for the Children's Workforce*. London: DfES

Doek, J.E., Krappman, L. and Lee, Y. (2006) *Introduction to the General Comment, in Implementing Child Rights in Early Childhood: a guide to General Comment 7*. The Hague: Bernard van Leer Foundation

Donaldson, M. (1978) *Children's Minds*. London: Fontana

Einarsdottir, J. (2007) 'Children's voices on the transition from preschool to primary school'. In A. Dunlop and H. Fabian (eds) *Informing Transitions in the Early Years: Research, Policy and Practice*. London: McGraw-Hill

Greene, S. (1998) 'Child development: old themes and new directions'. In M.Woodhead, D. Faulkner and K. Littleton (eds) *Making Sense of Social Development*. London: Routledge

Hockey, J. and James, A. (1993) *Growing Up and Growing Old*. London, Sage

Hodgkin, R. and Newell, P. (1998) *Implementation Handbook for the Convention on the Rights of the Child*. New York: UNICEF

Kagitcibasi, C. (1996) *Family And Human Development Across Cultures: A View From The Other Side*. London: Erlbaum

Lancaster, Y. J. (2006) *RAMPS: a Framework for Listening to Children*. London: Day Care Trust

Lansdown, G. (2005) *The Evolving Capacities of Children: Implications for the Exercise of Rights*. Florence: UNICEF Innocenti Research Centre

MacNaughton, G., Hughes, P. and Smith, K. (2007) 'Young children's rights and public policy: practices and possibilities for citizenship in the early years', *Children & Society*, 21(6), 458–469

Malaguzzi, L. (1993) 'History, ideas and basic philosophy'. In C. Edwards, L. Gandini and G. Forman (eds) *The Hundred Languages of Children*. Norwood, NJ: Ablex

Mallory, B.L. and New, R. (1994) *Diversity and Developmentally Appropriate Practices: Challenges for Early Childhood Education*. New York: Teachers College Press.

Moss, P., Dillon, J. and Statham, J. (2000) 'The "child in need" and "the rich child": discourses, constructions and practice', *Critical Social Policy*, 20(2), 233–254

Myers, R. (1992) *The Twelve who Survive*. London: Routledge

Parton, N. (2006) *Safeguarding Childhood: Early Intervention and Surveillance in a Late Modern Society*. London: Palgrave/Macmillan

Prout, A. (2000) 'Children's participation: control and self-realisation in British late modernity', *Children & Society, 14*, 304–15

Richter, L., Foster, G. and Sherr, L. (2006) *Where The Heart Is: Meeting the Psychosocial Needs of Young Children in the Context of HIV/AIDS.* The Hague: Bernard van Leer Foundation

Rogoff, B. (2003) *The Cultural Nature of Child Development.* New York: Oxford University Press

Rogoff, B., Mosier, C., Mistry, J. and Goncu, A. (1993) 'Toddlers' guided participation with their caregivers in cultural activity'. In *Contexts For Learning: Socio-Cultural Dynamics In Children's Development.* New York: Oxford University Press

Singer, E. (1998) 'Shared care for children'. In M. Woodhead, D. Faulkner and K. Littleton (eds) *Cultural Worlds of Early Childhood.* London: Routledge

Smith, A.B. (2002) 'Interpreting and supporting participation rights: contributions from sociocultural theory', *International Journal of Children's Rights, 10*, 73–88

Super, C. and Harkness, S. (1986) 'The developmental niche: a conceptualisation at the interface of child and culture', *International Journal of Behavioral Development, 9*, 545–69

Thomas, N. (2005) 'Interpreting children's needs: contested assumptions in the provision of welfare'. In J. Goddard, S. McNamee, A. James, and A. James (eds) *The Politics of Childhood: International Perspectives, Contemporary Developments.* Basingstoke: Palgrave Macmillan

Trevarthen, C. (1998) 'Children's need to learn a culture'. In M. Woodhead, D. Faulkner and K. Littleton (eds) *Cultural Worlds of Early Childhood.* London: Routledge

UNCRC (1989) *United Nations Convention on the Rights of the Child.* Geneva: Office of the United Nations High commissioner for Human Rights

UNCRC/UNICEF/Bernard van Leer Foundation (2006) *A Guide to General Comment 7: 'Implementing child rights in early childhood'.* The Hague, The Netherlands: Bernard van Leer Foundation

UNICEF (2006) *Every Child Matters: The Five Outcomes and the UN Convention on the Rights of the Child (UNCRC),* PDF downloaded at www.unicef.org.uk/tz/resources

Uprichard, E (2008) 'Children as "being and becomings": Children, childhood and temporality', *Children & Society, 22* (doi:10.1111/j.1099-0860.2007.00110.x)

van Oudenhoven, N. and Wazir, R. (2006) *Newly Emerging Needs of Children: An Exploration.* Garant: Antwerp

Whiting, B. and Edwards, C. (1988) *Children of Different Worlds – the Formation of Social Behaviour.* Cambridge, Massachusetts: Harvard University Press

Woodhead, M. (1996) *In Search of the Rainbow: Pathways to Quality in Large Scale Programmes for Young Disadvantaged Children.* The Hague: Bernard van Leer Foundation

Woodhead, M. (1997) 'Psychology and the cultural construction of children's needs'. In A. Prout and A. James (eds) *Construction and Reconstruction of Childhood* (2nd Edition). London: Falmer

Woodhead, M. (2002) 'Work, play and learning in the lives of young children'. In L.Miller, R. Drury and R. Campbell (eds) *Exploring Early Years Education and Care.* London: David Fulton

Woodhead, M. (2006) 'Changing perspectives on early childhood theory, research and policy' (Background paper to UNESCO EFA Global Monitoring

Report 2007), *International Journal of Equity and Innovation in Early Childhood,*
4(2), 5–48

Woodhead, M. and Faulkner, D. (2008) 'Subjects, objects or participants? Dilemmas of psychological research with children'. In A. James and P. Christensen (eds) *Research with Children: Perspectives and Practices* (2nd Edition). London: Falmer Routledge

Further reading

Maybin, J. and Woodhead, M. (2003) 'Socializing children'. In J. Maybin and M. Woodhead (eds) *Childhoods in Context*. Chichester: Wiley

MacNaughton, G., Hughes, P. and Smith, K. (2007) 'Young children's rights and public policy: practices and possibilities for citizenship in the early years', *Children & Society, 21(6)*, 458–469

UNCRC/UNICEF/Bernard van Leer Foundation (2006) *A Guide to General Comment 7: 'Implementing child rights in early childhood'*. The Hague, The Netherlands: Bernard van Leer Foundation

Woodhead, M. (2006) 'Changing perspectives on early childhood theory, research and policy' (Background paper to UNESCO EFA Global Monitoring Report 2007), *International Journal of Equity and Innovation in Early Childhood, 4(2)*, 5–48

LOOKING TO THE FUTURE

15

Carrie Cable and Linda Miller

INTRODUCTION

In this chapter we reflect on the earlier chapters in this book, discuss some of the key themes which have arisen and look to the future. As the chapters in this book clearly demonstrate, the field of early years is rapidly changing; as the Red Queen said to Alice in *Through the Looking Glass*, 'it takes all the running you can do, to keep in the same place' (Carroll 1927: 44). Early years is now firmly high on government agendas in many countries and the need to develop a professional workforce is generally agreed. The means of achieving this is the subject of much debate amongst policy makers, academics, researchers and, increasingly, practitioners. As a relatively 'new profession' we have a unique opportunity to influence the framing of the discourses around qualifications and training, provision, child development, pedagogy, leadership, partnerships with parents and the knowledge base that individuals (who make up any profession) need to draw on in their interactions with children.

A NICE LADY IS NOT ENOUGH: LOOKING BACK

In 1997 one of us, Linda, was fortunate to hear a conference address by Tiziana Filippini (1997), a pedagogista in the Reggio Emilia nurseries in Italy, who accompanied *The Hundred Languages of Children* exhibition in London. In her opening statement she challenged the audience that 'A nice lady is not enough' to ensure the best care and education for young children, a statement reflected in the focus of this book about developing professionalism in the early years.

The early years workforce is a feminised workforce and not only in the United Kingdom. In the 20 countries surveyed in the OECD report, men represent less than 1 per cent of the workforce in Early Childhood Education and Care (ECEC) (OECD 2006). Thus it is viewed as 'women's work', and this, some writers would argue, is the reason for it not being recognised as of sufficient importance to be properly remunerated and valued; the English Government has set a target of increasing male childcare and education workers to 6 per cent.

The notion of quality is one of the key concepts underpinning developments over the last 20 years and, as with other concepts, its interpretation varies from country to country. Research over the last decade supports the view that quality in the ECEC field requires adequate training and fair working conditions for staff (OECD 2006) and that the quality of provision is linked to the quality of staff that work in them (Sylva et al. 2003).

In 1994 the RSA *Start Right Report* concluded that: 'The calibre and training of the professionals who work with children are the key determinants of high quality provision'. (Ball 1994, para 6: 13). In 1996 Hevey and Curtis, in a book on *Training to Work in the Early Years,* identified three main professional groups working with young children and their families in the UK: teachers, health visitors and social workers; but they noted that the majority of day care and pre-school services were staffed by more than 200,000 largely unqualified childcare and education workers. There was no statutory training or qualification requirement for employment in early years services. The *Starting Strong II* report (OECD 2006) notes that governments often fear the funding consequences of raising qualifications in the workforce. Higher qualifications lead quite rightly to higher expectations relating to pay and conditions of work, which in turn contributes significantly to the costs of services.

The 2001 OECD report said:

Staff working with children in the ECEC programmes have a major impact on children's early learning and development. Research shows the link between strong training and support of staff – including appropriate pay and conditions – and the quality of ECEC services. In particular, staff that have more formal education and more specialised early childhood training provide more stimulating, warm and supportive interactions with children.

(OECD 2001:158)

The 2006 OECD report identified two main approaches to staffing in ECEC services.

1 In countries with split regimes, i.e. where care and education are seen as separate services, qualified teachers work with children over 3 years of age, while in the childcare sector a mix of less highly trained staff are employed. This broadly reflects the position in the UK until relatively recently, and the divide between the maintained and private, voluntary and independent (PVI) sectors.
2 In countries with integrated services, a core lead professional works in a more holistic way to support children and families. The development of a core lead professional and more integrated service has been identified as the way forward in the UK but has yet to be realised in practice.

What we have seen over the last decade is a welcome move towards raising the level of qualifications in the early years, but without the recognition through status and pay for the new higher-level workforce roles that are being developed.

PROFESSIONALISING THE EARLY YEARS WORKFORCE ACROSS THE UNITED KINGDOM

The chapters in this book have focused mainly on England, as we stated in the Introduction, but developments in each country of the UK reflect moves towards the professionalisation of the early years workforce. Finding reliable statistics and information that reflect the picture across the United Kingdom is not easy, as many documents and publications use the term the United Kingdom for Britain or refer to the UK, when in fact the information may relate to England only; this includes the recent OECD (2006) report *Starting Strong II*. Below we offer a brief snapshot of some recent developments relating to raising the qualification levels of the early years workforce across the UK.

The *Starting Strong II* report cites England as having made most progress of all countries in children's services since the first OECD review in 1999 (OECD 2006), although others have suggested that this was from a low baseline. As we saw in Chapter 1, since the election of a Labour Government in 1997 early years has been high on the reform agenda and there has been increased spending and moves towards integrated care and education provision, and higher quality provision through workforce reform (HM Treasury 2004). Chapter 2 charted the development of a new Early Years Professional to lead on the Foundation Stage curriculum for children from birth to 5 in all children's centres by 2010, and in every full-day care setting by 2015 (DfES 2005, CWDC 2006). Chapters 2 to 6 discussed the rise of Early Childhood Studies Degrees, developments in teacher education, the increasing professionalisation of childminders and the opportunities open to teaching assistants to improve their knowledge and skills.

Developments in Northern Ireland parallel many of the developments in England. The National Childcare Strategy (1999) emphasised the need for early years practitioners to be appropriately educated. According to Walsh (2007) there is a wide variety of qualifications within the childcare/pre-school sector and estimates suggest that 30 per cent of staff have no qualifications. Teachers cover the age range 4 to 12 and only some teacher education programmes have a core of child development. Nursery schools and classes are required to have a qualified teacher, and providers in the private and voluntary sector are required to arrange support from a qualified teacher. The importance of a suitably trained workforce was reinforced by the Effective Provision of Preschool Education Project in Northern Ireland (Melhuish et al. 1999), which recommended there should be a good proportion of trained teachers or equivalent. However, an issue for debate, as has been noted in relation to the EYP role and Qualified Teacher Status in England, is what constitutes equivalence. There is to be a scoping of the Childcare and Early Years workforce led by the Northern Ireland Social Care Council (NISCC) (http://www.niscc.info/intro. htm).

There is in Northern Ireland also a distinct role of an Early Years Specialist to support providers without a qualified teacher in early years settings (http://www. deni.gov.uk/index/pre-school-education_pg/16-pre-school_education-curricular guidance_pg/16-pre-school_education-qualifications_pg.htm). Qualifications regarded as suitable for this role include:

- 'acceptable' units from NVQ Level 4 in Early Years Care and Education;
- BA (Hons) Early Childhood Studies (Stranmillis College);
- Diploma in Early Childhood Studies (Stranmillis College);
- HND in Early Childhood Studies; or
- BA Ed (Hons) [Early Years Specialist] (University College, Worcester);

and also two years' experience in a leadership role and relevant organisational skills. The Early Years Organisation (formerly The Northern Ireland Pre-School Playgroups Association [NIPPA]) (http://www.early-years.org/) is committed to a graduate workforce based on a pedagogue tradition, rather than a teacher-led profession.

The Scottish Executive consultation on the National Review of the Early Years and Childcare Workforce (http://www.scotland.gov.uk/Publications/2006/07/10140823/0) advocates both work-based and academic routes towards a qualified workforce. Qualified teachers cover the age range 3 to 12 in primary schools. Workforce plans include developing leadership in the early years sector through a degree or a work-based equivalent, with programmes offering the new qualifications by 2008. As in England, it was suggested that a new term for a new qualified professional was needed, but in a language that works for Scotland and the term manager/lead practitioner has been adopted. Standards for lead practitioners/managers have been developed and specify the expectations of programmes. It is stressed that the standards are not intended as a national curriculum but seek to encourage programme and service providers to work collaboratively in the design and delivery of their curricula (QAA Scotland 2007). As in England, there are plans to develop an Integrated Qualifications Framework.

The teacher training curriculum in Wales is weighted towards the National Curriculum, with little or no focus on child development (Wynn Siencyn and Thomas 2007). The Flying Start programme for birth to 3-years-olds will be delivered from integrated centres or community focused schools by 'trained professionals'. A Children's Workforce Strategy is to be produced by 2008 and includes research into the capacity to deliver Level 4 and higher qualifications. A review of Initial Teacher Training (Furlong et al. 2006) proposes a move to graduate entry and the development of 'Pre-professional' degrees offering specialist routes such as Early Years.

What we see across the UK is a commitment to develop the early years workforce and new graduate roles, but in contexts which vary in terms of degrees of regulation and the specification of standards and outcomes. As the OECD (2006) report points out, the choice between the educator and the pedagogue for the lead role in early childhood is a complex one and may not be an 'either/or' choice. In the UK we can see the emergence of different roles which relate to the different ways early childhood education and care have been viewed and regulated in the past. If the future emphasis is to be on integrated education and care and increasingly on work in multi-agency teams, it is likely that different practitioners will form part of new professional teams. However, regulating for multi-professional working is one thing; it is the practitioners involved who will need to make it work and, in doing so, transform themselves as individuals and as members of communities of practice. This will require a commitment not only to achieving graduate-level qualifications and further and continuing professional development programmes, it will also require appropriate recognition through status and pay.

PROFESSIONALISM IN THE EARLY YEARS WORKFORCE

Defining professionalism

The development of a more professional workforce is an important part of the agenda for reform in the four countries described above and in the countries covered in section three of this book. Workforce reform is opening up new routes to training and professionalism for a diverse and under-qualified workforce. However, any discussion of professionalism or professionalisation cannot avoid consideration of the motivations on the part of governments and policy makers for the envisaged changes. The decisions that are made and the structures that are put in place are unique to each country. As has been discussed in a number of chapters in this book, they emerge from the specific social, cultural and historical contexts of the various countries and are influenced by political and ideological considerations and discourses, individual and collective values and beliefs, views of childhood, pedagogy and learning and views of the child and the role of parents.

For example, in England reform has been driven by the agenda outlined in *Every Child Matters* (DfES 2003) and a strong focus on protecting and safeguarding children from harm, together with economic policy objectives to encourage women into the workforce. Curriculum guidance in England, while contradictory in some of its theoretical underpinnings, can be viewed as embodying a highly structured approach to children's learning and the experiences that are provided for them, with an emphasis on preparing children for school in terms of knowledge, attitudes and behaviours. Hence children are not viewed as being in 'the now' but as being prepared for the next stage, and reporting and inspection arrangements endorse and encourage this view. These perspectives inevitably impact on the way that practitioners interpret their roles and the degree of autonomy they feel they have, and help to form the notions of professionalism in a particular context.

'Professionalism' is not an easy concept to define in the early years. The term 'profession' encompasses: professional knowledge, skills and competencies, dispositions, values and beliefs, the 'tools' of a profession and notions of professional expertise (Oberhuemer 2005; Osgood 2006). Both authors of this chapter are members of a Special Interest Group on Professionalism within the European Early Childhood Education Research Association (EECERA), representing over 12 countries. For the last two years we have been attempting to reach a definition of professionalism in the context of the early years workforce and to explore what this means. The diversity of this workforce in relation to roles, qualifications, settings and the regulations that govern these, together with debates and discussions around pedagogy, child development and views of the child have made it difficult to reach agreement on what should constitute a body of professional knowledge (Moss and Penn 1996). These discussions are also reflected in a number of chapters, and particularly in Chapter 3, in the efforts of the Early Childhood Studies network in England to develop and agree subject benchmarks.

One of our aims in drawing together chapters for this book was to reflect the diversity in the understanding of professionalism in the early years in the UK and elsewhere. However, we would want to suggest that this diversity is a strength and one that we need to hold on to because it allows for future learning and change. Diversity encourages us to be open to challenge – of our assumptions and beliefs and practices. Our recent conversations with other European professionals and academics suggest that there are common themes underpinning notions of professionalism that, although open to local interpretation, provide secure ground for ongoing debate and transformative action. We consider some of these in the following section.

Quality

Quality is one of the key concepts underpinning notions of professionalism. Parents have a right to expect that provision for their children meets certain standards and that children will be able to grow, develop and learn in a safe and secure environment, guided and supported by suitably qualified and skilled practitioners. All parents want the best for their children, irrespective of their social or economic situation and wherever they are in a country. Interpretations of quality will vary and be determined in each country and framed by the political, historical and socio-cultural context and they will also change over time. Quality is related to the development of regulatory frameworks, standards guidance documents and registration and inspection regimes, but also to the interpretation of these contributory facets and the conditions in which they have to be enacted and implemented. In order to do this, practitioners need to understand the political and ideological purpose behind the drive towards quality, be able to question these in terms of equity and social justice and negotiate and agree what it means, particularly with parents and carers.

Standards

Professional standards provide markers of what can and should be expected of those working in the early years. They help to define professional competence, not just in terms of skills or functional abilities but in terms of knowledge, values, attitudes, dispositions and relationships. Standards can and do provide structures, frameworks and expectations for courses of study and qualifications, and there is evidence that practitioners feel they provide benchmarks that help them to reflect on and evaluate their own performance, knowledge and skills (Fenech and Sumsion 2007). However, they can also be viewed as externally imposed, a regulatory device, criteria for making judgements or enforcement (see Chapter 11). Where professional standards are effective, they will enable negotiation, interpretation and provide for development and progression. They will be linked to ongoing training and qualifications and to recognised pay and conditions structures.

Expertise

Expertise linked to a body of knowledge is another important component of professionalism in the early years, gained through study and through experience, both individually and collectively. As professional roles change and develop so, too, will the body of knowledge. As new ideas and interpretations of theory arise and new research studies are made available, time must be made to consider these. The ability to interpret and apply knowledge in the interests of children in practice, provision and policy development is a key aspect of professional expertise. Expertise can also be viewed as encompassing attitudes and dispositions underpinned by knowledge, the values and beliefs that enable questions to be asked, that enable practice, provision and policy to be analysed and other viewpoints to be considered.

Reflection

Reflection is generally acknowledged as a key professional attribute. It is also generally acknowledged that reflection on practice is an ongoing process through which practitioners learn to critically examine their own practice and that it can support the development of communities of practice both within and across settings. Reflection associated with research, and action research in particular, can contribute to the process through which new ideas and practices are explored, beliefs are challenged and individuals and groups develop cooperative and collaborative working with and for children. It can also be a means of empowerment, leading to change at the individual and societal level.

Osgood (2006) has argued that we need to recognise the complex work that practitioners undertake and the importance of deep and sustained engagement between children and adults, which goes beyond technical competence to encompass enquiry and critical reflection. According to Oberheumer (2005), informed professional action requires a willingness to reflect on one's own taken-for-granted beliefs and an understanding that knowledge is not fixed but is contestable. She explores the concept of 'democratic professionalism' as an alternative way of conceptualising professional roles in the face of increased control and regulation; a concept which embraces ideas around participatory relationships and cooperation and collaboration between professional colleagues and stakeholders.

Identity

A sense of belonging to, and being recognised as belonging to, a profession is an important aspect of professional identity. At an individual level, a professional identity will be influenced by an individual's 'self-concept' and self-esteem' which are in turn influenced by external factors such as qualifications, training, roles, responsibilities, knowledge and experience, as well as the way society views work in the early years. Identities are not, however, fixed; they evolve and change through participation and active involvement in learning experiences. Recognised titles and status can be an important part of professional identity for individuals and for the profession as a whole. However, a collective professional identity is also fundamentally about how work with young children is viewed by society.

Social status

To be considered a professional is a mark of social status for workers in most countries and is a reflection of the value of the work they do and the esteem in which they are held by other members of the community and society. The value placed on work in the early years varies from country to country, but a desire to professionalise the workforce through training and qualifications indicates a move towards providing greater social status for the workforce. However, it can also be argued that for this to become a reality it will need to be accompanied by a change in the way that young children and work with young children are viewed.

LOOKING TO THE FUTURE

We need a new type of worker for these services: a worker who can combine many tasks and work with the whole child and her family; a worker who is a reflective practitioner, able to think and act for herself, rather than a technician trained to do as she is told; a worker on a par with teachers in terms of training and employment conditions.

(Moss 2003: 5)

In looking back over the last decade, it is clear that one consequence of moving towards a more professional workforce is that in some countries the workforce is becoming increasingly regulated and outcomes-and-standards based, a move that has been particularly prevalent in England. Critics of this approach (see Chapter 11) (see also Dahlberg and Moss 2005; Osgood 2006) argue that underpinning this model is a discourse of technical practice and of 'governing at a distance' by deploying 'technologies of performance in order to regulate agencies' (*and practitioners working within them*) (our italics) so that they are increasingly accountable, controlled and audited (Dahlberg and Moss 2005: 46, citing Dean 1999).

However, as authors in this book have argued (see Chapter 2 and above) standards, outcomes and regulations may help to inform professional practice. Dahlberg and Moss (2005), although discussing pre-schools, acknowledge the place of goals (which for this discussion might be referred to as standards or outcomes) but note the need for 'space' for the unexpected. As Moss says (2006: 9), 'Outcomes are important. But we need to be open to outcomes that are new, different and unexpected'.

The political context in each of the UK countries and beyond presents different tensions and challenges for those charged with developing and implementing professional development programmes for early years practitioners. Dahlberg and Moss's (2005) discussion of 'minor politics' (141) and of resisting dominant discourses, offers possibilities for change within what they term 'cramped spaces' (153). In their discussion, they cite the example of a pre-school as a cramped space, but for the purpose of this discussion, requirements for professional development courses within Higher Education Institutions (HEIs) could be viewed as such. Minor politics, according to Dahlberg and Moss (138–139, citing Rose: 277) is about 'seeing matters differently and making loud voices stutter'. It is about contesting, questioning and developing a critical attitude and about opening up space to think about how it might be possible to do things differently.

MacNaughton proposes three questions for practitioners to consider:

- Do you want to belong to a profession that works to conform to a particular body of specialised knowledge and practise this knowledge in the same way with all communities?
- Do you want to belong to a profession that works to reform how a particular body of knowledge is practised with different communities?
- Do you want to belong to a profession that works to transform how a particular body of knowledge is understood and practised with different communities? (MacNaughton 2003: 283)

These discussions and questions offer a challenge to providers to recognise their own agency in developing new programmes and interpreting regulatory standards, frameworks and benchmarks in creative ways. As Osgood (2006) notes, practitioners (*and providers*) (our italics) need not be passive recipients of the reform process, but can be active in rising to the challenge by negotiating where they are 'positioned and defined' and thus take on the role of autonomous professionals. At the same time, we need to acknowledge that it is a limited freedom bound and moulded by norms, standards, benchmarks and regulations and by societal constructions of child development, pedagogy and views of the child.

In this book we have attempted to explore professionalism in the early years at both a macro and a micro level, covering changes in government policy, regulatory frameworks, training and qualifications and the contexts and constraints under which these are being articulated and developed. We have sought to cover what these changes mean for practitioners in terms of developing their professional knowledge, skills, attributes, dispositions and behaviours. We have also tried to explore some of the debates and perspectives around what kind of profession and what kind of professional workforce we might want to see in the twenty-first century.

SUMMARY

To quote Sylva and Pugh (2005: 24), although writing broadly about the early years in England, 'Much has been achieved. . .Yet the vision is still hazy'. The development of a more professional workforce for the early years is an evolving process, subject to policy changes, budget constraints, government targets, often with short time-scales for implementation and dependent on the dominant discourse within a particular country. The discussion about professionalism in this book reminds us of a piece of work by the artist Cornelia Parker, titled *Cold Dark Matter: an Exploded View* which was exhibited in the Tate Gallery in London in 1991. A garden shed filled with objects was safely blown apart. The fragments of the shed and its contents were brought to the Tate, suspended from the ceiling and illuminated by a light bulb. For Parker, this work is a metaphor that marks not destruction but a transformation and the beginning of something new. For us, this image is symbolic of the opportunities that present in relation to the development of a new, more professional workforce in the UK and beyond. We do not have the luxury of taking apart what we have, but we can make choices about how we want to see it develop and engage critically in a process of transformation.

Questions/points for discussion/reflection

1 In what ways, if any, has your understanding of professionalism in the early years changed as a result of reading this book?
2 What are the next steps for your own professional development and how will you begin this process?
3 What do you see as the possibilities and challenges for the development of early years services in the twenty-first century?

REFERENCES

Ball (1994) *Start Right: The Importance of Early Learning.* London: RSA

Children's Workforce Development Council (CWDC) (2006) *Early Years Professional Prospectus.* Leeds: CWDC

Carroll, L. (1927) *Through the Looking Glass* (children's edition). London: Macmillan and Company Limited

Dahlberg, G. and Moss, P. (2005) *Ethics and Politics in Early Childhood Education.* London and New York: Routledge Falmer

Department of Education Northern Ireland (DENI) http://www.deni. gov.uk/index/pre-school-education_pg/16-pre-school_education-curricular guidance_pg/16-pre-school_education-qualifications_pg.htm (accessed 15/11/ 2007)

Department for Education and Skills (2003) *Every Child Matters – Summary.* London: DfES

Department for Education and Skills (2005) *Children's Workforce Strategy, Consultation Paper.* London: DfES

Early Years Organisation http://www.early-years.org/ (Northern Ireland) (accessed 15/11/2007)

Fenech, M. and Sumsion, J. (2007) 'Early childhood teachers and regulation: complicating power relations using a Foucauldian lens', *Contemporary Issues in Early Childhood, 8(2),* 109–122

Filippini, T. (1997) *The Reggio Approach.* Paper delivered at The Hundred Languages of Children Exhibition Conference, The Picture Gallery, Thomas Coram Foundation for Children, London, 11 July.

Furlong, J., Hagger, H. and Butcher, C. (2006) *Review of Initial Teacher Training Provision in Wales.* Oxford: Oxford University, Department of Educational Studies

Hevey, D. and Curtis, A. (1996) 'Training to work in the early years'. In G. Pugh (ed.) *Contemporary Issues in the Early Years* (2nd edition). London: Paul Chapman Publishing Ltd

HM Treasury (2004) in conjunction with Department for Education and Skills (DfES), Department for Work and Pensions (DWP), Department for Trade and Industry (DTI) *Choice for Parents, the Best Start for Children: a Ten Year Strategy for Childcare.* London: HMSO www.surestart.gov.uk/aboutsurestart/strategy/ (accessed 21/12/2004)

MacNaughton, G. (2003) *Shaping Early Childhood Learners, Curriculum and Contexts.* Maidenhead: Oxford University Press

Melhuish, E., Quinn, L., McSherry, K., Sylva, K., Sammons, P., Siraj-Blatchford, I., Taggart, B. and Gummares, S. (1999) *Effective Pre-School Provision in Northern Ireland.* Belfast: Stranmillis University College

Moss, P. (2003) *Beyond Caring: the Case for Reforming the Childcare and Early Years Workforce.* London: Daycare Trust, The National Childcare Campaign

Moss, P. (2006) 'Contesting early childhood . . .and opening for change.' Paper given at the Contesting early childhood . . .and opening for change conference at the Institute of Education, University of London, London, UK, 11 May 2006

Moss, P. and Penn, H. (1996) *Transforming Nursery Education*. London: Paul Chapman Publishing Ltd

National Review of the Early Years and Childcare Workforce: report and consultation (http://www.scotland.gov.uk/Publications/2006/07/10140823/0) (accessed 15/11/2007)

Northern Ireland Social Care council http://www.niscc.info/intro.htm (accessed 15/11/2007)

Oberheumer, P. (2005) 'Conceptualising the early childhood pedagogue: policy approaches and issues of professionalism', *European Early Childhood Education Research Journal, 13(1),* 5–15

OECD (2001) *Starting Strong. Early Childhood Education and Care.* Paris: Organisation for Economic Co-operation and Development

OECD (2006) *Starting Strong II. Early Childhood Education and Care.* Paris: Organisation for Economic Co-operation and Development

Osgood, J. (2006) 'Deconstructing professionalism in early childhood education: resisting the regulatory gaze,' *Contemporary Issues in Early Childhood, 7(1),* 5–14

QAA Scotland (2007) *Scottish Subject Benchmark Statement: The Standard for Childhood Practice.* Glasgow: QAA

Sylva, K., Melhuish, E., Sammons, P., Siraj-Blatchford, I., Taggart, B. and Elliot, K. (2003) *The Effective Provision of Pre-School Education (EPPE) Project: Findings from the Pre-School Period: Summary of finding.* London: Institute of Education/Sure Start

Sylva, K. and Pugh, G. (2005) 'Transforming the early years in England', *Oxford Review of Education, 31(1),* 11–27

Walsh, G. (2007) 'Northern Ireland'. In M. Clark, M. and T. Waller (eds) *Early Childhood Education and Care: Policy and Practice.* London: Sage Publications

Wynn Siencyn, S. and Thomas, S. (2007) 'Wales'. In M. Clark and T. Waller (eds) *Early Childhood Education and Care: Policy and Practice.* London: Sage Publications

Further reading

Baldock P., Fitzgerald, D. and Kay, J. (2005) *Understanding Early Years Policy.* London: Paul Chapman Publishing Ltd

Clark, M. and Waller, T. (eds) (2007) *Early Childhood Education and Care: Policy and Practice.* London: Sage Publications

http://www.cwdcouncil.org.uk/index.asp (Children's Workforce Development Council)

www.sssc.uk.com (Scottish Social Services Council)

www.wales.org.uk (Care Council for Wales)

www.niscc.info (Northern Ireland Social Care Council)

INDEX